Ginn English

Consultants
Richard L. Venezky
Carol J. Fisher

Ginn and Company

Acknowledgments: Grateful acknowledgement is made to the following publishers, authors, and agents for permission to use and adapt copyrighted materials:

Atheneum Publishers, Inc., for the poem "Winter Dark" by Lilian Moore, in *I Thought I Heard the City.* Copyright © 1969 Lilian Moore. Reprinted with the permission of Atheneum Publishers.

Doubleday & Company, Inc., for the information about meat consumption in Section A on page 90, about trees in Section B on page 180, about toothbrushes in Section B on page 182, about the first alarm clock on page 286, and about the toothpaste tube in Section A on page 287. All adaptations from *The People's Almanac* by David Wallechinsky and Irving Wallace. Copyright © 1975 by David Wallace and Irving Wallace. Reprinted by permission of Doubleday & Company, Inc.

Harcourt Brace Jovanovich, Inc., for the excerpts from "Arithmetic" in *The Complete Poems of Carl Sandburg,* copyright 1950 by Carl Sandburg; renewed 1978 by Margaret Sandburg, Helga Sandburg Crile and Janet Sandburg. Reprinted by permission of Harcourt Brace Jovanovich, Inc.

Harper & Row, Publishers, Inc., for "Hughbert and the glue" (Text only) from *Dogs and Dragons, Trees and Dreams: A Collection of Poems* by Karla Kuskin. Copyright © 1964 by Karla Kuskin. Reprinted by permission of Harper & Row, Publishers, Inc.

Curtis Brown, Ltd., New York, for the poem "Accidentally" from *No One Writes a Letter to the Snail* by Maxine Kumin. Reprinted by permission of Curtis Brown Ltd. Text Copyright © 1962 by Maxine Kumin.

Chelsea House Publishers, New York, for the poems or excerpts from poems by fourth-graders on page 95, all from *Wishes, Lies, and Dreams* by Kenneth Koch. Copyright © 1970 by Kenneth Koch. All reprinted by permission of the publisher.

The Christian Science Monitor for the poem on page 325, "Unfolding Bud" by Naoshi Koriyama (7/13/57). Reprinted by permission from *The Christian Science Monitor.* © 1957 The Christian Science Publishing Society. All rights reserved.

William Morrow & Company, Inc., for the poem "The Best Street" in *City Sandwich* by Frank Asch. Copyright © 1978 by Frank Asch. By permission of Greenwillow Books (A Division of William Morrow & Company). Also for the sentences in Section C on page 321, based on "25 Things That Fell From the Sky" from *The Book of Lists* by David Wellechinsky, Irving Wallace, and Amy Wallace. Copyright © 1977 by David Wallechinsky, Irving Wallace and Amy Wallace. By permission of William Morrow & Company.

Prince Redcloud for "And Then." Used by permission of the author who controls all rights.

Scholastic Inc. for "You Can't Get Rags from Ragweed" by Kaye Starbird. Reprinted by permission of Four Winds Press, a division of Scholastic Inc. from *The Covered Bridge House and Other Poems* by Kaye Starbird Jennison. Copyright © 1979 by Kaye Starbird Jennison.

Workman Publishing Company, Inc., for information about treating burns in Section A on page 117 and about making a bendable bone in Section A on page 152. Both from *The Kids' Kitchen Takeover,* copyright 1975 Sara Bonnett Stein. Workman Publishing, New York. Reprinted with permission of the publisher.

The dictionary entries and guide words on page 110 are abridged from *Scott, Foresman Beginning Dictionary* by E. L. Thorndike and Clarence L. Barnhart. Copyright © 1979, Scott, Foresman and Company.

Photographs: Animals, Animals, 119; The Bettmann Archive, Inc., 289; Bruce Coleman, Inc./Jen & Des Bartlett, 21, 155, G. D. Ploge, 293, B. & C. Alexander, 297; Elias P. Coulouras, 200; Grant Heilman Photography, 117; Stephen Maka, 29, 284–285, 291; NASA, 98, 123; Peter Arnold, Inc./Richard Choy, 54; Photo Color, 209; The Picture Cube/James Simon, 33, Jennifer Cogswell, 126, P. Ellen, 128, Frank Siteman 147; Stock Boston, Inc./Abraham Russell, 59, Donald Dietz, 130; Frank Siteman, 224, 315, 316.

Illustrators:

Bob Barner	Giles La Roche
Bettina Borer	Susan Lexa
Jon Buller	Robert Steele
Rosekrans Hoffman	

2

Contents

Winter Dark

Winter dark comes early
mixing afternoon
and night.
Soon
there's a comma of a moon,

and each street light
along the
way
puts its period
to the end of day.

Now
a neon sign
punctuates the dark
with a bright
blinking
breathless
exclamation mark!

—*Lilian Moore*

1

Giving
Directions

Sentences

A *sentence* is a group of words that tells a complete thought.

Sentence: My shirt is new.   **Not a sentence:** my shirt

A *sentence* states a complete thought or idea. A sentence begins with a capital letter. It ends with a period or other punctuation mark. A capital letter and a period alone do not make a sentence. The words must also be in the right order and make sense.

Which group of words is a sentence?

The stores were crowded.

The crowded were stores.

Both groups start with a capital letter and end with a period. But only one makes sense. The first group is a sentence. The words are in the right order.

Make a sentence with these words.

In a box the shirt put the person.

To be a sentence, a group of words must tell a complete thought. A sentence *fragment* does not tell a complete thought. It is only part of a sentence.

Why is this a sentence fragment?

The person at the counter.

What did the person at the counter do? How can the fragment become a sentence? You need to add more words.

Now it is a sentence.

The person at the counter wrapped the package.

PRACTICE

A. (Oral) Tell whether each group of words is a *sentence* or a *fragment*.

> **Example:** I saved my allowance for a month.
> **sentence**

1. Earned money in the summer.
2. Dad paid me to paint the fence.
3. Mowed my neighbor's lawn.
4. Shoveled driveways in the winter.
5. The Youth Club held a car wash on Saturday.
6. We raised money for the club.
7. I bought a birthday present for my brother.

B. (Written) Put each group of words in the right order. Use the capital letters and periods as clues. Write each sentence.

> **Example:** need a new sweater. I
> **I need a new sweater.**

1. on sale. I bought a pair of pants
2. my size. The salesperson helped me find
3. for the shirt. Mom looked in two stores
4. returned The customer the shirt.
5. wanted to buy We roller skates.
6. brother tried on the coat. My
7. The salesperson the money. took
8. happy. was He

APPLY

Write three sentences about ways to earn money. Be sure each sentence tells a complete thought.

Kinds of Sentences

There are four kinds of sentences.

Statement: You are here.   Question: Are you here?

Exclamation: You're here!   Command: Be here at noon.

Each kind of sentence does a different job. A *statement* tells something. A *question* asks something. An *exclamation* shows surprise or strong feeling. A *command* gives an order or direction.

Look at these examples.

The trail on the right is for experts. (statement)

Have you climbed this trail? (question)

That view is just beautiful! (exclamation)

Stand over here. (command)

What punctuation marks are used with the examples?

Some commands also show strong feeling. In this way, a command can be like an exclamation.

See how these commands are different.

Hold onto the railing. (command)

Don't touch that switch! (command)

REMINDERS

1. Use (.) with statements.
2. Use (?) with questions.
3. Use (!) with exclamations.
4. Use (.) or (!) with commands.

PRACTICE

A. (Oral) Tell what kind of sentence each of these is. Use the Reminders for help.

> **Example:** Find out more about Johnny Appleseed.
> **command**

1. Who planted apple trees over the country?
2. John Chapman was nicknamed Johnny Appleseed.
3. He walked from Massachusetts to Ohio.
4. He had a sack of apple seeds on his back.
5. Think of all the trees he planted!
6. Where did he get the seeds?
7. Why did he plant apple trees?

B. (Written) Write each group of words as a sentence. Add a capital letter. Add the correct punctuation mark.

> **Example:** what kind of apple do you like best
> **What kind of apple do you like best?**

1. apples grow ripe in the fall
2. they fall to the ground when they are ripe
3. have you ever gone apple picking
4. is it cheaper to pick your own apples
5. pick up the apples on the ground
6. we filled a basket with apples
7. be careful on the ladder
8. did you pick more apples
9. our apples are sweet

APPLY

Write four sentences about your favorite fruit. Use all four types of sentences. Label them.

Simple and Complete Subjects

> The *subject* of a sentence tells **whom or what the sentence is about.**
>
> "The seed grew." What grew? The seed did.

Every sentence must have a subject. The *subject* tells whom or what the sentence is about. The subject can be one word or a group of words.

Look at these sentences.

> The **bread**|is homemade.
> Fresh wheat **bread**|is delicious.
> **Bread** from the oven|is warm and tasty.

The *simple subject* is the main word in the subject part of each sentence. The word *bread* is the simple subject in each sentence.

The *complete subject* includes all the words that tell about the bread. Look back at each sentence. *The bread* is the complete subject in the first sentence. Name the complete subject in each of the next two sentences.

Now look at these sentences.

> Plums on the tree are sweet if ripe.
> A plum seed forms in a pit.
> The hard pit covers the seed.
> The seed inside the pit is soft.

Name the simple and complete subjects in each.

PRACTICE

A. (Written) Write each sentence. Underline the complete subject. Circle the simple subject.

Example: Flour(mills)grind the grain.

1. Tiny seeds are planted in the spring.
2. Rain in the spring helps the seeds grow.
3. Wheat fields in the Midwest stretch for miles.
4. The wheat fields are like "waves of grain."
5. The grain is the top part of the wheat.
6. Machines are used to cut the ripe wheat.
7. The machines cut the grain from the wheat.
8. The golden grain is stored in a grain elevator.

Bread

simple subject

B. (Written) Write a complete subject for each sentence.

Example: _____ eats corn.
      My family

9. _____ grows quickly.
10. _____ need water and sunlight to grow.
11. _____ are planted in the spring.
12. _____ tastes best right from the garden.
13. _____ tastes good cooked.
14. _____ is a breakfast cereal made from corn.
15. _____ is a good snack to make at home.
16. _____ eat corn for dinner.

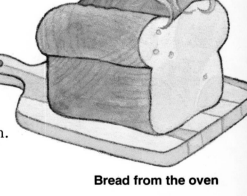

Bread from the oven

complete subject

APPLY

Write three sentences about plants you can grow in a garden. Underline the complete subjects. Circle the simple subjects.

Simple and Complete Predicates

> **The *predicate* of a sentence tells what the subject does, is, or has.**
>
> "Seals swim with ease." What do seals do? They swim with ease.

A sentence must have more than a subject. It must have a predicate, too. The *predicate* tells something about the subject. It tells what the subject does, is, or has. The predicate can be one word or a group of words.

Look at these sentences.

> The seal|**barks.**
> The seal|**is a good diver.**
> The seal|**has a thick coat of fur.**

What does the seal do? The first predicate is *barks*. It tells what the seal does. The next predicate tells what the seal *is*. The third tells what the seal *has*.

Now find the predicate in these sentences.

> The people|fish in the pond.
> The dogs|bark loudly at the geese.

In the first predicate, the main word is *fish*. In the second predicate, the main word is *bark*. These are called the *simple predicates*.

Look at the words *in the pond* and *loudly at the geese*. These words tell more about the simple predicates. Taken

all together, *fish in the pond* and *bark loudly at the geese*
form the *complete predicates.*

PRACTICE

A. (Written) Write each sentence. Underline the complete
predicate. Circle the simple predicate.

Example: Many creatures (live) in the Arctic.

1. Arctic summers are very short.
2. Seals and bears live well in the Arctic winter.
3. Thick fur protects the seals.
4. The polar bears hunt for seals to eat.
5. Some bears fish through holes in the ice.
6. They wait for a seal or fish.
7. Young bears learn from their mothers.
8. The mother bears help their cubs.

B. (Written) Write a complete predicate for each
sentence.

Example: The long winters _____ .
        are very cold

8. Noisy seals _____ .
9. Dogs by the sled _____ .
10. Alaskan homes _____ .
11. The fat walrus _____ .
12. Ice in the ocean _____ .
13. Warm clothing _____ .
14. Heavy snows _____ .
15. Friendly people _____ .

APPLY

Write three sentences about winter where you live. Tell
what you like about it. Then underline the complete
predicates. Circle the simple predicates.

Review the Basics I

A. Sentences

Write *sentence* or *fragment* for each group of words. *(pages 10–11)*

1. Railroad tracks stretch across the country.
2. Carry people to many places.
3. Things from here to there.
4. The caboose is the last car on the train.
5. A conductor checks your ticket.
6. The train at the railroad station.
7. Some people ride trains to work each day.
8. The passenger near the window.
9. Called out the name of the next stop.
10. A conductor helped them off the train.
11. Smiling people.
12. The ride was smooth.

B. Kinds of Sentences

Write each group of words as a sentence. Add a capital letter. Each group needs a correct punctuation mark. *(pages 12–13)*

1. have you ever been on a raft
2. some rivers have raft rides
3. put on your life jacket
4. the water is too cold for swimming
5. watch out for the rocks
6. melted snow runs down the mountain
7. have you seen a picture of the falls
8. don't rock the raft
9. use your oars to move the raft

C. Simple and Complete Subjects

Write each sentence. Underline the complete subject. Circle the simple subject. *(pages 14–15)*

1. Special plants grow in the hot desert.
2. A cactus keeps water in.
3. The roots of the plant take in water.
4. Spring rain makes desert flowers bloom.
5. Very little rain falls in the desert.
6. Nights in the desert are very cold.
7. The small animals need little water.
8. Some deserts are in the Southwest.
9. The daytime temperature is very high.
10. Some people travel at night.

D. Simple and Complete Predicates

Write each sentence. Underline the complete predicate. Circle the simple predicate. *(pages 16–17)*

1. Coyotes howled at night.
2. Stars in the night sky sparkled.
3. The tired cowboys sat near the campfire.
4. The youngest cowboy sang softly.
5. He sang songs of the Old West.
6. Cattle along the trail listened to the songs.
7. The songs helped the herd stay calm.
8. The herd stopped for water.
9. Cowboys moved the cattle slowly.
10. The herd moved to the train.
11. The tracks stretched for miles.
12. A pale moon made no shadows.

Sentences in a Paragraph

You have learned that words must be in the right order for a sentence to make sense. In the same way, sentences must be in the right order for a paragraph to make sense.

A *paragraph* is a group of sentences about one idea. All the sentences tell about that one idea. All four kinds of sentences can appear in a paragraph.

Paragraphs have a special form. They make a page easier to read. The first line of a paragraph is set in from the left margin. This is called *indenting.* An indented sentence is easy to find. It tells where a paragraph begins.

Read this paragraph.

> We get wool from sheep. Wool is used to make clothes and blankets. After the winter, the wool is cut from the sheep. Does it hurt? No, don't worry! This does not hurt the sheep. The wool soon grows back.

Each sentence is a complete thought. See how the order of the sentences helps make the meaning clear.

PRACTICE/APPLY

A. **(Oral)** Read the next two paragraphs. The first one is correct. Find the six errors in the second one.

> A legend says that on February 2 the groundhog comes out of its hole. If it sees its shadow, it goes back to sleep. This means there will be six more weeks of winter. If it does not see its shadow, it stays out. This means that spring will come soon.

A legend says that on February 2. The groundhog comes out of its hole. If it sees its shadow, it goes back to sleep? This means there will be six more weeks of winter. If it does not see its shadow. It stays out. This means that spring will come soon.

B. (Written) Rewrite this paragraph. Fix the two sentence fragments.

Cows give us milk. We use milk as a drink. And for butter and cheese. Cows on a dairy farm are milked by machine! A cow must be milked. Twice a day. Otherwise, it stops giving milk.

Sentence Punctuation and Capitalization

The first word of any sentence must start with a capital letter. A sentence must end with a period, a question mark, or an exclamation mark. If there were no punctuation marks, sentences would just run together.

Read this paragraph.

> my family chops wood for our stove in the fall we stack the wood in the winter we burn the wood to keep us warm

Did you get confused? What would help you?

Now read this paragraph.

> My family chops wood for our stove. In the fall, we stack the wood. In the winter, we burn the wood to keep us warm.

Now read each paragraph out loud. Notice how different they sound. In the first one, you cannot easily tell which words belong together. What makes the second paragraph so much easier to read?

REMINDERS

1. Use (.) with statements.
2. Use (?) with questions.
3. Use (!) with exclamations.
4. Use (.) or (!) with commands.

PRACTICE

A. (Written) Make two sentences from each group of words. Add capital letters and punctuation marks.

> **Example:** I have an energy project it shows ways to heat homes
> **I have an energy project. It shows ways to heat homes.**

1. the sun heats some homes does it heat yours
2. other homes use oil oil comes from the ground
3. some homes use coal instead coal comes from the ground
4. do you use wood wood is burned in stoves
5. some homes use the wind they have windmills
6. what fuel heats your home why should we save fuel

B. (Written) Rewrite this paragraph. There are five sentences in it. Use capital letters and punctuation marks. Be sure to indent the first line.

my house is snug and warm in the winter is yours we keep all the windows shut tight no wind can come in the cracks we make sure the heat stays in the house.

APPLY

Write three sentences about ways to keep warm when the weather is cold. Use capital letters and punctuation marks correctly.

Words That Organize

You have studied word order in sentences. You have learned to use punctuation marks and capital letters, too. You have learned to keep the meaning clear in all sentences.

Clear meaning is important in paragraphs, too. Certain kinds of words help to keep the meaning clear. They organize thoughts. They help to keep sentences in order. They show the sequence of what happened.

Look for the words that organize this paragraph.

> I like to make fruit shakes. **First** I put bits of fruit into the blender. **Then** I add a cup of milk. **Last** I press the middle button on the blender. A fruit shake is delicious!

Organizing words hold the thoughts together. They keep the sentences in order. Each thought follows the one before. The thoughts are in sequence. Their meaning is clear.

Words that organize do not have to come at the beginning of sentences. Sometimes they are used within sentences.

Where are the organizing words here?

> Cut up the fruit before you make the shake.
> Clean up the mess around the blender.

These words are important. The meaning will change if the organizing word is changed. Replace *before* with *after*. How is the sentence different? How does the meaning change?

PRACTICE

A. **(Oral)** Complete each sentence with an organizing word. Use the Word Bank.

Here's how to give a dog a bath.

1. _____ catch the dog and hose it down with water.
2. _____ scrub the dog with soap.
3. _____ rinse off the soap with more water.
4. _____ run away before the dog shakes water all over you!

B. **(Written)** Rewrite the paragraph. Add organizing words for the blanks. Use the picture and the Word Bank if you need help.

I always set the table _____ dinner. _____ I put down the placemats. _____ I put the plates in the _____ of the placemats. _____ I put napkins and forks on the _____ of the plates. _____ I put knives and spoons on the _____ of the plates.

APPLY

Write four sentences about a game you like to play. Use organizing words.

Directions

Think how often you use directions. You tell people how to get from one place to another. You tell people how to make things. If you cook, you follow recipes. You follow directions if you make model airplanes or cars.

To make sense, directions need to be in order. Organizing words help, too.

Read these directions.

To make scrambled eggs, **first** crack the eggs and put them in a bowl. **Next** add one tablespoon of milk for each egg. **Then** beat the eggs. **Finally** pour the eggs and milk into a frying pan.

What can happen if the directions are out of order? If the eggs are in the pan, you may forget to beat them.

Good directions give all the steps in the correct order. Good directions are clear and easy to understand. The next two sets of directions are from the map.

Why is the first set of directions easier to follow?

Turn right at the first set of lights. Walk two blocks. Next take the left at the traffic lights. Then turn right onto Maple Street. The library is on the left.

Go up to the lights and turn right. Follow the road a little way past the curves to the next set of lights. Go through the lights. Go all the way down the street, after you take the first left at the corner. Turn right. The library is on the left.

PRACTICE

A. (Oral) Study the street map. The footprints show how to get from the school to the library. The directions shown below are in the wrong order. Give them in the correct order. Add an organizing word to each sentence.

1. Walk two blocks to Maple Street.
2. Turn right onto Maple Street.
3. Walk north on Elm Street for two blocks.
4. Turn left onto Pine Street.
5. The library is on the left.

B. (Written) Use the map to write directions telling how to get from the library to the school. Be sure to use organizing words.

APPLY

Write directions telling how to go from your home to a friend's home. Remember to use organizing words.

Compound Subjects

> **A *compound subject* has two or more simple subjects.**
>
> Seeds and nuts are food.

You have studied simple and complete subjects. You know that the subject of a sentence tells whom or what the sentence is about.

Name the subjects in these sentences.

Chipmunks|eat seeds.   Red squirrels|eat seeds.

A sentence may have more than one subject. Often the subjects are joined by the word *and.* The subjects share the same predicate.

Look at this sentence.

Chipmunks and red squirrels eat seeds.

The two subjects are *chipmunks* and *red squirrels.* They share the predicate *eat seeds.* Two subjects with the same predicate are called a *compound subject.*

Combine these sentences. Use a compound subject.

Birds eat nuts. Squirrels eat nuts.

A compound subject may have more than two subjects. Put commas after the first and second subjects.

Look how commas are used here.

Chipmunks, red squirrels, and rabbits eat seeds.

PRACTICE

A. (Oral) Name each compound subject.

> **Example:** Maine and Oregon have large forests.
> **Maine and Oregon**

1. Pines, fir trees, and spruce trees grow there.
2. Pines and fir trees are softwood trees.
3. Squirrels, owls, and raccoons live in the trees.
4. Chipmunks and rabbits live on the ground.
5. Ducks, geese, and beavers have water homes.
6. Deer, moose, and bears use the forests, too.
7. People and animals need the forests.

B. (Written) Combine each pair of sentences. Write one sentence with a compound subject.

> **Example:** Campers use the forests. Hikers use the forests.
> **Campers and hikers use the forests.**

1. Pine seeds and spruce seeds grow in cones. Fir seeds grow in cones.
2. Moose live in forests. Deer live in forests.
3. Lumberjacks work in forests. Rangers work in forests.
4. Charcoal is made from wood. Paper is made from wood.
5. Fires kill trees. Diseases kill trees.
6. Scouts learn to save trees. Students learn to save trees.
7. Fire fighters help to put out fires. Foresters and scouts help to put out fires.

APPLY

Write three sentences of your own. Tell what you might see in a forest. Use compound subjects in your sentences. Underline them.

Compound Predicates

> **A *compound predicate* has two simple predicates.**
>
> Some cars | are small. Some cars | save gas.
> Some cars | are small and save gas.

Two sentences that tell about the same thought can often be combined. Both sentences should have the same subject. The new sentence will have one subject and two predicates joined by the word *and*.

See how these sentences are joined.

Bus drivers | **know their routes**.
Bus drivers | **drive safely**.
Bus drivers | **know their routes and drive safely**.

In the new sentence, the predicates share the same subject. Two predicates with the same subject are called a *compound predicate*. The new sentence is more interesting. It tells more about the subject. In the next example, the subject is *This engine*.

What is the compound predicate?

This engine carries a crew and pulls the train.

Not all sentences can be joined this way. When the ideas are quite different, they should not be joined.

Should these sentences be joined?

Pilots study for years. Bus drivers smile often.

The first sentence is about pilots. The second one is about bus drivers. The ideas in each one are different. The sentences should not be joined.

PRACTICE

(Written) Join each pair of short sentences. Write the new one.

Example: Some buses have soft seats. Some buses are comfortable.
Some buses have soft seats and are comfortable.

1. Bus travel is fun. Bus travel shows you the country.
2. The school bus stops near my home. The school bus carries me to school.
3. City buses bring people to work. City buses carry people back home again.
4. A bus runs at certain times. A bus follows a special route.
5. Bus drivers check the tickets. Bus drivers help the passengers.
6. Some buses give tours. Some buses carry tourists.
7. Bus stops have signs. Bus stops are easy to find.

APPLY

Join the two pairs of short sentences. Write the new paragraph.

An airport is a great place to visit. Planes take off. Planes land. Control tower staff help. People arrive. People leave. Ticket agents are busy.

Correcting Run-on Sentences

> A *run-on sentence* contains two or more complete thoughts that should not be connected.
>
> Run-on: May is a spring month and roses bloom in summer.
> Corrected: May is a spring month. Roses bloom in summer.

In Lessons 9 and 10, you learned that some short sentences should be joined. A longer sentence can be nicer to listen to. It can be easier to understand. You must be careful, though. Some short sentences should not be joined.

Read this run-on sentence. See how it is fixed.

Run-on: Bear Paw Trail starts at the lake and it is the prettiest trail and the steepest trail.

Corrected: Bear Paw Trail starts at the lake. It is the prettiest trail and the steepest trail.

The run-on sentence above joins two sentences that have different thoughts. One thought tells where the trail starts. The other thought tells what the trail is like (pretty and steep). These two thoughts should not be joined.

How would you fix this run-on sentence?

Run-on: The Rockies are steep and we drove through sixteen states last June.

Always read a sentence after you write it. Check to be sure that it makes sense. Check that it says what you meant to say. Check for run-on sentences.

PRACTICE

(Oral) Fix each run-on sentence. There are three of them.

1. Mountains cover about one-fifth of all land and some mountains have train tunnels.
2. Most climbers are experts for mountain climbing takes skill.
3. Mountain climbers try to climb the highest peaks. The trails are marked on small mountains.
4. Mountain climbers carry ropes and the rock is slippery.
5. Beginners climb easy trails and some people see deer and moose in the mountains.

APPLY

This paragraph contains two run-on sentences. Rewrite the paragraph. You will have six sentences.

The Rocky Mountains are in eight states and the mountains cover one-fourth of America and the Rockies have snow at the top and the snow melts to make rivers. Parts of the Rockies get rain and the high peaks are cool in summer and it is very cold in the winter.

Yes-No and WH-Questions

> **A Yes-No question needs a yes or no answer. A WH-question asks who, what, when, where, why, or how.**
>
> Yes-No question: Is Jake a good player? (Yes.)
> WH-question: Who plays first base? (Jake plays first base.)

There are two kinds of questions. One is a Yes-No question. It needs only a *yes* or *no* answer. When you answer a Yes-No question, you can also write the question as part of the answer. Then you must put a comma after *yes* or *no*.

Both answers are correct.

> **Question:** Do you like to exercise?
> **Answer:** Yes.
>
> Or: Yes, I like to exercise to feel healthy.

The other kind of question starts with a WH-word. There are six WH-words. They are *who, what, when, where, why,* and *how.* The words *yes* and *no* do not answer WH-questions.

Look at these WH-questions and answers.

> **Who** helps you exercise? A gym teacher helps me.
> **What** kind of exercise do you do? I do pushups.
> **When** do you exercise? I exercise every day.
> **Where** do you exercise? I exercise at home.
> **Why** do you exercise? I exercise to stay healthy.
> **How** long do you exercise? I exercise for thirty minutes a day.

PRACTICE

A. (Oral) Tell whether the sentence is a WH-question or a Yes-No question.

   Example: When should you brush your teeth?
      WH-question

1. Who can help you exercise?
2. Can you touch your toes?
3. What is a jumping jack?
4. Where is the school gym?
5. Is milk good to drink?
6. Do you eat the right foods?

B. (Written) Write the correct answer for each question.

   Example: Can you catch a ball?
      It's easy.   Yes.
      Yes.

1. Where is your glove?
   I have it in my gym bag.   Yes, I just got a new one.
2. Who is up at bat next?
   I can't wait!   I am up next.
3. Did you hit a home run?
   I tried.   No, I struck out.
4. How far can you hit the ball?
   I can hit the ball past first base.   Yes, I can hit the ball.
5. What position do you play?
   Yes.   I play first base and shortstop.
6. Do you like to play ball?
   Hockey is my favorite sport.   Yes, I like to play ball.

APPLY

Pretend you want to learn about a sport. Write four questions about the game or the skills needed. Label the questions *WH* or *Yes-No*. Then write the answers.

Review the Basics II

A. Compound Subjects
Join each pair of sentences. Use a compound subject. *(pages 28–29)*

1. Schools have libraries.
   Towns have libraries.
2. Magazines are kept in libraries.
   Newspapers are kept in libraries.
3. Children use libraries.
   Adults use libraries.
4. Librarians help you find books.
   Library assistants help you find books.
5. Authors are listed in the card catalog.
   Book titles are listed in the card catalog.
6. The title is on the book.
   The author's name is on the book.

B. Compound Predicates
Join each pair of short sentences. Write the new one. *(pages 30–31)*

1. Cotton comes from a plant.
   Cotton grows into soft bolls.
2. Seeds grow in the cotton bolls.
   Seeds have to be picked out.
3. Cloth is made from cotton.
   Cloth is used for clothes.
4. Cotton needs sun.
   Cotton grows in warm climates.
5. Cotton is planted in the spring.
   Cotton is picked at the end of the summer.
6. Cotton mills clean the cotton.
   Cotton mills spin the fibers.

C. Correcting Run-on Sentences

Fix each run-on sentence. *(pages 32–33)*

1. Camping is popular and many people camp in national parks every year.
2. Campers have to bring enough food and equipment and the right equipment is important.
3. The right clothing is important and long pants and boots should always be worn.
4. Campers build fires for cooking and a fire must be put out carefully.
5. Camping is a good way to see plants and animals and campers should avoid poison ivy.
6. Many kinds of trees are in a forest and campers should learn about them.

D. Yes-No and WH-Questions

Write *WH-question* or *Yes-No question* for each sentence. *(pages 34–35)*

1. Where is the Milky Way?
2. Why do we like to look at the stars?
3. Can you find the Big Dipper?
4. Are stars hot?
5. Who uses stars to tell directions?
6. Are stars closer to Earth or to the moon?
7. Are stars really as small as they look?
8. How far away are the stars?
9. What are stars made of?
10. When can we see the stars?

A Paragraph: Topic and Detail Sentences

A *paragraph* is a group of sentences about one main idea. One sentence can tell the main idea. It is called the *topic sentence.* The rest of the sentences tell more about the main idea. They are called *detail sentences.*

Read this paragraph.

> **It is easy to make a stencil painting.** First get a piece of heavy paper. Draw shapes on it, spaced apart. Next cut out the shapes. The paper with the cut-out shapes is the stencil. Put the stencil on a clean piece of paper. Color in the shapes with paint.

The topic sentence is the first sentence in the paragraph. It tells that you will read about making a stencil painting. That is the main idea. The detail sentences tell the steps. In some paragraphs, the detail sentences give examples.

Find the topic and detail sentences.

> People like to know what happens in the world. They read newspapers and magazines to stay up to date. They watch the news on television. They read history books to find out why things happened the way they did.

A paragraph must be about one topic or main idea. All the details must tell about that one topic. The topic sentence is very important. It tells what the paragraph is about. Some details seem to fit with more than one topic.

These detail words fit both topic sentences.

     bus   car   train   airplane

There are many ways to go across the country.

Wheels come in many shapes and sizes.

PRACTICE

A. (Oral) Give a topic sentence for each group of words.

> **Example:** pitcher catcher outfielder manager
> **Members of a baseball team have their own special jobs.**

1. jacket parka sweater coat
2. sheets pillow blanket bedspread
3. crosswalk red light green light
4. cereal juice milk
5. paper pencil pen ruler
6. library card card catalog book

B. (Written) Find the topic sentence. Next find four details that go with it. Write them as a paragraph.

Winter is the time to shovel snow.

In each season there is work to do.

People swim in the summer.

Spring is the time to plant gardens.

Leaves must be raked each fall.

Families go on vacations in the summer.

In summer the lawn must be mowed.

APPLY

Make a list of chores people have at home, such as washing dishes. Then write a topic sentence for the list.

A Whole-Class Paragraph

You know now that a paragraph is made up of a topic and detail sentences. In this lesson, your teacher will help you write a paragraph as a class. You will write about the picture on this page.

Study the picture now.

All the things in the picture can be used in arts-and-crafts projects. You could make a drawing with them. You could press flowers or wax leaves. You could sew a puppet. You will tell about the picture in the topic sentence.

Begin a list of topic sentences with these.

> Hand puppets are easy to make.
> A rainy day is great weather for arts and crafts.

Think of some other topic sentences. Each one should tell about the picture. As a class, choose one topic sentence. Your teacher will write it on the chalkboard.

Now think of details for the topic. Choose three or four from the class list. State those details in sentence form. Your teacher will write them on the board after the topic sentence.

REMINDERS

1. A paragraph is about one main idea.
2. It has a topic sentence.
3. Detail sentences give steps or examples.
4. The first line is indented.

PRACTICE

(Oral) One word in each group is more general than the others. It could be used in a topic sentence. The other words could be used in detail sentences. Name the general word from each group.

Example: shoes clothes jacket pants
  clothes

1. meat groceries grapes corn
2. pitcher catcher team outfielder
3. sewing needle thread cloth
4. washing floors mop bucket soap
5. weeding planting watering gardening
6. ice snow cold winds winter
7. bank dollar penny dime

APPLY

From the Practice, write a topic sentence for the general word. Write three detail sentences for the other words.

A Paragraph of Directions: Plan, Write, Edit

By now, you have learned a lot about paragraphs. You are ready to write one on your own. Writing has three parts. The first part is to plan what you want to write. The second part is to write it. The last part is to edit what you wrote, to correct mistakes.

PLAN

You will write a paragraph that tells how to get from one place to another. The first step in planning is to stop and think.

Study the map for a few minutes.

You can write how to get from the school to the library. You can write how to go from the theater to the police station. Decide which places you will use.

Now make a list of all the steps you need to use in your directions. You do not need to use sentences in this list. Just list the names of streets and any special markers along the route, such as a street light.

Read your list out loud as you find the parts on the map. Are the steps in the right order? Pretend that your reader will not see the map. Be sure that your list includes all the names and markers your reader will need.

WRITE

Begin with a sentence that tells where the directions start and end.

Look at this example.

>   You will go from the school to the library.

Next look over your list of steps. Turn the steps into sentences. Use organizing words from the Word Bank.

Be sure to tell each step one at a time. Tell your reader where to turn. Use the names of streets. Point out special markers. Tell things to look for on the way. Your directions should be simple and complete.

WORD BANK

first
second
next
last
in front of
across from
after
before
behind
right
left
turn
cross
pass

EDIT

Now that you have written your paragraph, you need to edit it. This part is as important as the first two parts. Now you should check for mistakes. Editing shows that you care about what you have written.

When you edit, mark where you need corrections. Use the editing marks on page 44.

¶ You will go from the ~~libery~~ *library* to the theater. (Turn right at the bakery.) First, cross at the traffic lights and turn west on Pine Street. Go past the corner store. ✗Walk two blocks and then take the second left at South Street. Walk one block to the movie theater. The theater ∧is on the left.

Now read your own paragraph. Pretend that this is the first time you are reading the directions. Do they seem to make sense? Look back at the map to check each step.

✔ Are any words missing?

✔ Are the detail sentences in order?

Read your paragraph again now to check its form.

✔ Is the first line indented?

✔ Does each sentence begin with a capital letter and end with the right punctuation mark?

✔ Are all words spelled correctly?

Finally copy your paragraph in your best handwriting.

Your teacher may also hand out an *Editing Checklist.* Use it to check all the writing you do. Some items on that list may not make sense yet. You will understand them all as you go further in this book.

16 COMMUNICATING

Giving Oral Directions

Have you asked people for directions? Did they give you good ones, or did you get confused? Clear directions tell what you need to know. They leave out nothing important. They are easy to follow.

When you give someone directions, put yourself in that person's place. He or she may not know the area as well as you do. Always try to give street names. Tell markers or signs to look for. Also, just like written directions, oral directions must be in order.

When you give oral directions, speak clearly and slowly. If the person does not seem to understand what you said, repeat it. Add details that might help.

Follow the Guidelines.

GUIDELINES

1. Speak clearly.
2. Tell the steps one at a time.
3. Tell the steps in order.
4. Make sure the listener understands.

PRACTICE/APPLY

Think of how to get from your classroom to some other place in the school. Tell the directions to a classmate. Do not tell where the directions lead. When you are done ask, "Where are you?" Be sure to follow the Guidelines. If you do, your friend should be able to name the place.

Unit 1 Test

A. Sentences

Write *sentence* or *fragment* for each group of words. *(pages 10–11)*

1. Maria Tallchief was born in Oklahoma.
2. Called her Betty Marie.
3. Her father was an Osage.
4. Saw the dancing of the Osage tribe.
5. Betty Marie studied piano and dancing.
6. She went to New York.
7. Studied hard with a dance company.
8. One of the best dancers in the world.
9. She is well known.
10. Do you like ballet?

B. Kinds of Sentences

Write each group of words as a sentence. Add a capital letter. Add the correct punctuation mark. *(pages 12–13)*

1. do you write letters to friends
2. mail moves fast today
3. letters traveled slowly in earlier times
4. today letters take less time
5. how do letters get from place to place
6. list some ways that letters travel
7. are trucks, trains, and airplanes on your list
8. good for you
9. you named them all
10. that job was not easy
11. at first traders carried mail
12. how much did a stamp cost then

C. Subjects and Predicates

Write each sentence. Underline the complete subject.
Circle the simple subject. *(pages 14–15)*

1. Some small animals are called amphibians.
2. Two amphibians are the toad and the frog.
3. Their lives are spent in water and on land.
4. The meaning of amphibian comes from this fact.
5. These two animals are different in some ways.

Write each sentence. Underline the complete predicate.
Circle the simple predicate. *(pages 16–17)*

6. A frog's skin is smooth and moist.
7. Toads have bumps on their skins.
8. The bumps hold a bad-tasting liquid.
9. This liquid saves toads from danger.
10. Hungry animals leave toads alone.

D. Correcting Run-on Sentences

Fix each of these run-on sentences. *(pages 32–33)*

1. My uncle was born in Italy in 1893 and he was one of the most famous baseball players of all time.
2. In 1913 Uncle Curly played in New York and he stayed there for seventeen years.
3. Curly played in St. Louis and he traveled all over this country.

E. Writing

Look at the map on page 42. Choose a route that you have not yet written about. Write a paragraph of directions. Be sure you have a topic sentence. Check that your directions are complete and in the right order. *(pages 42–44)*

Writing on the Job

Angel Sanchez owns a small toy store. Each month he counts the games and toys in his store. He starts at the top shelf and works toward the bottom shelf.

He fills in an inventory form. This form lists everything on the shelves. It tells how many of each thing there is. It also shows where each thing is. By comparing the numbers on the list, Angel can tell what he has sold.

The numbers are details. They help Angel. They tell him what to buy for next month. They also tell him what not to buy. Read the inventory form. Look for the details.

Which toy was the best seller?
Why will Angel order more baseballs?
Why will Angel put the Solar Space Suits on sale?

Write Away!

Pretend you own a store. Think of the kind of store you would like to own. Think about what you would sell.

Write an inventory list of the things you would sell. Write how many of each thing you have. Tell on which shelf you keep each thing. Here are some ideas to help you.

A Pet Supply Store
20 rubber mice
15 fish tanks
6 dog beds

A Joke Store
20 leaking cups
5 squirting pens
10 sets of chattering teeth

June / July

		June 30	July 31
top shelf	Ronny Robots	20	14
top shelf	Wild Wands	16	9
top shelf	talking dolls	5	4
middle shelf	baseball bats	13	8
middle shelf	baseballs	22	9
middle shelf	roller skates	7 pairs	3 pairs
bottom shelf	Grape Gorilla Games	17 sets	12 sets
bottom shelf	Solar Space Suits	82	82
bottom shelf	Mummy Masks	12	8

Remember to order baseballs!
Put Solar Space Suits on sale next week!

You Can't Get Rags from Ragweed

If you're a true believer,
I'll warn you in advance:
You can't get rags from Ragweed
Or milk from Milkweed plants.

You can't use Lady's Slippers
For shoes or dancing pumps,
And—as for Johnny-jump-ups—
There isn't one that jumps.

Such names of weeds and blossoms
Are harmless, I expect,
But since they're only pretty
And not a bit correct. . .

Don't ever set your wristwatch
When Four o'Clocks say four
Or think that Tiger Lilies
Will rush at you and roar.

And never wait for Bluebells
To ring outside your gate,
For—if you do—you're likely
To have a long, long wait.

—*Kaye Starbird*

50

2

Writing
Messages

SKILLS TO BUILD ON

Singular and Plural Nouns
Common and Proper Nouns
Possessive Nouns
Abbreviations

PRACTICAL APPLICATIONS

Writing a Letter
Taking Messages

Nouns

> **A *noun* is a word that names a person, place, or thing.**
>
> The <u>singer</u> on the <u>stage</u> held a <u>microphone</u>.

Different people have different jobs. Words have different jobs, too. The job of a noun is to name. *Nouns* name people, places, and things.

Study the chart.

Nouns

People	Places	Things
teacher	airport	tree
firefighter	city	cloud
woman	kitchen	fog
father	yard	raccoon
dentist	farm	truck
student	desert	money

Look around you. Make a list of things that you see. The words on your list are nouns. Which nouns name people? Which name places? Which name things?

Which nouns name people? places? things?

A **cowhand** works the **cattle** on a **ranch.**
A **pilot** flies an **airplane** through the **sky.**
A **clown** does **tricks** at the **circus.**

PRACTICE

A. (Oral) Name the nouns in each sentence.

> **Example:** A lumberjack cuts down a tree.
> **lumberjack, tree**

1. A truck takes the tree to a sawmill.
2. Workers at the sawmill cut the tree into boards.
3. The leftover wood is ground into pulp.
4. The pulp is made into paper.
5. The paper may be taken to a printer.
6. The printer prints the news on the paper.
7. Then the newspapers are taken to newstands.
8. Many people buy the newspapers.
9. People like to read the news daily.

B. (Written) Make three columns labeled *People, Places,* and *Things.* Write each noun in the correct column. Four nouns name people. Four nouns name places. Eight nouns name things.

Example:	**People**	**Places**	**Things**	
	dentist	town	balloon	
farmer	zoo		oven	city
tools	brush		painter	saw
corn	country		tractor	baker
bakery	doctor		bread	paint

APPLY

Think of a job you would like to have. Write three sentences about the job. Underline each noun. Label each noun *person, place,* or *thing.*

Singular and Plural Nouns

> A *singular noun* names one person, place, or thing.
> A *plural noun* names more than one person, place,
> or thing.
>
> <u>Singular:</u> jogger   <u>Plural:</u> joggers

Singular means "one." A singular noun names one
person, place, or thing. *Plural* means "more than one." A
plural noun names more than one person, place, or thing.

Find the nouns in these sentences.

What is your number in the race?
Each runner starts slowly.
Cameras clicked and lights flashed.
The cheers filled the streets.

Which nouns are singular? Which are plural? Form the
plurals of most nouns by adding -*s.*

Look at these examples.

sock→socks   number→numbers
shoe→shoes   runner→runners

PRACTICE

A. (Oral) Name *singular* or *plural* for each underlined noun.

> **Example:** The <u>circus</u> is in town.
> **circus—singular**

1. The life of a circus <u>clown</u> is not all fun.
2. <u>Clowns</u> are hard workers.
3. Most clowns go to a <u>school</u> for clowns.
4. The clowns plan their <u>acts</u>.
5. <u>Animals</u> join the act, too.
6. Some clowns make their own <u>costumes</u>.
7. They work hard to plan new <u>tricks</u>.
8. Some become famous <u>stars</u>.

B. (Written) Use the noun at the end of each sentence to fill in the blank. Write a singular noun if the blank is marked *S*. Write a plural noun if the blank is marked *P*.

> **Example:** A zoo needs many different <u>P</u>. (helper)
> **helpers**

1. The <u>S</u> runs the zoo. (director)
2. You pay admission to a <u>S</u>. (clerk)
3. Guides may take <u>P</u> around. (visitor)
4. Zoo keepers clean and feed the <u>P</u>. (animal)
5. A <u>S</u> keeps the animals healthy. (doctor)
6. Nursery <u>P</u> care for small animals. (worker)
7. College <u>P</u> may study the animals. (student)
8. One baby <u>S</u> grew two inches last month. (chimp)

APPLY

Write three sentences about a large animal. Circle the plural nouns. Draw a line under each singular noun.

More Plural Nouns

> **For some singular nouns, you must do more than add -s to form the plural.**
>
> wish→wishes   loaf→loaves
> ruby→rubies   child→children

You have studied singular nouns that need an -s to be plural. For some nouns you must do more than add -s. For some nouns you must add -es. For other nouns you must change or drop letters in the word. For words like *beach, puppy, knife,* and *woman* you must do more than add -s. See how the plurals of some nouns are formed.

Look at the chart.

Forming Plural Nouns

Some nouns end with *ch, sh, ss, zz, x,* or *s*. Add *-es*.	peach→peaches box→boxes buzz→buzzes glass→glasses fish→fishes bus→buses
Some nouns end with a consonant letter and *y*. Change the *y* to *i* and add *-es*.	bakery→bakeries fly→flies cherry→cherries lady→ladies daisy→daisies berry→berries
Some nouns end in *f* or *fe*. Change the *f* or *fe* to *ve* and add *-s*. Or simply add *-s*.	leaf→leaves cliff→cliffs roof→roofs calf→calves life→lives chief→chiefs
Some special nouns change their forms completely.	man→men goose→geese child→children ox→oxen tooth→teeth mouse→mice

PRACTICE

A. (Oral) Tell whether each noun is *singular* or *plural*.

> **Example:** The beach was crowded with children.
> **beach—singular, children—plural**

1. The men arrived with the box.
2. Gail stands near the edge of the cliffs.
3. A strawberry is larger than a cherry.
4. Our bus left for lunch first.
5. My glasses were lost in the bushes.
6. Daisies have long, pointed leaves.
7. Peaches have fuzz on them.
8. Children have fun at the beach.
9. The dog chased foxes.
10. My tooth is loose.
11. Her geese honk at cars.

B. (Written) Write each singular noun. Then write its plural form.

1. chief	8. dish	15. guess
2. ox	9. branch	16. watch
3. woman	10. child	17. baby
4. knife	11. daisy	18. leaf
5. dress	12. goose	19. half
6. sandwich	13. lady	20. roof
7. bus	14. fox	21. fish

APPLY

Write three sentences using nouns from Practice B. Use one singular noun and one plural noun in each sentence. Underline them.

Common and Proper Nouns

A *common noun* names any person, place, or thing.
A *proper noun* names a particular person, place, or thing.

Common noun: island   Proper noun: Long Island

There are two kinds of nouns, common and proper. A *common noun* names any person, place, or thing. A *proper noun* names a particular person, place, or thing. A proper noun starts with a capital letter. Look at the difference between the two. Study the chart.

Common and Proper Nouns

	Common Nouns	Proper Nouns
People	president aunt judge	President Johnson Aunt Ellen Judge Sandra Day O'Connor
Places	city country state zoo	Washington Canada Texas San Diego Zoo
Things	day month holiday street building	Monday June Labor Day Beacon Street Empire State Building

How are the two lists of nouns different? A common noun, such as *day,* names any day. A proper noun names a special day. *Monday* is a proper noun.

PRACTICE

A. (Oral) Name a proper noun for each common noun.

1. school	**5.** day	**9.** country
2. street	**6.** state	**10.** holiday
3. city	**7.** friend	**11.** month
4. dog	**8.** girl	**12.** boy

B. (Written) Write each sentence correctly. Add capital letters to the proper nouns. Underline the common nouns.

> **Example:** There is one holiday in october.
> **There is one <u>holiday</u> in October.**

1. Our school was closed on columbus day.
2. That day was on a monday in october.
3. Uncle raul took us to a museum.
4. We took a train to new york city.
5. We went to the museum of modern art.
6. We saw paintings by artists from france.
7. One artist was named paul gauguin.
8. He painted scenes of the island of tahiti.
9. Tahiti is in the pacific ocean.

APPLY

Think of a place you would like to visit. Pretend you are at that place with your best friend. Write three sentences about your trip. Use proper nouns.

Empire State Building

Possessive Nouns

> A *possessive noun* shows ownership. An apostrophe
> (') is used to form a possessive noun.
>
> one cat—the cat's tail   two dogs—the dogs' ears

Possession means that a person or thing has or owns
something. Something belongs to someone. Words can show
ownership in several ways.

Look at these sentences.

This is the tractor **that belongs to the farmer.**
This is the tractor **of the farmer.**
This is **the farmer's** tractor.

Each sentence gives the same message. Which sentence
seems easiest to say? Which one is shortest?

The word *farmer's* takes the place of more than one
word. *Farmer's* is a possessive noun. A *possessive noun* lets
you say the same thing in a short, easy way. You need to
learn three rules to spell possessive nouns. Study the chart.

Forming Possessive Nouns

For a singular noun, add an apostrophe and *s* (*'s*).	For a plural noun that ends in *s*, add only an apostrophe (').	For a plural noun that does not end in *s*, add an apostrophe and *s* (*'s*).
teacher→teacher's Chris→Chris's	cooks→cooks' Bells→Bells'	women→women's mice→mice's

PRACTICE

A. (Written) Give the same message. Use a possessive noun.

> **Example:** the hat <u>that belongs to the ranger</u>
> **the ranger's hat**

1. the chair <u>of a dentist</u>
2. the ship <u>of the sailors</u>
3. the nurse <u>of Dr. Levy</u>
4. the trainer <u>of the dogs</u>
5. the helmet <u>that belongs to a worker</u>
6. the meal <u>of the chef</u>
7. the books <u>that belong to Miguel</u>
8. the pen <u>that belongs to a writer</u>

B. (Written) Add an apostrophe to each group of words.

> **Example:** the riders horse
> **the rider's horse**

9. a doctors chart
10. two cooks kitchens
11. one cats whiskers
12. the childrens teacher
13. Brendas job
14. one pilots plane
15. the captains ship
16. three teachers books
17. the Browns house
18. the students desk

APPLY

Three friends own funny masks. In three sentences, tell about the masks. Use possessive nouns. Underline them.

Review the Basics I

A. Nouns
Write the nouns in each sentence. *(pages 52–53)*

1. Reference books are helpful.
2. A dictionary has lists of words.
3. The words are spelled for us.
4. An atlas has maps in it.
5. An atlas shows rivers and mountains.
6. Special maps tell about rain and crops.
7. Some books have many volumes.
8. These books are encyclopedias.

B. Singular and Plural Nouns
Use the noun at the end of each sentence to fill in the blank. Write a singular noun if the blank is marked S. Write a plural noun if the blank is marked P. *(pages 54–55)*

1. A _S_ shows facts. (graph)
2. There are different kinds of _P_ . (graph)
3. A bar graph uses _P_ of different lengths. (bar)
4. It is easy to compare _P_ on a bar graph. (thing)
5. On a line graph, a _S_ is drawn from point to point. (line)
6. A circle graph is marked in pie-shaped _P_ . (piece)
7. Each piece looks like a _S_ of pie. (slice)

C. More Plural Nouns
Write each singular noun. Then write its plural form. *(pages 56–57)*

1. calf
2. crash
3. box
4. woman
5. bakery
6. child
7. class
8. leaf

D. Common and Proper Nouns

Write each sentence correctly. Add capital letters to the proper nouns. Underline the common nouns. *(pages 58–59)*

1. maria lives in a city called el paso.
2. El paso is in texas.
3. Her house is on olvera street.
4. maria has a little dog named paco.
5. maria goes to the brook school.
6. el paso is in the united states near mexico.
7. A river named the rio grande forms the border.
8. Sometimes maria's family goes shopping in mexico.
9. A bus takes them to the city of juarez.
10. juarez is just a few miles from el paso.

E. Possessive Nouns

Change each group of words. Use a possessive noun to give the same message. *(pages 60–61)*

1. the tunnel of the ants
2. the roar that belongs to a lion
3. the cave of two bears
4. the bed of the dog
5. the dens of the lions
6. the nest of a bird
7. the home of the people
8. the hive that belongs to the bees
9. the web of a spider
10. the holes of the foxes
11. the collar of the cat
12. the pet that belongs to a neighbor

Nouns in a Paragraph

You have learned that nouns name people, places, and things. Nouns can be singular or plural. They can be common or proper. You have also seen that nouns can show possession. A noun may do more than one job at a time.

Look at this paragraph.

A **doctor** may work in a **hospital.** Some **doctors** have their own **offices.** My **doctor's office** is in the **County Medical Center.** Many other **doctors' offices** are in the same **building.**

Each word in dark print above is a noun. The word *doctor's* is a possessive noun. It is also singular. How is the word *doctors'* different?

Which nouns name places? Which places are singular? The word *offices* names a place. It is a common noun. Is there a proper noun that tells a place? These nouns do more than one job at a time.

PRACTICE/APPLY

A. (Written) Make three columns on your paper. Label them *People, Places, Things*. Write each noun from the next paragraph below the correct label. Ten nouns name people. Two name places. Four name things.

    José Ruiz and Ana Ruiz are ranchers. The Ruizes raise cattle on their ranch. Many cowhands care for the Ruizes' cattle. A cowhand spends long days out on the range. A cowhand's job is not easy. The Ruizes pay their workers well.

B. (Written) Now make four columns on your paper. Mark them *Singular, Plural, Common, Proper*. Each noun from the paragraph above fits in two of the columns. Write each noun in the two correct columns.

Abbreviations

An *abbreviation* is a short way to write a word. An abbreviation may end with a period. It may start with a capital letter. If it does, it stands for a proper noun.

Forming Abbreviations

The days of the week have short forms.	Sun. Tues. Thurs. Sat. Mon. Wed. Fri.
So do all the months except May, June, and July.	Jan. Mar. Aug. Oct. Dec. Feb. Apr. Sept. Nov.
Times of day can also be abbreviated.	A.M.-between midnight and noon P.M.-between noon and midnight
Some people use titles with their names.	Ms.→any woman Mrs.→a married woman Mr.→any man Jr.→junior Sr.→senior

Names of states can be abbreviated in two ways. One form is used in general writing. The other form is known as *postal abbreviation.* Use it with a ZIP Code.

Abbreviations for States

State	Common Abbreviation	Postal Abbreviation
California Florida	Calif. Fla.	CA FL

Addresses may have abbreviations, too.

Avenue→Ave.   Boulevard→Blvd.   Drive→Dr.

These are abbreviations for units of measure. Most of them have periods. Which one does not?

inch→in.	foot→ft.	miles per hour→mph
ounce→oz.	pound→lb.	gallon→gal.
pint→pt.	quart→qt.	mile→mi.

PRACTICE

A. (Written) Write the abbreviations for the underlined words.

Example: Memphis, Tennessee   Salem Drive
Memphis, Tenn.   **Salem Dr.**

1. October 17, 1984
2. Doctor Ann Hill
3. Miami, Florida 33101
4. Paul Ames, Junior
5. Tuesday

6. Mister Carlos Sanchez
7. 23 Grove Street
8. San Diego, California 92199
9. April 1, 1984
10. 1613 Second Avenue

B. (Written) Rewrite this paragraph. Use abbreviations where possible.

On January 17, 1984, Mister Jones asked his class this question. A car will go from Brooklyn, New York, to Tampa, Florida. That is 1205 miles. How long will the trip take at 55 miles per hour?

APPLY

Write three sentences. Use four abbreviations from this lesson. You might write about people and addresses or months and measures. You might tell about a friend or a famous person.

Letter Parts

A letter is like a surprise package. You must open it to learn what is inside. A friendly letter has five parts. They are the *heading, greeting, body, closing,* and *signature.*

Look at each part of this letter.

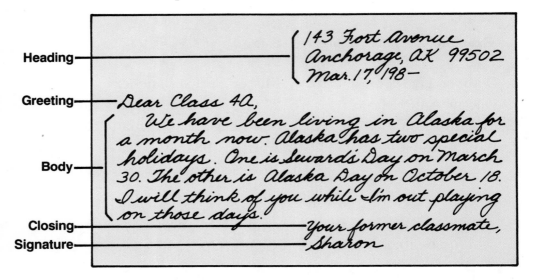

Heading — 143 Fort Avenue
Anchorage, AK 99502
Mar. 17, 198—

Greeting — Dear Class 4A,

Body — We have been living in Alaska for a month now. Alaska has two special holidays. One is Seward's Day on March 30. The other is Alaska Day on October 18. I will think of you while I'm out playing on those days.

Closing — Your former classmate,
Signature — Sharon

GUIDELINES

1. The heading tells where and when the letter was written. Capitalize all proper nouns in the heading.
2. The greeting tells to whom the letter is written. Capitalize the first word of the greeting.
3. The body tells the reason for the letter.
4. The closing says good-by. Capitalize the first word in the closing.
5. The signature tells who wrote the letter.

PRACTICE

A. (Oral) Name each letter part. Tell what is wrong with each one. Remember to look at the punctuation.

> **Example:** yours truly,
> **closing; capital letter missing, Yours truly,**

1. 13689 grant avenue
   raleigh, nc 27602
   july 7, 19-
2. dear liz,
3. your friend,
4. ricardo

5. peter
6. dear Ray
7. Yours truly
8. 195 James st
   dallas Texas
   sept 26 19-

B. (Written) This letter is mixed up. Rewrite it. Put the parts in the right order. Use capital letters and punctuation marks correctly.

blue hill, me 04614
sept. 9, 198-

dear lily,
suzanne

    I'm happy that you want to be my pen pal. I would love to see Hawaii someday. Maine is not as warm as Hawaii. We get a lot of snow. Snow is great if you like to ski!

your pen pal,
16 river road

APPLY

    Write three sentences for the body of the letter above. Tell why you want to see Hawaii. Ask questions about that state. If you live in Hawaii, write about Maine.

Punctuating Letters and Envelopes

A *comma* is a punctuation mark. It can help you understand what you read. Commas are used in special places in a letter.

Using Commas

Use a comma in an address. Put it between the city or town and the state.	Pawtucket, RI 02860 Yuma, AZ 85364
Use a comma in a date. Put it between the day's date and the year.	Feb. 28, 198- May 17, 198-
Use a comma after the greeting and the closing.	Dear Ms. Seeto, Your friend,

A letter is mailed in an envelope. The envelope shows who is sending the letter to whom. Punctuation marks are needed on an envelope, too.

Where are commas used on this envelope?

Return Address — Jean Washington
43 Royal St.
New Orleans, LA 70113

Mailing Address — Mr. Ralph Gardner
78 Placer Ave.
Tuskegee, AL 36083

The *mailing address* tells where and to whom the letter is being sent. The mailing address goes in the middle of the envelope. The *return address* tells who is sending the letter. Put the return address in the upper left. Put the stamp on the upper right.

PRACTICE

(Written) Rewrite each letter part correctly. Use commas and abbreviations where needed.

Example: Hudson nh 03051
Hudson, NH 03051

1. Anoka, mn 55303
2. november 23, 198-
3. Dear Jeff
4. Your grandmother
5. Los Angeles California 90052
6. Your uncle
7. Dear Doctor march
8. February 18 198-

APPLY

Address an envelope you would send to your teacher at your school.

Noun Endings

> **Noun endings -er and -or mean "someone who."**
>
> <u>Someone who reads</u>: reader   <u>Someone who acts</u>: actor

An ending can change a word. The ending makes the word do a different job. A word ending is called a *suffix*.

The letters *-er* and *-or* are noun endings, or noun suffixes. The suffixes *-er* and *-or* can change some words into nouns.

See how these words were changed into nouns.

work + er = Someone who works: worker.
climb + er = Someone who climbs: climber.
sail + or = Someone who sails: sailor.
act + or = Someone who acts: actor.

PRACTICE

(Written) Add *-er* or *-or*. Write each word as a noun.

Example: talk
  talker

1. lead	**4.** sing	**7.** climb	**10.** spell
2. farm	**5.** work	**8.** act	**11.** paint
3. walk	**6.** teach	**9.** sail	**12.** clean

APPLY

Choose one of the new nouns you have made. Write three sentences that tell what this person does.

Using *A, An,* and *The*

> ***Articles*** **are small words that mark nouns. The words *a, an,* and *the* are articles.**
>
> <u>A</u> light gleamed in <u>an</u> open window of <u>the</u> house.

The articles *a, an,* and *the* tell you that a noun is coming. Use *a* or *an* with singular nouns. *A* is used before consonants. *An* is used before vowels. *A* or *an* mark any person or thing. Use *the* with singular or plural nouns. A particular person or thing is marked by *the.*

What nouns go with the articles?

> **An** ambulance has **a** siren.
> **The** flashing light
> warns people, too.

PRACTICE

(Written) Rewrite the paragraph. Use the correct articles.

(A/An) bike rider should follow (a/the) safety rules. Stop at (a/an) red light. Wear (a/an) orange or white hat at night. (An/The) color helps people see you.

APPLY

Write three sentences about safety rules you follow at home. Use articles and underline them.

Using *This, That, These,* and *Those*

> **This, that, these, and those often mark a noun.**
>
> **These** shoes fit <u>those</u> feet.   **This** sock matches <u>that</u> sock.

This and *that* are used with singular nouns. *These* and *those* are used with plural nouns. *This* and *these* tell about things nearby. *That* and *those* tell about things far away.

Look at these examples.

I like **this** car.   **That** car near the curb is ours.

These rolls go in the oven.   **Those** rolls are hot.

PRACTICE

(**Written**) Choose the correct word. Write each sentence.

1. (This/These) book is mine.
2. (Those/That) books are yours.
3. (These/That) tools are Bud's.
4. (Those/These) tools in the truck are his.
5. (That/This) bite of toast is crisp.
6. (That/This) toast yesterday was soft.

APPLY

Write two pairs of sentences about a holiday. In the first pair, use *this* and *that*. In the second, use *these* and *those*.

Using *Some, Many,* and *Several*

> ***Some, many*** and ***several*** **may point to a noun.**
>
> **Some** rooms have <u>several</u> doors. <u>Many</u> rooms have none.

The words *some, many,* and *several* point to plural nouns.

To find a plural noun, ask "Some what?" "Many what?" or "Several what?"

Name the plural nouns.

> **Some** detectives found **many** clues in **several** places.

PRACTICE

(**Written**) Write the plural noun from each sentence.

1. There are many shops in the mall.
2. Some friends of mine work there.
3. My mother owns several shops.
4. I have some favorite stores.
5. Many pets at that shop are for sale.
6. This store sells several tasty snacks.

APPLY

In sentences 4, 5, and 6, change all the words that tell when a noun is coming. Write the new sentences.

14 MORE BASIC SKILLS

Expanding Sentences Using Nouns

> **Nouns appear in many parts of a sentence. Adding nouns can make sentences grow.**
>
> **Sal talks.**
> **Sal, my new parrot, talks to strangers.**

Nouns are important in sentences. You know that a noun can be used as the subject in a sentence. It tells whom or what the sentence is about. Another noun can be used to tell more about the subject.

Look at these examples.

| Paul|rides. | Erica|flies. |
| Paul, my **brother,**|rides. | Erica, a **pilot,**|flies. |

What details were added to each short sentence? What nouns were used to add the details?

A noun can be used to tell more about the action in a sentence. The action, remember, is in the predicate part of a sentence.

What details are added here?

Paul, my brother,|rides bucking horses.
Paul, my brother,|rides bucking horses in a rodeo.
Erica, a pilot,|flies a plane.
Erica, a pilot,|flies a plane for an airline.

What nouns were used to add the details? Can you think of other details that could have been added using nouns?

PRACTICE

A. (Written) Add nouns to complete these sentences. Write each new sentence.

> **Example:** _____ drives a _____ .
> **Alex drives a car.**
> Or: **Auntie drives a motor home.**

1. _____ sails.
2. My _____ , a _____ , teaches _____ .
3. The _____ wrote a _____ .
4. _____ acts in a _____ .
5. _____ , my _____ , sawed _____ .
6. _____ grows _____ in her _____ .
7. _____ , my _____ , danced in a _____ .
8. _____ makes _____ .

B. (Written) Make these sentences grow. Add nouns and any other words you need.

> **Example:** Rags sleeps.
> **Rags, my aunt's cat, sleeps on the rug by the stove at night.**

9. The miner dug gold.
10. Firefighters climbed.
11. Everett hammered nails.
12. Chuck drives.
13. Marilyn fixed the car.
14. The clerk added.
15. Pam cooks.
16. The dentist drills.
17. The quarterback threw.
18. A diver explored.
19. Mom takes pictures.
20. Dan fishes.

APPLY

Write three expanded sentences. Use at least four nouns in each one. You might tell a joke or a riddle. You might write a good reason for doing something.

Review the Basics II

A. Noun Endings

Add *-er* or *-or* to change each word to a noun. Write the nouns. *(page 72)*

1. build
2. help
3. dream
4. own
5. swing
6. walk
7. sail
8. play
9. watch
10. act
11. talk
12. sleep
13. sing
14. climb
15. train

B. Using *A, An,* and *The*

Choose the correct article for each sentence. Write each sentence. *(page 73)*

1. You can make music with (a/an) old bottle.
2. Cut the bottom out of (a/an) plastic bottle.
3. Sing through (the/an) bottle.
4. Fill (a/an) glass bottle with water.
5. Hit the bottle with (a/an) spoon.
6. Listen to (an/the) sound you make.
7. Fill a second bottle to (a/an) different height.
8. (The/An) sound will be different.

C. Using *This, That, These,* and *Those*

Choose the correct word. Write each sentence. *(page 74)*

1. Cut (that/those) old plastic bottles in half.
2. Attach (this/these) piece of tubing to the neck.
3. Blow into (that/those) piece of tubing.
4. You will make (this/these) noises like a trumpet.
5. (This/That) tube in my hand is too long.
6. (That/Those) tube in the box is the right size.

D. Using *Some, Many,* and *Several*

In each sentence the word *some, many* or *several* points to a noun. Write that noun. *(page 75)*

1. Some sandwiches are made on rolls.
2. Submarine sandwiches use several meats.
3. The sandwiches have many names.
4. Some people call them torpedoes.
5. In many cities, subs are called heroes.
6. Only heroes or heroines can eat several subs!
7. In some places, subs are called grinders.
8. Where did some words come from?
9. Many customers made up new names.
10. Several guesses may be right.

E. Expanding Sentences Using Nouns

Add nouns to complete these sentences. Write each new sentence. *(pages 76–77)*

1. The _____ swung the _____ .
2. _____ skated.
3. _____ , the _____ , threw the _____ .
4. _____ , my _____ , runs.
5. _____ swims in a _____ .
6. _____ hit the _____ .
7. _____ delivers _____ to _____ .
8. _____ coaches _____ .
9. A _____ uses _____ .
10. The _____ shines at _____ .
11. The _____ barks at the _____ .
12. _____ grow in the _____ .

15 COMMUNICATING

Friendly Letters

You have learned about the five parts of a friendly letter. One part, the *body*, tells the reason the letter was written. Friendly letters are written for different reasons. You may invite someone to a party. You may thank someone for something. Each letter gives different facts.

An *invitation* should answer these questions: Who is doing the inviting? What will happen? When? Where? An invitation should give any other needed facts.

Look at the invitation.

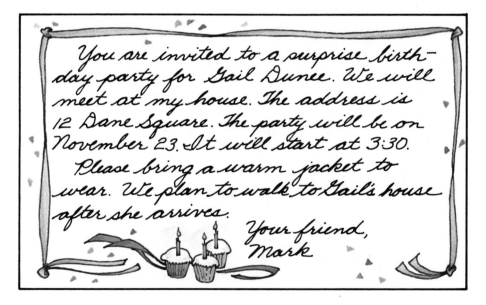

You are invited to a surprise birthday party for Gail Dunee. We will
meet at my house. The address is
12 Dane Square. The party will be on
November 23. It will start at 3:30.
Please bring a warm jacket to
wear. We plan to walk to Gail's house
after she arrives.
Your friend,
Mark

Does the invitation answer all the questions? What else does it tell?

You write a *thank-you* letter to thank someone. It should be short and polite. It should tell the person what you are thanking him or her for.

Read this thank-you letter.

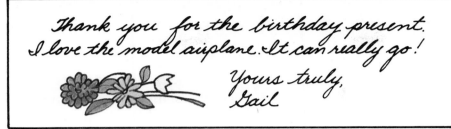

*Thank you for the birthday present.
I love the model airplane. It can really go!*
Yours truly,
Gail

Does it have all the facts? What ideas could you add?

PRACTICE

(Written) What type of letter would you write for each event? Answer by writing *invitation* or *thank-you letter*.

Example: You loved the book your aunt sent.
      thank-you letter

1. You are having a Fourth of July picnic.
2. Your class is giving a play.
3. A pen pal wants you to visit.
4. Your friend sent you a frog.
5. A poster from your grandfather arrived.
6. You want to take some friends to a park.
7. You want your uncle to help your team.
8. You and your friends are putting on a circus.
9. You had a good time at a friend's party.
10. A friend sent you a coconut from Hawaii.

APPLY

Pretend that a friend has given you a new record for your birthday. Write three sentences you would put in a thank-you letter.

Business Letters

Business letters often are sent to people you do not know. A business letter may ask for something. You may want information. You may want to buy something. You may want help with a complaint. A business letter is more formal than a letter to a friend.

A business letter has six parts. You learned about the five parts of a friendly letter in Lesson 8. A business letter has the same parts plus an *inside address.* The inside address shows the company you are writing to. It also tells who will read the letter. In the greeting, write this person's name. If you do not know the name, write *Dear Sir or Madam.* Use a colon (:) after the greeting.

Study this business letter.

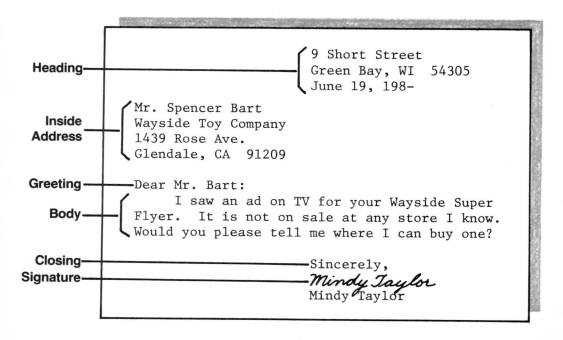

Heading
```
                              9 Short Street
                              Green Bay, WI   54305
                              June 19, 198-
```

Inside Address
```
Mr. Spencer Bart
Wayside Toy Company
1439 Rose Ave.
Glendale, CA   91209
```

Greeting — Dear Mr. Bart:

Body
```
        I saw an ad on TV for your Wayside Super
Flyer.  It is not on sale at any store I know.
Would you please tell me where I can buy one?
```

Closing — Sincerely,

Signature — *Mindy Taylor*
Mindy Taylor

PRACTICE

(**Written**) Correct this business letter. One part is missing. Fix six punctuation errors and seven missing capital letters.

```
                              4321 branch St.
                              pontiac MI  48053
                              march 12 198-

mr. George harris
Fishing Life Company
2002 Park Ave.
New York NY  10016

dear Mr harris
     I want to buy some new fishing tackle.  Please
send me a list of your rods and reels.  I read
about them in the newspaper.  The ad said that the
list was free.

                    Fred Walsh
                    Fred Walsh
```

APPLY

Write two sentences for a business letter. Order skates.

Letters: Plan, Write, Edit

In this lesson, you will write a letter. It will be either a friendly letter or a business letter.

Letters are written for many reasons. A friendly letter may be an invitation or a thank you. A business letter is often written to ask for something.

There are three steps in writing. You need to plan, write, and then edit. Follow the steps one at a time.

PLAN

Imagine that your grandfather sent you an ant farm. You have never seen one before. You like to watch the ants dig. They make tunnels. The ant farm was made by the Living Toy Company. Its address is 29 Pond Road, Berlin, NH 03570. Which kind of letter will you write?

You may write a friendly letter to thank your grandfather. You think the farm is a great birthday gift. You may ask him to visit so that he can watch with you.

You may want to write a business letter to the Living Toy Company. Ask how you can buy an ant farm. You may want to know about other farms.

Choose which kind of letter you will write. Are you writing a friendly letter? Or, will it be a business letter? Plan your letter.

WRITE

Now you are ready to write. For a friendly letter, tell why you are writing. Be polite. Remember to punctuate each letter part. Use the Guidelines on page 68 as a guide.

If you write a business letter, be sure to include the six letter parts. Check the Guidelines on page 83. Look at the model business letter on page 82. Use it as a guide. It will help you put each part in the correct place.

EDIT

When you edit your own letter, pretend that you are seeing it for the first time. Is each part in the right place? Read the body of the letter.

✔ Does each sentence make sense?
✔ Are any words missing?
✔ Are the sentences in order?

Now look at each part again to check the form.

✔ Is the punctuation correct?
✔ Are capital letters used when needed?
✔ Are all words spelled correctly?
✔ Are abbreviations correct?
✔ Are plural and possessive nouns spelled correctly?
✔ Is your handwriting neat and easy to read?

Before you edit your letter, practice on the business letter below.

It has twelve errors. There is at least one error in each part. Look at the Guidelines on page 83. They will help.

39 Pratt st.
derby KS 67037
Oct. 15 198—

Ms Ina barton
Space Center
Cape canaveral, FL 32920

Dear Ina
How are you doing? My class is doing a project on the space program. I would like to know about the space center. Please send me any pamphlets you have

your friend
Kip

18 COMMUNICATING

Taking Messages

Rita took a telephone message for her brother Rick. She took a good message. She listened carefully to what the caller said. She gave all the information Rick needed.

This is the message she wrote.

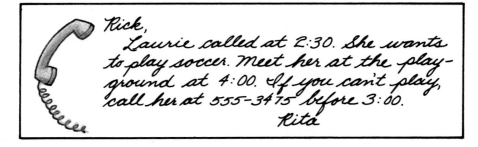

Rick,
Laurie called at 2:30. She wants to play soccer. Meet her at the playground at 4:00. If you can't play, call her at 555-3475 before 3:00.
Rita

Rita's message tells who the message is for. Does it tell who called? Rita wrote the time of the call and the reason. Should Rick call back? How can he reach the caller? Rita signed the message. Now, if Rick has any questions he knows whom to ask.

PRACTICE/APPLY

(Oral) Look at this list of people. Think of a message one person might leave for the other. Choose a partner. Exchange messages.

1. school principal
2. astronaut
3. fourth-grade student
4. movie or TV star
5. grandparent
6. TV reporter
7. parent
8. President of the U. S.

Unit 2 Test

A. Singular and Plural Nouns

Use the noun at the end of each sentence to fill in the blank. Write a singular noun if the blank is marked with an S. Write a plural noun if the blank is marked with a P. *(pages 54–57)*

1. A _S_ asked a fox to dinner. (crane)
2. She wanted to play a _S_ on the fox. (trick)
3. Cranes have long _P_ . (beak)
4. _P_ have short noses. (fox)
5. The crane served some _P_ in a tall bottle. (berry)
6. The poor fox could not get one _S_ . (berry)
7. Then the fox asked the crane to _S_ . (lunch)
8. The fox put the food on flat _P_ . (dish)
9. The crane could not pick up any _P_ . (piece)
10. That taught the crane a _S_ . (lesson)

B. Common and Proper Nouns

Write each sentence correctly. Add capital letters to the proper nouns. Underline the common nouns. *(pages 58–59)*

1. The rockers, a new band, will hold a concert.
2. The concert is set for next friday, june 8.
3. Come to the bates school on central avenue.
4. Tickets went on sale last monday.
5. gina and frank bought tickets first.
6. Their brother, mike, is a part of the band.
7. He and bruce are guitar players.
8. ella plays the drums.
9. The singers are maryann, ruben, and tony.
10. The rockers want to roll next friday.

C. Possessive Nouns
Write each group of words. Add an apostrophe to make the underlined words show possession. *(pages 60–61)*

1. a <u>cats</u> tail
2. a <u>workers</u> tools
3. the <u>peoples</u> faces
4. two <u>dogs</u> bites
5. a <u>friends</u> name
6. those <u>childrens</u> toys
7. a <u>girls</u> name
8. each <u>boys</u> partner
9. the <u>principals</u> office
10. these <u>owls</u> ears
11. some <u>players</u> injuries
12. two <u>babies</u> dreams
13. a <u>teams</u> captain
14. two <u>writers</u> pencils
15. a <u>turkeys</u> wings
16. my <u>arms</u> elbow
17. <u>Kims</u> voice
18. two <u>horses</u> tails
19. some <u>families</u> home
20. those <u>girls</u> friends

D. Using *A, An,* and *The*
Rewrite the paragraph on your paper. Choose the correct article for each sentence. *(page 73)*

Most countries use (<u>an/the</u>) metric system. This is (<u>a/an</u>) easy system. The metric unit of length is (<u>a/an</u>) meter. (<u>An/A</u>) meter is a little longer than a yard. There are 100 centimeters in (<u>a/an</u>) meter. Is (<u>a/an</u>) inch longer or shorter than (<u>a/an</u>) centimeter?

E. Writing
Write a friendly letter to a student in your class. In your letter, tell why you chose to write to that person. Be sure to include all five parts of a friendly letter. Check that punctuation marks are used correctly. Be sure to use capital letters on all proper nouns. *(pages 84–86)*

Keep Practicing

A. Sentences
Write *sentence* or *fragment* for each group of words.
(Unit 1, Lesson 1)

1. People eat a lot of meat in a lifetime.
2. Think of all the kinds of meat.
3. People eat beef, pork, ham, lamb, fowl, and fish.
4. The average person eats twelve sheep.
5. Fourteen cattle and two calves.
6. Eats twenty-three pigs.
7. That person will eat 880 chickens.
8. Thirty-five turkeys eaten.
9. Close to 770 pounds of fish of all kinds.
10. How much meat will you eat?

B. Kinds of Sentences
Write each group of words as a sentence. Each group needs a capital letter. Add the correct punctuation mark.
(Unit 1, Lesson 2)

1. our language borrows words from other languages
2. can you think of any borrowed words for foods
3. *tea* is from the Chinese word *t'e*
4. from Italian we get *spaghetti* and *pizza*
5. be careful when you spell these words
6. the Germans gave us *noodle* and *hamburger*
7. where do you think we got *chili* and *taco*
8. what an interesting language we have
9. the spelling of some words changes
10. what other words can you name
11. ask a friend to spell *quiche*

C. Simple and Complete Subjects

Write each sentence. Underline the complete subject. Then circle the simple subject. *(Unit 1, Lesson 3)*

1. Rules about the American flag were made in 1923.
2. The flag should be shown on all days.
3. It should never touch the ground or floor.
4. All persons should salute the flag in a parade.
5. Men wearing hats should take them off.
6. Women should put their right hands on their hearts.
7. Our flag should never be used in an ad.
8. Flags may not be used on clothing.
9. Many people do not know the rules.
10. A book of the rules would be helpful.

D. Simple and Complete Predicates

Write each sentence. First underline each complete predicate. Then circle each simple predicate. *(Unit 1, Lesson 4)*

1. Sound is made by objects moving fast.
2. The moving object sends out waves.
3. These waves travel through the air.
4. Our ears hear the waves as sounds.
5. Sound travels faster in water than in air.
6. Some planes fly faster than sound.
7. You see the plane first.
8. You hear the sound it makes last.
9. Some whistles make silent sounds.
10. Only animals hear those sounds.
11. Most dogs hear silent sounds.

E. Compound Predicates

Join each pair of short sentences. Write the longer one.
Each new sentence will have a compound predicate.
(Unit 1, Lesson 10)

1. A reporter does not stay in an office.
   A reporter does not just sit at a desk.
2. A newspaper reporter moves around the city.
   A newspaper reporter has to look for a story.
3. The reporter talks to many people.
   The reporter makes notes of things people say.
4. A photographer may go with the reporter.
   A photographer may take pictures.
5. The reporter goes back to the office.
   The reporter writes the story.
6. An editor reads the reporter's story.
   An editor may change it.
7. Then the reporter rewrites the story.
   Then the reporter sends it to be set in type.
8. The story is printed in the newpaper.
   The story is read by many people.

F. Correcting Run-on Sentences

Fix each of these run-on sentences. *(Unit 1, Lesson 11)*

1. Maria Montoya Martinez was a Pueblo and she was the most famous Native American potter.
2. Maria wanted to make pottery in the old way and she and her husband worked until they found the secret.
3. Maria worked with her children and grandchildren and the Pueblo people soon had an important craft business.

G. Sentence Punctuation and Capitaliziation

Rewrite this paragraph. There are five sentences in it. Use capital letters and punctuation marks. Be sure to indent the first line. *(Unit 1, Lesson 6)*

one Vermont town came up with a new idea to save energy they want to cover the town with a dome what an idea the dome would keep the heat in and the snow out would you like to live in a domed city

H. Words That Organize

Each sentence needs an organizing word. Complete each sentence with a word from the list. Use each word once. *(Unit 1, Lesson 7)*

first	bottom	in
after	next	then
last	soon	down
second		

1. _____ take a clean sponge.
2. _____ cut the sponge into a shape you like.
3. _____ soak the sponge until it is wet.
4. Put the sponge in the _____ of a dish.
5. _____ sprinkle grass seed on the sponge.
6. _____ keep the sponge damp.
7. The grass will sprout _____ about a week.
8. The grass roots will grow _____ into the sponge.
9. The lawn will die _____ a while.
10. _____ you can start a new lawn!

Something Extra

Poetry in Motion

Some poems smile as wide as the sky. Other poems frown like an empty heart. Some poems compare things. They tell how different things are alike. A comparison helps a reader see a sharp image. For example, a poem might compare a garden hose to a snake. They are alike in many ways. Here are two ways.

> The curled garden hose rests **as** calmly **as** a tired snake.

> Water from a hose flicked **like** a snake's tongue.

These two comparisons use the words *like* and *as*. A comparison that uses *like* or *as* is called a *simile.* Read the comparisons on page 95. What things are compared? Does each one contain *like* or *as*? Is each one a simile?

Write Away!

The poems on page 95 are alike. They each use similes. They are alike in another way. Fourth-graders wrote them. Write a comparison poem. Complete each of these similes. Then add at least four more similes to the poem.

> (Something) shines as bright as (something else).
> (Something) roars like (something else).

Now write a comparison poem about yourself. First tell what you used to be. In the next line tell what you are now. Use a simile in each line. Here is an example.

> **I used to** sing like a frog.
> **Now I** croak like a crooked record.

The snow is as white as vanilla custard.
A bumpy mattress is just like a camel's back.
A deer is as graceful as a ballerina.
—*Melanie Popkin*

Snowflakes are like shining diamonds.
A breeze is like the sky is coming to you.
The sun is like golden bright earrings.
—*Iris Torres*

The thunder is as loud as a beating drum.
The rain is as cold as ice cubes.
—*Martin Freihofer*

A cat's paw touching grass sounds like
a cloud floating.
—*Lisa Jill Braun*

Accidentally

Once—I didn't mean to,
but that
was that—
I yawned in the sunshine
and swallowed a gnat.

I'd rather eat mushrooms
and bullfrogs' legs,
I'd rather have pepper
all over my eggs

than open my mouth
on a sleepy day
and close on a gnat
going down that way.

It tasted sort of salty.
It didn't hurt a bit.
I accidentally ate a gnat
and that
was
it!

—*Maxine W. Kumin*

96

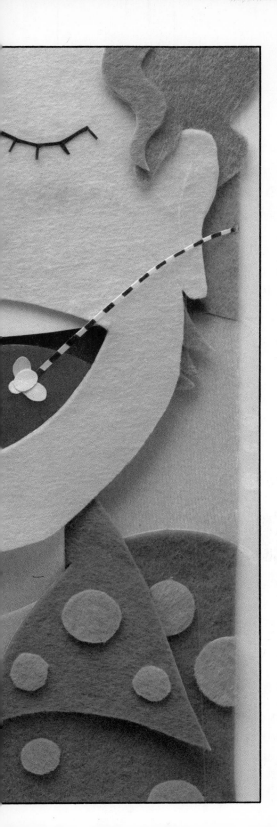

3

Telling
What
Happened

SKILLS TO BUILD ON

Verbs and Verb Tenses
Subject-Verb Agreement
Time and Space Order
Contractions with *Not*

PRACTICAL APPLICATIONS

Writing an Order Paragraph
Telling What Happened

Action Verbs

> A *verb* may tell an action. The most important part of the predicate is the verb.
>
> Planets|<u>spin</u>. Astronaut Ed White|<u>walked</u> in space.

The *verb* is the most important part of the predicate. An *action verb* tells what the subject does.

Look at the action verb in each sentence.

Two engines|**roar**.   The rocket|**rises** into space.

PRACTICE

(**Written**) Write the action verb from each sentence.

Example: Rockets move at amazing speeds.
 move

1. He stepped out of the spacecraft.
2. A 25-foot lifeline held him to the ship.
3. The lifeline fed air to the astronaut.
4. White twisted in space.
5. He saw Earth 120 miles away.
6. He talked to the crew.
7. White returned to the ship.

APPLY

Think about something you can make with paper and paste. Write three sentences about it. Underline each verb.

Other Verbs

> **A *verb* may tell what the subject is, was, or will be.**
>
> The sun|<u>is</u> very hot. Ed White|<u>was</u> an astronaut.

   Some verbs tell what a person or thing is. They do not show action. The verbs *am, is, are, was, were,* and *will be* do not show action.

Look at the verb in each sentence.

   I|**am** here. The bus|**was** late. The seats|**were** full.
   Cal|**is** alone. The rooms|**are** empty. I|**will be** there.

PRACTICE

(Written) Write the verb from each sentence. Circle the verbs that do not show action.

Example: Beets are vegetables.

1. The towels were wet.
2. The ball rolled to the side.
3. A walk in the rain is fun.
4. Earth spins in space.
5. Our sun is very hot.
6. I am tired.
7. Each class was small.
8. Fred cooked dinner.
9. They are ready.
10. Alice will be here.

APPLY

   In three sentences, tell what your favorite food is like. Do not use action verbs.

Subject-Verb Agreement

> Use the *s-form* of the verb with a singular subject that means *he, she,* or *it.* Use the *plain form* with *I, you,* or a plural subject.
>
> s-form   plain form
>
> <u>Singular</u>: That girl|runs.   <u>Plural</u>: Those girls|run, too.

The subject of a sentence can be singular or plural. The verb in a sentence must agree with the subject. Verbs have two forms. These are the *s-form* and the *plain form.* If the subject is singular, use the *s*-form. If the subject is plural, use the plain form.

Look at these examples.

> One boy|**rides.**   Three boys|**ride.**
>
> Kate|**jogs.**   Her brothers|**jog,** too.

For many verbs such as *ride* and *jog,* you just add *-s.* For some verbs, you need to follow other rules. Study the chart.

Forming the *s*-form of Verbs

Some verbs end with *ch, sh, ss, zz, s,* or *x.* Add *-es.*	touch→touches fix→fixes buzz→buzzes miss→misses wish→wishes bus→buses
Some verbs end with a consonant letter and *y.* Change the *y* to *i* and add *-es.*	hurry→hurries fly→flies try→tries
The singular subjects *I* and *you* do not use the *s*-form.	I } walk. He You She } walks. It

PRACTICE

A. (Oral) Name the form of the verb that best completes each sentence.

> **Example:** The doorbell (<u>ring/rings</u>).
> **rings**

1. Mary (<u>rush/rushes</u>) to the door.
2. She (<u>open/opens</u>) the door.
3. The children (<u>cry/cries</u>) "Surprise!"
4. Mary's friends (<u>smile/smiles</u>) at her.
5. "What is this?" she (<u>ask/asks</u>).
6. "It is a surprise birthday party!" they (<u>say/says</u>).
7. Then they (<u>give/gives</u>) Mary her presents.

B. (Written) Use the correct form of the verb to complete each sentence. Use the plain form if the subject is plural. Use the *s*-form if the subject is singular. Write each sentence.

> **Example:** Our bodies ——— the right foods. (need)
> **Our bodies need the right foods.**

1. Milk, meat, and grains ——— us protein. (give)
2. People ——— energy from fat. (get)
3. Fat ——— from oils, meat, and milk products. (come)
4. Vitamins ——— people healthy. (keep)
5. Vegetables and fruit ——— many vitamins. (contain)
6. Calcium ——— bones and teeth. (build)
7. Milk products ——— calcium. (provide)

APPLY

Think of some foods you like. Write four sentences about the foods. Draw a line under each verb. Circle each simple subject.

Verb Tenses

> **The *tense* of a verb tells the time of the action.
> Three tenses are *present*, *past*, and *future*.**
>
> <u>Present:</u> glows <u>Past:</u> glowed <u>Future:</u> will glow

Verbs show time. A *present tense* verb shows an action that is happening now. A *past tense* verb shows an action that already happened. A *future tense* verb shows an action that has not happened yet. However, the action is expected to happen. Future tense verbs use *will* or *shall*.

Read these sentences.

Present: The spacecraft **roars.**

Past: The rocket **leaped** into space.

Future: Soon we **will travel** in space. I **shall go** there, too.

To form the past tense of most verbs, add *-ed* to the plain form of the verb. Other past tense verbs follow different rules. Study the chart.

Forming Past Tense Verbs

Some verbs end with *e*. Drop the *e* and add *-ed.*	wave→waved skate→skated love→loved
Some verbs end with a consonant letter and *y*. Change the *y* to *i* and add *-ed.*	carry→carried hurry→hurried spy→spied
Some verbs end with a short vowel sound and a single consonant letter. Double the final consonant and add *-ed.*	drag→dragged hop→hopped rub→rubbed

PRACTICE

A. (Oral) Give the verb from each sentence. Name its tense, *present, past,* or *future.*

> **Example:** Many spacecraft explore our solar system.
> **explore—present tense**

1. Their cameras look at the planets.
2. The cameras return pictures to Earth.
3. Voyager 2 lifted off from Earth in 1977.
4. It reached Saturn in 1981.
5. Voyager's pictures show Saturn's rings close up.
6. Voyager will visit other planets far from the sun.
7. It will reach Neptune in 1989.

B. (Written) Write the past tense form of these verbs.

1. sail	**5.** chip	**9.** like	**13.** race
2. worry	**6.** save	**10.** cry	**14.** bury
3. stop	**7.** try	**11.** watch	**15.** laugh
4. blast	**8.** fan	**12.** dare	**16.** beg

APPLY

Write three sentences about a day in school. In one, tell something you did last week. In one, tell what you are doing this week. In one, tell something you will do next week. Use past, present, and future verb tenses.

Helping Verbs

A verb that helps another verb is called a *helping verb.* The helping verb comes before the *main verb.*

helping verb main verb

The crew can stay on the ship.

WORD BANK

can	shall
could	will
may	
would	should
might	
am is	do
are	was
were	have
had	does
did	has

Some verb forms are used alone. Others need help. A verb that helps another verb is called a *helping verb.* The helping verb comes before the main verb. A verb can have more than one helper.

Look at the helping verbs here.

> This spacecraft **is** going to Mars.
> The workers **did** check it thoroughly.
> The craft **may have** lost power.

The complete verb in the first sentence is *is going.* The verb is made up of the helping verb *is* and the main verb *going.* Find the complete verb in the second sentence. What is the helping verb? The main verb? Name the two helping verbs in the third sentence.

Some verbs are always helping verbs. They should never be used alone. Other verbs may sometimes be used as helping verbs.

Name the complete verbs here.

> Voyager 2 **is touring** the solar system.
> Voyager **is** on its way to Uranus.

PRACTICE

A. (Oral) Name the complete verb from each sentence. Then name the main verb.

> **Example:** Scientists can learn much from rocks and soil.
> **complete verb: can learn; main verb: learn**

1. A spacecraft has landed on Mars.
2. It has lifted samples of the crust with a special scoop.
3. Scientists will have tested the crust.
4. This crust can give us information.
5. Tests might show living things in the crust.
6. Rocks can provide information,too.
7. A rock may tell a planet's age.
8. A test will give the date.

B. (Written) Write the complete verb from each sentence. Circle each helping verb.

> **Example:** Scientists will work for years!
> (will) work

1. The craft had traveled for eighteen months.
2. Scientists were waiting for its arrival at Jupiter.
3. It might save the trip.
4. It could tell them much about the huge planet.
5. At last the spacecraft has arrived.
6. Its cameras are working perfectly.
7. Pictures have arrived on Earth.
8. We all can see the pictures.

APPLY

Write three sentences that tell how to help a new student feel comfortable in your class. Use helping verbs.

Review the Basics I

A. Verbs

Write the action verb from each sentence. *(page 98)*

1. I made a color wheel from a small paper plate.
2. First I colored the wheel in pie shapes.
3. Then I poked it through the center with a pencil.
4. The wheel turns easily.
5. The colors blend into one.

Write the verb from each sentence. Circle the verbs that do not show action. *(page 99)*

6. Sequoya lived long ago.
7. He was a Cherokee.
8. There were no written letters in his language.
9. Then he made symbols for the sounds.
10. People studied his written language.
11. Sequoya was a clever person.
12. Samples of his work are in a history book.

B. Subject-Verb Agreement

Write the form of the verb that best completes each sentence. *(pages 100–101)*

1. Emma (want/wants) to be a detective.
2. She (look/looks) for mysteries to solve.
3. Rico and Lucy (give/gives) her a new mystery.
4. Things (keep/keeps) disappearing.
5. Emma (watch/watches) their house.
6. Emma (sit/sits) under a tree in the yard.
7. She (see/sees) a magpie fly in an open window.
8. "Magpies (steal/steals) things," Emma says. "That's the thief!"

C. Verb Tenses

Write the past tense form of these verbs. *(pages 102–103)*

1. cry
2. dip
3. carry
4. envy
5. guide
6. blaze
7. visit
8. squeeze
9. mark
10. haunt
11. crunch
12. wrap
13. trade
14. jam
15. brag
16. arrive
17. jump
18. invite
19. wash
20. call

D. Helping Verbs

Write the complete verb from each sentence. Circle each helping verb. *(pages 104–105)*

1. Film makers do get awards each year.
2. An award is called an "Oscar."
3. The first Oscar was given in 1928.
4. The best film should win the award.
5. The Sound of Music was picked in 1965.
6. Many films have won Oscars.
7. An Oscar can make money for a film.
8. Most people have seen the films.
9. Actors and actresses will win Oscars, too.
10. An Oscar can help them.
11. They may get better parts.
12. They might be seen on television.
13. An Oscar is made with gold.

Verbs in a Paragraph

You have learned how to use verbs. You know that a verb tells a present, past, or future action. You know that a verb should agree with its subject. A verb also can make your sentences interesting.

Some verbs do not tell much. Some verbs do not tell as much action as other verbs. They sound dull.

Which sentence is more interesting? Why?

The roller coaster went around the curve.
The roller coaster screeched around the curve.

Verbs are also important in a paragraph. Do not use the same verb over and over. Use different verbs that show action in interesting ways. Read these paragraphs.

WORD BANK

splashed
soared
sailed
flew
hopped
skipped
somersaulted
bounced

Super Frog jumped out of the water. She jumped onto a tall tree. Then she jumped from the tree to a passing plane. Next she jumped right over a mountain. Last she jumped back into the water.

Super Frog leaped out of the water. She bounded onto a tall tree. Then she sprang from the tree to a passing plane. Next she hurdled right over a mountain. Last she vaulted back into the water.

In the first, the same verb is used too many times. The second paragraph has different verbs. They show more action. Which is more interesting? Why?

You can choose new verbs from the Word Bank to replace *jumped*. By changing the verbs, you will make a new paragraph.

PRACTICE/APPLY

Choose interesting verbs from the Word Bank. Replace the underlined verbs. Write the paragraph with the new verbs.

The trapeze artist <u>went</u> back and forth. She <u>went</u> over and over in the air. She <u>went</u> over the crowd. Her fingertips <u>went</u> near her partner's. His hands <u>went</u> around hers tightly. Together, they <u>went</u> back to the platform.

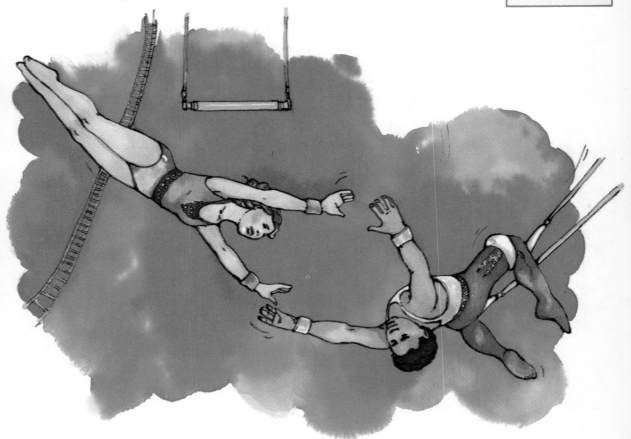

Now rewrite the paragraph above. This time, use interesting verbs in the future tense.

The Dictionary

A *dictionary* is a valuable tool. It shows how to spell words and how to say them. It also gives the meanings of words. A dictionary is easy to use. Use one often.

The words in a dictionary are in *alphabetical order.* To find a word, first decide if it will be close to the front, the back, or the middle of the book. See how the letters show the three parts.

Next use the *guide words* at the top of the page. They give the first and last *entry words* on the page. The entry words are the words that are defined. The guide words tell if an entry word is on the page.

Look at the guide words and entry words.

---

lily of the valley | line   339

lily of the valley, plant having tiny, sweet-smelling, bell-shaped white flowers arranged up and down a single flower stem. *plural* lilies of the valley.

lima bean (lī′mə bēn′), a broad, flat, pale-green bean, used as a vegetable.

limb (lim), **1** leg, arm, or wing. **2.** a large branch: *They sawed the dead limb off the tree. noun.*

line¹ (līn), **1** piece of rope, cord, or wire: *a telegraph line.* **2** cord for measuring or making level. A plumb line has a plumb at the end of a line and is used to find the depth of water or to see if a wall is vertical. **3** a long narrow mark: *Draw two lines here.* **4** anything that is like a long narrow mark: *the lines in your face.* **5** mark with lines: *Please line your paper with a pencil and ruler.*

Only part of the page is showing. The first entry word is *lily of the valley.* What is the last entry word?

PRACTICE

A. (Written) Write these three pairs of guide words on your paper.

loan|main   make|moan   moat|more

Then list the numbered words under the right pair of guide words.

Example: loan|main   make|moan   moat|more
             mail   **meek**   **money**

1. mail
2. meek
3. mast
4. money

5. mare
6. mean
7. mole
8. mild

9. moon
10. mist
11. maid
12. mark

13. mile
14. meal
15. mob
16. mad

B. (Written) Read the meanings for each word. Then read each sentence. Write the meaning that fits the underlined word in each sentence.

> **Example:** The <u>line</u> showed two feet of water under the boat.
> **2. cord for measuring or making level**

17. See the <u>lines</u> on the palm of your hand.
18. Telephone <u>lines</u> stretch between poles.
19. We made a <u>line</u> in the dirt.
20. We <u>lined</u> our paper with a pencil.
21. The <u>limb</u> of the tree broke.
22. Which <u>limb</u> did you break Alex?
23. My Dad loves <u>lima bean</u> soup.

APPLY

Write three sentences using different meanings of the word *line*.

Time Order and Space Order

When you write about an event, you tell things in the order they happened. You use *time order.* When did the event happen? What happened before? What happened later?

Notice the words that tell *when.*

> **On Monday** Jeri made yogurt. **First** she heated milk until it almost boiled. **Then** she let the milk cool for fifteen minutes. **After** the milk cooled, she added a little plain yogurt. **Next** she poured the mixture into clean jars and capped them. **Finally** she put the jars into a pot of hot water. **After** five hours the mixture had turned into yogurt.

Use *space order* to tell where an event takes place. Use it to tell about the place where an event happens. Words like *near* and *far, left* and *right, top* and *bottom* give clues to where something is.

Notice the words that tell *where.*

> Greg could not find the cat anywhere. He called **outside** the house. He looked on the **top** closet shelf. He hunted in the **bottom** of the closet. He peeked **under** the couch. Then he heard a meow **far off.** Greg walked **toward** the sound. He went **into** his room. The meow sounded **nearer.** The cat was **inside** a drawer!

The Word Bank shows time-order and space-order words.

WORD BANK	
Time Order	
second	first
next	last
finally	then
before	after
Space Order	
near	far
bottom	top
right	left

PRACTICE

(Oral) Read these events. Tell which is important, space order or time order.

Example: The ball came flying toward Raul. If he moved to the right spot, he could catch the ball.
space order

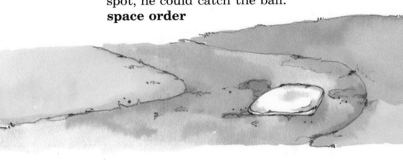

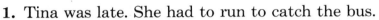

1. Tina was late. She had to run to catch the bus.
2. Jane was writing as fast as she could. "You have two minutes left to finish," the teacher said.
3. The puck was sliding toward the goal. The goalie fell on the puck to stop the score.
4. Mrs. Wong wanted to get to the store. It would close in no more than ten minutes.
5. The children counted the number of blocks from their homes to school. Aaron lives the closest.
6. Mr. Green planted the seeds about a quarter of an inch into the soil. He made rows about ten inches apart. The seeds would have enough room.
7. Rain has fallen for a week. The water in the lake is rising. The forecast said two more days of rain.

APPLY

Write four sentences about a trip you would like to take. Use time-order words and space-order words. Underline the time-order words. Circle the space-order words.

Contractions with *Not*

> **A *contraction* is a word made from two other words. When a verb and *not* are combined, they form a contraction.**
>
> can + not = <u>can't</u>   were + not = <u>weren't</u>

A *contraction* is a short way of writing two words. When the two words are put together to form the contraction, one or more letters are left out.

A verb and the word not can be put together to make a contraction. An *apostrophe* (') takes the place of the missing letters. Study the chart.

Contractions with *Not*

is not→isn't	does not→doesn't	have not→haven't
was not→wasn't	did not→didn't	will not→won't
has not→hasn't	are not→aren't	do not→don't
can not→can't	were not→weren't	would not→wouldn't

What letter or letters are left out in each contraction? *Will not* is special. You must memorize *won't.*

REMINDERS

1. When you make a contraction with *not*, break *not* between the *n* and *t.*
2. Replace the dropped letter or letters with an apostrophe ('). Be sure to write the apostrophe.
3. You must memorize that *will not* becomes *won't.*

PRACTICE

A. (Oral) Give the two words that form each of these contractions.

1. weren't
2. wasn't
3. isn't
4. won't
5. can't
6. aren't

7. didn't
8. doesn't
9. wouldn't
10. don't
11. haven't
12. hasn't

B. (Written) Rewrite each sentence. Use a contraction for the underlined words.

> **Example:** I <u>have not</u> had such a bad day as today!
> **I haven't had such a bad day as today!**

1. Mom's car <u>would not</u> start.
2. I <u>could not</u> get to school on time.
3. The class <u>did not</u> like my being late.
4. We <u>were not</u> able to go on our museum trip.
5. The class <u>has not</u> been to the museum before.
6. Our teacher <u>can not</u> plan another trip for a while.
7. She <u>will not</u> have the time.
8. My friends <u>are not</u> mad at me, though.
9. They know it <u>was not</u> anyone's fault.

APPLY

Think of something you do not like to do. Write three sentences about it. Use contractions with *not.*

The Verb *Have*

> **As a main verb, the word *have* means "to own."**
> ***Have, has,* and *had* are also helping verbs.**
>
> I <u>have</u> my own violin.   I <u>had</u> rented one before.

The verb *have* and its other forms can be used in two ways. Sometimes, *have, has,* and *had* are main verbs. They can also be used as helping verbs.

Read these examples.

> We **had** two tickets to the space museum.
> The museum **has** moon rocks on display.
> The rocks **have** a gray color.
> The spacecraft **has traveled** a long way.
> The astronauts **have worked** long hours.
> Their trip **had taken** five days.

Have and *has* are the present tense form of the verb. Use *have* with a plural subject. Use *has* with a singular subject.

Had is the past tense form of the verb. Use *had* with both plural and singular subjects.

Have, has, and *had* help us ask questions. They are used with a main verb.

Where is *has* in each sentence?

> **Has** the spaceship **landed** on Mars?
> Yes, the spaceship **has landed** on Mars.

In a question, place *have, has,* or *had* before the subject. Put the main verb after the subject.

PRACTICE

A. (Oral) Tell the correct word to complete each sentence.

> **Example:** How (<u>have</u>/has) you tried to stop a burn from hurting?
> **have**

1. Long ago, people (have/<u>had</u>) used aloe plants.
2. An aloe plant (<u>has</u>/have) healing juice.
3. Many sunburn creams (<u>have</u>/had) aloe juice in them.
4. (Had/<u>Have</u>) you squeezed the juice onto a burn.
5. Most people (<u>have</u>/has) baking soda in their kitchens.
6. Baking soda and water also (<u>had</u>/has) helped burns.
7. The pain (have/<u>has</u>) gone away.
8. Some medicines (<u>have</u>/has) this juice, too.

B. (Written) Write each statement as a question. Write each question as a statement.

> **Example:** Russian spaceships have come down on land.
> **Have Russian spaceships come down on land?**

1. American space capsules had landed in the water.
2. Parachutes have slowed down the capsules.
3. Have Navy ships picked the capsules from the water?
4. Has the space shuttle changed this?
5. Has the space shuttle landed like a plane?
6. Astronaut John Young has piloted the shuttle.
7. Has the landing been perfect?
8. Our scientists have done a great job.

APPLY

Write three sentences that tell about a pet or a favorite toy you have had. Use *have, has,* and *had* in your sentences.

Verb Forms

> **The forms of a verb are its *basic parts*. Each verb has four basic parts.**
>
> ask   asking   asked   asked

The *basic parts* of a verb can help you form verb tenses. There are four basic parts of a verb. Study the chart.

Basic Parts of Verbs

Present	Present + ing with helping verb am/was	Past	Past with helping verb have/had
end	ending	ended	ended
slip	slipping	slipped	slipped
wave	waving	waved	waved
try	trying	tried	tried

The first column shows the plain form. This part is used alone. The third column shows the *-ed* form. This part is also used alone. The other parts are used with helping verbs. Use *am, is, are, was,* and *were* with the *-ing* form.

Forming the *-ing* Forms of Verbs

For most verbs, add *-ing*.	float→floating fry→frying
Some verbs drop the *e* and add *-ing*.	dance→dancing take→taking
Some verbs double the consonant and add *-ing*.	bud→budding win→winning dig→digging

For most verbs, the fourth part is spelled like the third. Both end in *ed.* You must remember, however, always to use a helping verb with the fourth part. Use *have, has,* or *had* with the fourth part.

PRACTICE

A. (Oral) Name each main verb and each helping verb.

> **Example:** Weather always has seemed important to people.
> **main verb: seemed; helping verb: has**

1. Early settlers had looked for weather clues.
2. They had noticed these things before rain.
3. Bees were staying near the hive.
4. A cow's tail was pointing east.
5. Flies were swarming together.
6. A seagull was sitting in the sand.
7. These things have predicted bad weather.

B. (Written) Write the correct form of each verb.

> **Example:** Many schools are (teach) art.
> **Many schools are teaching art.**

1. Children have (learn) how artists work.
2. Children are (paint) pictures in oil and watercolor.
3. Students are (make) sculptures.
4. Some artists have (combine) two or more art forms.
5. One artist is (mix) painting and sculpture.
6. Other artists have (glue) things onto surfaces.
7. They are (use) cloth, photos, wood, and plants.

APPLY

Imagine that you are an ant. Write three sentences that tell about your life. Underline each helping verb you use.

Irregular Vers

It goes off
at ten.

> **The spelling of an _irregular verb_ changes. The basic parts of an irregular verb do not end in _ed._**
>
> It <u>goes</u> off at ten. It <u>went</u> off at ten. It <u>has gone</u> off.

To spell the basic parts of an *irregular verb,* do not add *-ed* to the present part. The spelling of an irregular verb changes.

Irregular Verbs

Present	Present + ing with helping verb am/was	Past	Past with helping verb have/had
go	going	went	gone
run	running	ran	run
come	coming	came	come
see	seeing	saw	seen

Irregular verbs need helping verbs. Use *am, is, are, was,* or *were* with the *-ing* form. Use *have, has,* or *had* with *gone, run, come,* and *seen.*

Find the helping verbs.

> I **was going** away. She **has gone.**

Like regular verbs, irregular verbs must agree with the subject of a sentence. For *run, come,* and *see,* just add *-s* to match a singular subject. For *go,* add *-es.*

120 **GRAMMAR/USAGE:** Irregular Verbs

Irregular verbs also tell the time of an event.

Name the time of each verb.

> Josie goes to the park. Last week she went twice.

PRACTICE

A. (Oral) Name the verb that completes each sentence.

> **Example:** Carlos had (<u>went/gone</u>) to the school's field day.
> **gone**

1. His sister Ana will (<u>running/run</u>) in a race.
2. The time for the race was (<u>coming/come</u>) close.
3. Carlos (<u>see/saw</u>) Ana at the starting line.
4. The runners (<u>ran/run</u>) down the track now.
5. They are (<u>coming/came</u>) to the finish line.
6. Ana has (<u>ran/run</u>) faster than everyone.
7. Carlos had (<u>seeing/seen</u>) that and was very proud.

B. (Written) Write each sentence using the correct form.

> **Example:** We have _____ to the big game today. (go)
> **We have gone to the big game today.**

1. People have _____ from all over the city. (come)
2. Some people were _____ late. (come)
3. They are _____ to get tickets. (run)
4. We have _____ these teams play before. (see)
5. We _____ with our friends to their last game. (go)
6. We are _____ to this game, too. (go)

APPLY

Write four sentences about a game or race. Use different forms of the verbs *go, come, run,* and *see.*

The Verb *Do*

> As a main verb, *do* has many meanings. *Do, does,* and *did* are also used as helping verbs.
>
> **Do the dishes. We did like the meal.**

Do is an irregular verb. Its basic parts do not end in *ed*.

You will find many meanings for *do* in a dictionary.

> **Solving a puzzle:** I am **doing** the crossword.
> **Cooking a meal:** The chef has **done** a good job.

You know that a verb must agree with its subject. Use *do* with a plural subject. Use *does* with a singular subject. Use *did* with both singular and plural subjects.

Look at these sentences.

> The astronaut **does** her exercises. (singular subject)
> Astronauts **do** exercises in space. (plural subject)
> One astronaut **did** push-ups. (singular, past tense)
> Others **did** somersaults. (plural, past tense)

Remember that *do* and *did* never have helping verbs in front of them. *Doing* and *done* must be used with helping verbs. Which uses *am, is, are, was,* and *were?* Which uses *have, has,* or *had?*

Do, does, and *did* also help us ask questions. In a question, put *do, does,* or *did* before the subject. Put the main verb after the subject.

Find *did* in these sentences.

> Did the rocket go fast? The rocket did go fast.

PRACTICE

A. (Oral) Name the form of *do* that best completes each sentence.

> **Example:** (Did/Does) you know that a chimp was in space?
> **Did**

1. Ham, a chimp, (do/did) not know he was an astronaut.
2. He just (did/done) what he was trained to do.
3. He had (did/done) the same tasks over and over.
4. He would (doing/do) that task in space.
5. Scientists tested what space (done/did) to the brain.
6. Flight records showed what Ham was (doing/do).
7. Tests showed that Ham had (did/done) his task.
8. Ham (do/did) his job well.

B. (Written) Write each statement as a question. Write each question as a statement.

> **Example:** Did the astronauts exercise every day?
> **The astronauts did exercise every day.**

1. Each astronaut does work hard.
2. Does an astronaut run on a treadmill?
3. They do use exercise bikes.
4. Training does make the heart pump more.
5. Did they stay healthy?
6. Good health did help.
7. Did their hearts and muscles stay strong?
8. Their breathing did improve.
9. Did you know these facts?

APPLY

Write three sentences about what you might do in space. Use different forms of the verb *do*. Circle each verb.

Review the Basics II

A. Contractions with *Not*
Write the two words that form each of these contractions. *(pages 114–115)*

1. wasn't
2. won't
3. can't
4. isn't
5. weren't
6. hasn't
7. don't
8. didn't
9. haven't
10. doesn't
11. wouldn't
12. aren't

B. The Verb *Have*
Choose the correct word to complete each sentence. Write the word. *(pages 116–117)*

1. Paul (has/have) a toothache.
2. The beavers (have/has) constructed a new dam.
3. One year (have/has) passed since the last flood.
4. Who (have/has) the time?
5. Jane (had/have) baked bread yesterday.
6. You (has/have) not watered the plants today.
7. Dick (have/has) cooked his own lunch.
8. The trains (has/have) arrived late all week.

C. Verb Forms
Write each sentence. Underline the main verb. Circle the helping verb. *(pages 118–119)*

1. Kevin's dad has purchased a CB radio for his truck.
2. Then he had applied for a license.
3. Now he is learning CB language.
4. He has learned some funny things.

5. Truckers have called places by special names.
6. They have named Florida "Alligator Alley."
7. Kevin's dad is going to the Shaky Side.
8. That is what truckers are calling the West Coast.

D. Irregular Verbs
Write the form of the verb that best completes each sentence. *(pages 120–121)*

1. Our friends are (going/go) to be in the raft race.
2. Last year, we (gone/went) to watch them race.
3. Have you (come/came) to see Tom race?
4. Have you ever (saw/seen) a raft race?
5. The rafts (running/run) the river rapids.
6. Some rafts have (went/gone) very fast.
7. They have (come/came) down the river like bullets.
8. Last year, one raft (ran/run) the river backward!

E. The Verb *Do*
Write each sentence. Choose the verb that best completes each sentence. *(pages 122–123)*

1. Math is (did/done) in different ways.
2. The Incas (did/done) math with knotted ropes.
3. The Pueblos had (did/done) math with sticks and pebbles.
4. Some people still (does/do) math with an abacus.
5. An abacus (does/do) math as fast as an adding machine.
6. Computers are (do/doing) most math work today.
7. A computer (does/done) math faster than a person.
8. I (does/do) math by counting my fingers and toes.
9. How (do/does) you know the answer?

14 COMMUNICATING

Writing about an Event

Time and space are joined. All events have a time and a place. In our world, we cannot separate time from space. It is impossible.

When you write, you can do the impossible. You can keep time and space apart. Two writers can tell about one event in different ways. One writer may stress time order. Another may stress space order.

Look at the photograph.

Two different paragraphs can be written about the same event. One may stress time order. The other may stress space order.

Read each paragraph.

First the crews used burners to heat air in the balloons. The balloons swelled with hot air. Then the pilots climbed into the baskets of their balloons. When the starter's gun went off, the balloons rose slowly. For three hours they floated across the fields. Finally the first balloon reached the finish point.

What is stressed in the paragraph on page 126—time order or space order? What clue words did the writer use?

The balloons rose up from the field. On the ground below, watchers craned their necks to see. The balloons drifted past. They moved from left to right. The wind carried them. The pilot of the balloon nearest the watchers waved to the crowd. Behind that balloon, another was coming on fast. The farthest balloon already looked small in the distance.

Does the second writer focus on time or space? What clue words were used?

PRACTICE

(Written) Look at these photos. Think about writing a paragraph. Will you stress time order or space order? Make a list of the details you would put in your paragraph.

APPLY

How would you wash a car? Write three sentences to tell how. Stress either time order or space order.

Paragraphs of Action

A paragraph of action tells about an event. It gives the details of what happened. Verbs are very important in a paragraph of action. Verbs give life to the paragraph.

When you write, choose your verbs with care. Dull verbs will make your paragraph dull. Exact verbs give a true picture of the action.

Look at the words in dark print in these paragraphs.

Our whale-watching ship **sat** in the waves. Its engines **were** quiet. Suddenly a teacher **said,** "A whale to the right!" The great, gray body of the whale **came** out of the water. Then the whale **moved** in midair. Its body **hit** the surface. Water **went** up as the whale went into the sea.

Our whale-watching ship **rolled** in the waves. Its engines **remained** quiet. Suddenly a teacher **shouted,** "A whale to the right!" The great, gray body of the whale **rose** out of the water. Then the whale **twisted** in midair. Its body **struck** the surface. Water **sprayed** up as the whale **disappeared** into the sea.

The first paragraph has verbs that are dull. The second has verbs that are more interesting. The verbs are exact. Which paragraph gives a better picture of what happened?

PRACTICE

A. **(Oral)** Name the verb from each pair that is more exact or interesting.

Example: go—race
race

1. laugh—chuckle
2. ate—munched
3. jump—leap
4. drink—gulp
5. whisper—talk
6. walk—march
7. sit—squat
8. slumber—sleep
9. look—glare
10. wiggle—move

B. **(Written)** Rewrite this paragraph. Use the exact or interesting verb from each pair.

Ann, the new girl, (walked/bounded) over to the group of children. They were (huddled/standing) in a corner of the playground. As Ann (came/approached), the group walked away. Ann (walked/shuffled) sadly to the door. What a surprise the children had (done/prepared) for Ann! They had (taped/put) balloons and paper streamers all over the room.

"Welcome to our class!" the children (yelled/said).

APPLY

What do you like to do on a rainy day? Write three sentences to describe what you do. Use exact, interesting verbs.

An Order Paragraph: Plan, Write, Edit

A paragraph can make its readers feel they are at an event. The details can do this. They must tell about the event in the right order. They must be written in a lively, interesting way.

In this lesson, you will write a paragraph. You will tell about an event. Remember, there are three stages in writing. First you will plan what to write. Next you will write the paragraph. Then you will edit your work.

If you wish, you may write about the roller coaster ride shown in the picture. A ride on a roller coaster can be thrilling. Or, you might choose some other event to write about. Your first task is to choose an event.

PLAN

Start your paragraph with a topic sentence. It should tell the main idea of the paragraph.

Here is one topic sentence for the picture.

> Last week I rode my first roller coaster.

Think about the event you chose. Write a topic sentence about it. You may use the sample above.

Now you must plan the rest of the paragraph. Make a list of details about the event. What details will you give? Will you write them in time order or space order?

When your list is complete, reread it. Then number the details in the order you will write them. When your list is complete and in order, you are ready to write.

WRITE

Start your paragraph with the topic sentence. Then look over your list of details. Turn each detail into a sentence.

Here is an example.

> **Detail:** Roller coaster going up
> **Sentence:** The roller coaster climbed slowly up the steep track.

Write the sentences in the order in which you numbered the details. Add time or space clue words. Check the Guidelines. Use them as you write your paragraph.

GUIDELINES

1. Use lively, exact verbs. Make each of your sentences interesting.
2. Include time or space clue words in the right order.

EDIT

Editing takes skill. You must read your work with care. The following paragraph was not edited well. It contains many errors. One sentence is in the wrong place. Two need capital letters. Before you edit your own paragraph, practice on this one.

Check the punctuation marks. Some are missing and some are wrong. Also look at the verbs. Are they interesting? Are all words spelled correctly?

> on the last day of vacation, we went to an amusement part. First we went on the bumper cars Last we went down the giant slide? we climbed to the top and went all the way down Next we went in the fun house.

Now check your own paragraph. Look for errors like the ones in the practice paragraph.

✔ Does each sentence make sense?
✔ Are any words missing?
✔ Are the detail sentences in order?
✔ Are the verbs exact and interesting?

Now reread your paragraph. Check the form.

✔ Is the punctuation correct?
✔ Are capital letters used when needed?
✔ Are all words spelled correctly?
✔ Does each verb agree with its subject?
✔ Are irregular verbs used correctly?
✔ Is your handwriting neat and easy to read?

As the last step, copy your corrected paragraph. Use your best handwriting.

Telling What Happened

Have you ever been asked, "What happened to you?" Before you answer, think about what you will say.

When you start, make a general statement. Look at this example.

I fell off my bike after ball practice.

Next add the details. Time clue words will help your listeners know the order of events.

Look for time clue words in these details.

Before I got to the driveway, I heard a noise. I turned my head to see what had made the sound. Just **then** a dog leaped in front of my bike. I swerved. That is **when** I crashed into the trash can and fell.

GUIDELINES

1. Think things through before you speak.
2. Speak clearly. Look at the person as you speak.
3. First make a general statement.
4. Then add the details of the event. Put them in order with time clue words.

PRACTICE/APPLY

Decide what you will say if you are asked "What happened to you today?" Plan the general statement. Then think of the details you will add. Tell a classmate.

Unit 3 Test

A. Subject-Verb Agreement
Write the form of the verb that best completes each sentence. *(pages 100–101)*
1. The Holland Tunnel (go/goes) under the Hudson River.
2. Cars (travel/travels) 100 feet below the river.
3. Huge fans (move/moves) the tunnel air.
4. Almost 2400 cars an hour may (pass/passes) through the tunnel.
5. Sometimes a car (break/breaks) down.
6. Tunnel police (act/acts) quickly.
7. A tow service (remove/removes) the car.
8. This (prevent/prevents) big traffic jams.

B. Verb Tenses
Write the verb from each sentence. Name its tense. Write *present, past,* or *future. (pages 102–103)*
1. Many creatures eat wood.
2. You will see them in a crumbly dead log.
3. First you will notice a patchy gray plant.
4. Parts of the plant grow down into the wood.
5. You will find beetle tunnels next.
6. The beetles bored holes in the wood for their eggs.
7. The baby beetles then chewed their way along the log.
8. Carpenter ants also carve tunnels in wood.

C. Contractions with *Not*
Write the two words that form each of these contractions. *(pages 114–115)*

1. aren't	5. wouldn't	9. isn't
2. hasn't	6. won't	10. can't
3. doesn't	7. haven't	11. don't
4. wasn't	8. didn't	12. weren't

D. Irregular Verbs
Write the best verb for each sentence. *(pages 116–117)*

1. We (has had) a great time last night.
2. My friends and I (has/had) watched a play at school.
3. Joe said, "Carla (have/has) never seen a better play."
4. Carla said, "I (have/has) my own opinion."
5. They (have/has) not practiced enough.

Write the best verb for each sentence. *(pages 120–121)*

6. "You won't believe what I have (saw/seen)!" yelled Ann.
7. We (ran/run) after her.
8. We all (gone/went) to a big parking lot.
9. A flying saucer had (come/came) down in the lot!
10. I (saw/seen) what the others missed.

Write the best verb for each sentence. *(pages 122–123)*

11. "What are they (doing/did)?" asked Kim.
12. Lisa (did/done) a quick turn.
13. Then we all had (did/done) one.
14. At eight o'clock, the race for home was (did/done).
15. I (did/done) stop at the back door.
16. The visitors (doing/did) not follow us.

E. Writing
Imagine that you have come to school with a puppy. Write an order paragraph. Tell what happens when you walk into the classroom. Use a topic sentence. Use time-order or space-order words. Use exact verbs. Have each detail sentence tell about the topic sentence. *(pages 130–132)*

Keep Practicing

A. Singular and Plural Nouns

Use the noun at the end of the sentence to fill in the blank. Write a singular noun if the blank is marked *S*. Write a plural noun if the blank is marked *P*. *(Unit 2, Lessons 2, 3)*

1. A corn plant has many __P__ . (use)
2. Corn on the __S__ is a favorite food. (cob)
3. Cornmeal can be made into __P__ . (pancake)
4. Have you ever seen __P__ of corn on a farm? (box)
5. Early settlers stuffed mattresses with the __P__ . (leaf)
6. The settlers made a __S__ of corn cobs. (fire)
7. Pilgrim __P__ played with husk dolls. (child)
8. Today many __P__ are made from corn. (product)
9. Powder used for __P__ is one corn product. (baby)
10. Some __P__ of glue also contain corn. (kind)

B. Common and Proper Nouns

Write a proper noun for each common noun. Remember to begin each proper noun with a capital letter. *(Unit 2, Lesson 4)*

1. month	9. holiday	17. boy
2. building	10. street	18. automobile
3. friend	11. doctor	19. team
4. country	12. relative	20. album
5. woman	13. teacher	21. restaurant
6. day	14. road	22. girl
7. city	15. state	23. president
8. store	16. man	24. business

C. Possessive Nouns

Each group of words needs an apostrophe. Write each group correctly. *(Unit 2, Lesson 5)*

1. Sallys pumpkin seeds
2. Uncle Teds garden
3. Aunt Maes apples
4. Hatties garden
5. Peters squash blossoms
6. Ms. Riveras flowers
7. Mr. Wongs vegetables
8. two farmers fields
9. many farmers crops
10. a crows wings
11. several rabbits ears
12. the scarecrows hat
13. the chickens eggs

D. Noun Endings

Add *-er* or *-or* to change each word to a noun. Write the nouns. *(Unit 2, Lesson 10)*

1. bowl	9. dunk	17. sail
2. pitch	10. row	18. cream
3. block	11. golf	19. sign
4. kick	12. jump	20. drain
5. throw	13. creep	21. eat
6. raid	14. act	22. crunch
7. catch	15. fly	23. twist
8. pass	16. watch	24. turn

E. Using *A, An,* and *The*

Write the following paragraph on your paper. Choose the correct article for each sentence. *(Unit 2, Lesson 11)*

Look closely at (a/the) tips of your fingers. You can see that (the/a) designs are different. One kind of fingerprint is called (a/an) arch. (A/An) arch is like a doorway with a rounded top. (The/An) loop is another kind of fingerprint. The loop is shaped like (an/a) hairpin. The third kind of fingerprint is (the/an) whorl. A whorl is like (a/an) series of circles.

F. Using *This, That, These,* and *Those*

Choose the correct word. Write each sentence. *(Unit 2, Lesson 12)*

1. (These/That) animals are circus performers.
2. (Those/This) lions know how to roll over.
3. (Those/That) horse lets tigers ride on its back.
4. (This/These) bear can ride a bike.
5. (These/This) tricks are hard to do.

G. Using *Some, Many,* and *Several*

In each sentence, the word *some, many,* or *several* points to a noun. Write that noun. *(Unit 2, Lesson 13)*

1. Many small ponies can dance.
2. We saw some dogs walk on tightropes.
3. Several large tigers leaped through hoops.
4. We saw some chimps play basketball.
5. Each animal did many tricks.

H. Abbreviations

Rewrite this paragraph. Abbreviate as many words as possible. You should have twelve abbreviations.
(Unit 2, Lesson 7)

On April 5, I went to see Doctor Cohen for my checkup. Her office is at 260 Sumner Street, Tampa, Florida. She found out I was four feet three inches tall. I weighed seventy-eight pounds and three ounces. My next checkup will be on December 9 at four in the afternoon. It is a Monday. I will leave after school. the office is six miles from my house.

I. Punctuating Letters and Envelopes

Rewrite each letter part correctly. Use commas and abbreviations where needed. *(Unit 2, Lesson 9)*

1. Gary Indiana
2. Dear Aunt Flo
3. edwards street
4. Yours Truly:
5. February 12 198-
6. Dear Doctor lee
7. your Friend
8. september 14, 198-
9. Dear sir
10. Boston, ma 01432
11. Houston Texas 77008
12. Your uncle
13. Yours truly

Something Extra

In the News

James Jones is a reporter. He wrote a news story for the Fourth Grade Free Press. Read the story on page 141.

Who was at the fair?   When was the fair?

Where was the fair?   What events took place?

James answered all these questions in his news story. Reporters always give the most important facts in the beginnings of their stories. They tell *who* the story is about, *what* happened, *when* it happened, and *where* it happened.

James told about the events at the fair in the order in which they happened. He used time order. A good reporter tells a story in time order.

Write Away!

Write a news story about a Summer Fair. Tell who, what, where, and when in your first few sentences. Report the events in the order they happened.

Make up a headline. Here are some story ideas to help you start.

Who: students; fourth grade class; the winners

What: Summer Fair; won backward running contest; awarded prizes

Where: Case School Playground; around the track; judges' stand

When: June 20–21; Saturday, June 20; after each event

Fourth Grade Free Press

It's Snow Fooling!
It's Snow Fair!

It's snow fun this weekend at Pine Park. On Friday families from all over the city joined in the ice-float parade. The parade opened this year's snow fair at Pine Park.

After the parade, there was a tug-of-war. A team of fourth-graders, called the Powerful Peppermints, won this contest.

On Saturday there was a snow relay, a skating race, and a giant snowball roll.

The last event took place on Sunday at noon. Hundreds of families went to Pine Park for the January Gymnastics Show.

—*James Jones*

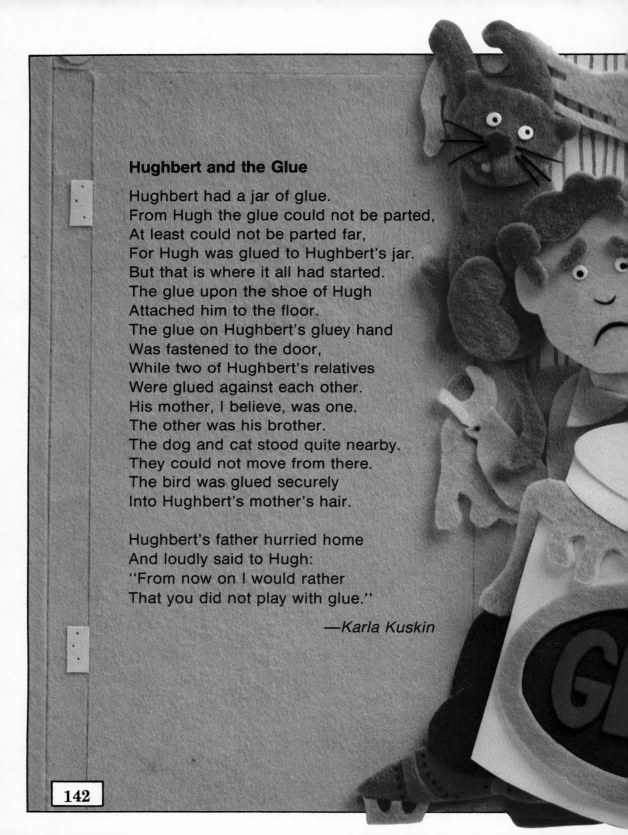

Hughbert and the Glue

Hughbert had a jar of glue.
From Hugh the glue could not be parted,
At least could not be parted far,
For Hugh was glued to Hughbert's jar.
But that is where it all had started.
The glue upon the shoe of Hugh
Attached him to the floor.
The glue on Hughbert's gluey hand
Was fastened to the door,
While two of Hughbert's relatives
Were glued against each other.
His mother, I believe, was one.
The other was his brother.
The dog and cat stood quite nearby.
They could not move from there.
The bird was glued securely
Into Hughbert's mother's hair.

Hughbert's father hurried home
And loudly said to Hugh:
"From now on I would rather
That you did not play with glue."

—*Karla Kuskin*

142

4

Looking at
Stories

SKILLS TO BUILD ON

Adjectives
Adverbs
Card Catalog
Dialogue

PRACTICAL APPLICATIONS

Writing a Story
Telling Stories

Adjectives

> An *adjective* is a word that describes a noun. An adjective may come before or after the noun.
>
> <u>careful</u> raccoons <u>wrinkled</u> monkeys <u>long, green</u> snakes

You know that a noun names a person, place, or thing. An *adjective* is a word that describes a noun. The adjective gives a detail about the noun.

Look at these sentences.

A fox hides in a den.

A **young** fox hides in a **warm** den.

The words *young* and *warm* are adjectives. They add details about the fox and den. They answer *What kind?*

An adjective may tell one of three things about a noun. Most adjectives tell *Which ones? How many?* or *What kind?* Look at the chart.

Adjectives Give Details

Which Ones?	How Many?	What Kind?
other lions	ten lions	hungry tigers
the last ant	some birds	a green moth
this buffalo	few whales	smelly skunks

More than one adjective can describe the same noun.

Find the adjectives in this sentence.

We saw a large, tan lion hide in the tall, green grass.

PRACTICE

A. (Oral) For each sentence, name the adjective and the noun it describes. Then tell the question each adjective answers: *Which ones? How many? What kind?*

> **Example:** Small animals have ways to be safe.
> **small animals—What kind?**

1. Porcupines have sharp quills.
2. Loose quills catch in an enemy.
3. An armadillo curls into a tight ball.
4. The hide of an armadillo is tough skin.
5. Most enemies will not get through.
6. A brown weasel may change color.
7. In the snow, those weasels are hard to see.

B. (Written) Add at least one adjective to each sentence. Write each new sentence.

> **Example:** Giraffes eat the leaves of trees.
> **Tall, graceful giraffes eat the leaves of trees.**

1. Lions eat meat.
2. Monkeys like fruits.
3. Moose eat meals of bark.
4. Beavers also chew bark.
5. Squirrels hide nuts.
6. Otters catch fish.

APPLY

Write about a friend. In three sentences, tell something nice. Use adjectives. Circle them.

Using Adjectives That Compare

> **An adjective is used to compare nouns. To compare two nouns, use *-er* or *more*. To compare three or more nouns, use *-est* or *most.***
>
> My cat is <u>quicker</u> and <u>more skillful</u> than a dog.
> My cat is the <u>quickest</u> and <u>most skillful</u> of all cats.

Adjectives can be used to compare nouns. To compare two nouns, add *-er* to the adjective. To compare three or more nouns, add *-est*.

See how *tall* changes.

A horse is **tall.**

An elephant **is taller** than a horse.

A giraffe is the **tallest** animal in the world.

For words like *playful,* do not add *-er* or *-est*. Use *more* and *most* instead. Look at these sentences.

Otters are **more playful** than lions.

Monkeys are the **most playful** of all.

Forming Adjectives That Compare

For some adjectives, change the *y* to *i* and add *-er* or *-est.*	happy	happier	happiest
For some adjectives, drop the final *e* and add *-er* or *-est.*	tame	tamer	tamest
For some adjectives, double the final consonant and add *-er* or *-est.*	big	bigger	biggest

PRACTICE

A. (Oral) Choose the correct word to complete each of these sentences.

> **Example:** Sharks are the (more/most) dangerous fish of all.
> **Sharks are the most dangerous fish of all.**

1. A white shark is the (more/most) fierce shark of all.
2. The white shark is (fast/faster) than the blue shark.
3. White sharks are (rarer/rarest) than whale sharks.
4. The whale shark is the (bigger/biggest) fish in the sea.
5. Whale sharks are the (more/most) harmless of all sharks.
6. A shark's sense of smell is (sharper/sharpest) than a person's.
7. A shark's skin is (rough/rougher) than sandpaper.
8. Sharks look the (meaner/meanest) of all fish.

B. (Written) For each sentence, write the adjective and the noun it describes. Write how many things are being compared in each one.

> **Example:** The smallest bird of all is a hummingbird.
> **smallest bird, all birds**

1. The bee hummer is smaller than a moth.
2. Ostriches are the biggest birds of all.
3. An ostrich can be taller than a horse.
4. Parrots may be the most colorful birds ever seen.
5. A hawk has sharper eyesight than a person.
6. A crow is more intelligent than an owl.
7. Parakeets are the most popular of all pet birds.
8. My pet bird is the prettiest one in town.

APPLY

Write three sentences. Compare a cat, a dog, and a bird. Use adjectives in each sentence. Circle them.

Details and the Senses

> **An adjective can tell how things look, sound, taste, smell, or feel.**
>
> <u>Large, crisp</u> apples have <u>cool, sweet</u> juices.

What we know about the world comes to us through five senses: *sight, hearing, taste, smell,* and *touch.*

Sight tells us what things look like. Hearing tells us what things sound like. We use these senses most often.

These adjectives describe what is seen and heard.

A **bright** light glared. The **shrill** siren shrieked.

You see that a light is bright. You hear that a siren is shrill. These details come to you through your senses.

Taste, smell, and touch are our other three senses. Look at these groups of words.

salty ocean   **burned** toast   **slippery** ice

Which adjective tells how something tastes? How something smells? How something feels?

Adjectives of the Senses

Sight	Hearing	Taste	Smell	Touch
yellow curly	loud coughing	peppery sour	flowery smoky	scratchy cool

Name some adjectives you could add to the chart.

PRACTICE

A. (Oral) Name one of the five senses for each adjective. Name *sight, taste, smell, touch,* or *hearing.* Some adjectives may fit with more than one sense.

1. sharp
2. loud
3. fresh
4. feathery

5. salty
6. tall
7. spicy
8. purple

9. furry
10. soft
11. bitter
12. striped

B. (Written) Look at the sense listed for each sentence. Add two adjectives to the sentence. Put a comma between them. Write the new sentence.

Example: June heard a dog. (hearing)
June heard a noisy, barking dog.

1. The dog's tongue licked Cruz's hand. (touch)
2. An elephant tossed dust onto his back. (touch)
3. Kit held a rose to her nose. (smell)
4. Paula cut a slice of watermelon. (taste)

5. The ambulance's siren shattered the quiet. (hearing)
6. We looked out over the ocean. (sight)
7. Ari sipped some soup. (taste)
8. The sound of the drum startled Tony. (hearing)

APPLY

Pretend you are creating a haunted house. What will you include? Write three sentences about the house. Use adjectives that tell about the senses.

The Adjectives *Good, Bad, Many,* and *Much*

> **The adjectives *good, bad, many,* and *much* change form when they are used to compare.**
>
> My lunch was <u>good</u>. Yours looked <u>better</u> than mine.
> Joe's lunch looked <u>best</u> of all.

You know that you add *-er* or *-est* to many adjectives to compare nouns. The adjectives *good, bad, many,* and *much* are different. They change form when used to compare.

Comparing *Good, Bad, Many, Much*

For One	For Two	For Three or More
good	better	best
bad	worse	worst
many		
much	more	most

Use *better, worse,* and *more* to compare two nouns. Use *best, worst,* and *most* to compare three or more nouns.

Notice that *much* and *many* both use *more* and *most* to compare. Use *many* to describe things you can count, such as letters, lunches, and leaves. Use *much* to describe things that are hard to count, such as mail, food, and trash.

Which of these sentences compare two things?

There was **more** rain than sunshine this week.
Monday's weather was **better** than Thursday's.
Tuesday's weather was the **worst** of all.

PRACTICE

A. (Oral) Choose the adjective that correctly completes each sentence.

Example: We had (much/more) rain this week than last.
more

1. This is Gail's (best/good) summer ever!
2. Her new camp is (better/best) than last year's.
3. Last year, Gail had the (worse/worst) time.
4. There were (more/many) rainy days than sunny ones.
5. Last year's weather was (worse/worst) than this year's.
6. Gail has the (best/better) counselors of all.
7. She is doing (more/many) crafts than last year.
8. Gail is having the (much/most) fun ever!

B. (Written) Decide which form of the adjective will best complete each sentence. Write each sentence.

Example: Eric thinks snowy weather is the (good) of all.
Eric thinks snowy weather is the best of all.

1. The class was talking about (good) and bad weather.
2. Pat thinks snowy days are the (bad) of all.
3. She likes (much) sun than snow.
4. Chip wants (many) foggy days than sunny ones.
5. Phil thinks hurricanes are the (bad) of storms.
6. Rita says a tornado is (bad) than a hurricane.
7. Cindy says any weather is (good) than no weather!

APPLY

Write three sentences that tell why you like one color more than the others. Use forms of the adjectives *good*, *bad*, *many*, and *much*.

Review the Basics I

A. Adjectives

For each sentence write three answers. Write the adjective and the noun it describes. Then write the question each adjective answers: *Which one? How many? What kind? (pages 144–145)*

1. You can make a bendable bone.
2. Save a bone from a chicken dinner.
3. Put that bone into a glass.
4. Fill that glass with vinegar.
5. Vinegar dissolves the hard part of the bone.
6. The bone becomes soft and it bends.
7. This takes two weeks for a drumstick.
8. A wishbone takes fewer days to soften.
9. It is a thinner bone.
10. This is a great trick.

B. Using Adjectives That Compare

Choose the correct word to complete each sentence. Write each sentence. *(pages 146–147)*

1. Many stars are (bigger/biggest) than our sun.
2. Many stars are also (hotter/hottest) than the sun.
3. The (hotter/hottest) stars of all are blue.
4. The (cooler/coolest) stars of all are red.
5. Some red stars are the (more/most) gigantic of all stars.
6. A red star is (dimmer/dimmest) than a yellow one.
7. A yellow star is (brighter/brightest) than a red one.
8. A blue star is the (more/most) brilliant of the three.
9. Some small stars look (whitest/whiter) than the others.
10. Of all the stars, which looks (bigger/biggest)?

C. Details and the Senses
Look at the sense listed for each sentence. Add two adjectives to the sentence. Put a comma between them. *(pages 148–149)*

1. The dragon came out of its cave. (sight)
2. The woman stood before the dragon. (sight)
3. "Will you light my barbecue grill?" she asked. (touch)
4. The dragon lit the fire for her. (hearing)
5. She cooked over coals. (smell)
6. The meat looked delicious. (sight)
7. The dragon looked at the meat. (touch)
8. It was a bite for him. (taste)
9. The dragon thought for a minute. (touch)
10. The woman looked at the grill. (sight)

D. The Adjectives *Good, Bad, Many,* and *Much*
Choose the adjective that correctly completes each sentence. Write each complete sentence. *(pages 150–151)*

1. Carrie is the (better/best) pitcher on the team.
2. She is a (worse/worst) hitter than Alex.
3. Alex is a (better/good) hitter than anyone but Liz.
4. Liz has hit (many/more) home runs than Alex.
5. Liz has the (most/more) hits of anyone.
6. Tim is the (worse/worst) fielder on the team.
7. He makes the (many/most) errors of all the players.
8. They think their team is the (better/best) of all.
9. We think they are (good/better) than last year.
10. Their pitchers are the (better/best) in the league.

Adjectives in a Paragraph

Adjectives can help us see things more clearly. You know that adjectives add details. They make a description come alive. Details can make things seem real.

Compare these two sentences.

I held a frog.
I held a damp and wiggly frog.

Which sentence makes the frog seem real? Which one helps you feel the frog in your hand?

A paragraph may describe something. Adjectives in the paragraph can make a place or thing seem real. The readers may feel that they are "there."

Which paragraph has adjectives?

Worms create a sky on the ceiling of a cave. The creatures dangle threads like lines. Insects are drawn to the worms' light. The bugs stick to the threads. The victims are reeled in to be eaten.

More than a thousand glowing worms create a starry sky on the ceiling of a cave. These tiny creatures dangle silken threads thinner than fishing lines. Insects are drawn to the worms' bluish light. The most careless bugs stick to the gummy threads. The unlucky victims are reeled in to be eaten.

Which paragraph makes the scene seem more real? Which is more interesting? When you write, use adjectives to improve your paragraphs.

PRACTICE/APPLY

(Written) Read this paragraph. It describes the picture on this page. Rewrite the paragraph. Add adjectives from the Word Bank.

   A flock of penguins waddles across the ice. The birds look like they have suits on. Are they going to a party? The birds are walking to the water.

WORD BANK

black
silly
foolish
plump
several
proud
those
playful
white
many
fancy
awkward
noisy
slippery
unusual
graceful

Forming Adjectives with Suffixes

You can change the meaning of a word by adding a suffix to it. A *suffix* is a word part that is added at the end of another word. It changes the meaning of that base word. Some suffixes change base words into adjectives. Study the chart.

Making Adjectives with Suffixes

Suffix	Meaning	Base Word + Suffix = Adjective
-able	able, likely to	comfort + able = comfortable
-ful	full of, marked by	help + ful = helpful
-ish	like a, somewhat	snap + ish = snappish
-less	without	care + less = careless
-y	full of, having	taste + y = tasty

By changing base words to adjectives, you can write the same message in a different way. Nouns from one sentence can become adjectives in another.

Both sentences in these pairs give the same message.

No **clouds** were in the sky. The day was **cloudless.**
There was a **breeze.** The day was **breezy.**
We could **enjoy** the day. The day was **enjoyable.**

With adjectives, one sentence can give the same message as three. Three short sentences can be joined.

What three sentences made this one?

It was a cloudless, breezy, enjoyable day.

PRACTICE

A. (Oral) Add *-able, -ful, -ish, -less,* or *-y* to these words. Make adjectives you know. (Some words could take more than one ending.)

Example: grace
        graceful

1. child	**6.** help	**11.** clown
2. wonder	**7.** play	**12.** sand
3. pain	**8.** noise	**13.** sun
4. beauty	**9.** bend	**14.** wash
5. age	**10.** cream	**15.** break

B. (Written) Make an adjective to fit each sentence. Add *-able, -ful, -ish, -less,* or *-y* to the word at the end of each sentence. Write each sentence.

Example: The _____ period ended. (score)
        The scoreless period ended.

1. We played an _____ game of soccer. (enjoy)
2. Both teams' players were _____ . (skill)
3. At first the crowd grew _____ . (noise)
4. Everyone tried not to make any _____ errors. (care)
5. One _____ player made a great shot. (fear)
6. He was _____ . (success)
7. The goalie's move was _____ . (point)
8. A _____ score was made. (wonder)
9. Then the other team made one more _____ mistake. (fool)
10. We were _____ when our team won. (thank)

APPLY

Make adjectives from the base words *spoon, hope,* and *break.* Use each new word in a sentence.

Finding Books in the Library

A library has two kinds of books, *fiction* and *nonfiction.* Fiction is a made-up story by a writer.

Fiction books are put on the shelf after checking the author's last name. They are in alphabetical order.

Nonfiction books tell about real places, people, and things. To find a *nonfiction* book, first look in the card catalog. You will find three cards for each nonfiction book. Each card shows the same information.

The cards in a *card catalog* are in alphabetical order. Look at the catalog drawer on page 159. There are two sets of letters on the front. All the cards in the drawer start with FRE to FRO. You would find a subject card on *freedom* in this drawer. A card on *fish* would be in another drawer.

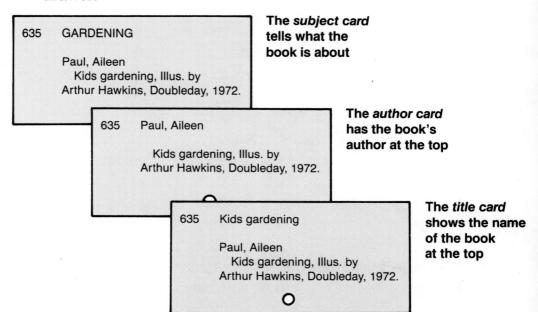

The *subject card* tells what the book is about

635 GARDENING

Paul, Aileen
    Kids gardening, Illus. by
Arthur Hawkins, Doubleday, 1972.

The *author card* has the book's author at the top

635 Paul, Aileen

    Kids gardening, Illus. by
    Arthur Hawkins, Doubleday, 1972.

The *title card* shows the name of the book at the top

635 Kids gardening

Paul, Aileen
    Kids gardening, Illus. by
    Arthur Hawkins, Doubleday, 1972.

PRACTICE

A. (Oral) Tell if each topic can be found in this catalog drawer. Tell *before* or *after* for other topics.

> **Example:** a book titled *The Frog Band*
> **yes**

1. a book written by John D. Frith
2. a book about France
3. a book titled *Friendly Dinosaurs*
4. a book about flying
5. a book written by Don Freeman
6. a book titled *Fun with Magic*
7. a book about freshwater fish

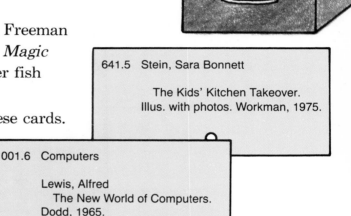

FRE-FRO

> 641.5 Stein, Sara Bonnett
>
> The Kids' Kitchen Takeover.
> Illus. with photos. Workman, 1975.

B. (Written) Look at these cards. Write the answers to the questions.

> 001.6 Computers
>
> Lewis, Alfred
>   The New World of Computers.
> Dodd, 1965.

1. What is the title of the book by Sara Stein?
2. Who wrote *The New World of Computers?*
3. What is the subject of Alfred Lewis's book?
4. What is the title of the book by Alfred Lewis?
5. What is the subject of *The New World of Computers?*
6. Who wrote *The Kids' Kitchen Takeover?*

APPLY

In a card catalog, look up kites. Write three sentences, name two books, their authors, and why you chose the books.

Punctuating Dialogue

Few people ever spend a whole day without speaking. On most days, you speak to many people. *Dialogue* is what people say to each other. When you repeat words spoken by another person, you quote them.

Written dialogue has two parts. One part is the *speaker tag.* It tells who spoke. It may also tell how the person spoke. The speaker tag may be first. It may come at the end. It may be in the middle.

Look at these examples.

Meg asked quietly, "What do you do when an

elephant sneezes?"

"You tell me," **said Phil with a smile,** "because

I don't know."

"Get out of the way!" **Meg answered laughingly.**

The other part of dialogue is the words that are spoken. That part is called the *quotation.* It is set off by quotation marks (" "). Inside these marks are put the exact words that were said. Find the quotations in each of the three examples above.

When you read dialogue, look for clues to find out who is talking and what is said. An indented line is one clue to look for. The start of each quotation is indented. When you write dialogue use the same clue. Indent the start of each new speaker.

Check the Guidelines with these examples.

"Where do you find elephants?" asked Mei Ling.

"I don't know," admitted Ron.

"It depends on where you lost them!" exclaimed Ana.

PRACTICE

(Written) Put the correct punctuation in these sentences.

Example: Can we go to the carnival asked Marge.
      "Can we go to the carnival?" asked Marge.

1. Dad announced happily Here we are at the carnival!
2. What do you want to do first asked Mom.
3. I want to ride the roller coaster shouted George.
4. Luisa pleaded May we ride the bumper cars?
5. I want to go on the ferris wheel said Carmen.

APPLY

Write three sentences of dialogue between a robot and yourself. Use quotation marks in each sentence.

Adverbs

> **An *adverb* tells more about a verb, an adjective, or another adverb.**
>
> A <u>very</u> small bird landed <u>here</u> <u>quite</u> <u>quietly</u>.

An *adverb* is one kind of describing word. An adverb describes a verb, an adjective, or another adverb. Adverbs answer the questions *Where? When?* and *How?*

Look at the adverbs in these sentences.

> The hawk dives **down.** It pounces **now.**
> It moves **very quickly.** It is a **very** fast bird.

The adverb *down* describes *dives.* It tells where the hawk dives. What does *now* tell about *pounce?*

The adverb *very* appears twice. In one sentence, it describes an adverb. In the other, it describes the adjective *fast.* What question does *very* answer? What question does *quickly* answer?

Adverbs can move around without changing the meaning of the sentence. Look at these sentences.

> **Now** I see it. I see it **now.**

Many adverbs end in *ly.* The chart shows how *-ly* is added to a word to make an adverb.

WORD BANK

Where?

here
away
forward
near

When?

later
soon
today
now

How?

bravely
fast
neatly
quite

Forming Adverbs

tame + -ly = tamely slow + -ly = slowly	kind + -ly = kindly bad + -ly = badly

PRACTICE

A. (Oral) Name the adverb from each sentence. Tell the question it answers: *When? Where?* or *How?*

> **Example:** An otter can easily catch a fish.
> **easily—How?**

1. Sea otters live mainly on shellfish.
2. A sea otter floats peacefully.
3. Now the otter holds a rock.
4. The otter soon breaks a clamshell.
5. The otter lazily eats the clam.
6. Otters sometimes eat fish.
7. An otter is a very good swimmer.
8. It can dive deeply.
9. The otter chases fish there.

B. (Written) Write two new sentences for each sentence. In one sentence, add an adverb. In the next sentence change the adverb.

> **Example:** Frogs leap.
> **Frogs leap quickly.**
> **Frogs leap high.**

1. A whale dived.
2. Geese honked.
3. Fish swim.
4. Horses run.
5. Birds fly.
6. Seals play.
7. Children sing.
8. Babies sleep.
9. The wind blows.
10. A bell rings.
11. The cat purrs.
12. Balloons pop.

APPLY

Write three sentences about an activity you enjoy. Use adverbs to tell where, when, and how. Circle each adverb.

Adverbs for *When, Where,* and *How*

> An adverb answers the question *When? Where?* or *How?* A group of words may act as an adverb.
>
> <u>After dark</u>, a moth flew <u>to the lamp.</u>

A group of words can act as an adverb. The group of words can tell more about a verb.

Read these examples.

The bat left its cave **after dark.** (when)
The bat flew **through the air.** (where)
The bat's wings flapped **with great speed.** (how)

The words *after dark* tell *When? Through the air* tells *Where?* What does *with great speed* answer?

Look at the words in darker type below. *In, at, before,* and *after* are not adverbs. They mark a group of words that may act as an adverb.

Three word groups begin with *in.* Each answers a different question. What questions can the word *at* answer?

WORD BANK		
When?	**Where?**	**How?**
at noon	**in** the house	**with** a friend
during dinner	**to** the door	**in** a low voice
in an hour	**at** school	**without** any books

PRACTICE

A. (Oral) Name the group of words from each sentence that answers: *When? Where?* or *How?*

> **Example:** Many animals sleep through the winter.
> **through the winter—When?**

1. Some animals change in a strange way.
2. Their temperatures drop after a short time.
3. Their heartbeats slow during the sleep.
4. At this time, the animals hardly breath.
5. They get energy from their body fat.
6. These animals sleep until warm weather.
7. They awaken in the spring.

B. (Written) Add a group of words to each sentence to answer the question. Write the sentence.

> **Example:** Juan was walking. (Where?)
> **Juan was walking near the river.**

1. Juan saw a snake. (When?)
2. The snake crawled. (Where?)
3. Its tongue flicked. (How?)
4. The snake's body slithered. (Where?)
5. The snake stopped. (When?)
6. The snake turned. (How?)
7. The snake went. (Where?)

APPLY

Write three sentences about something you once did in school. In your sentences, use groups of words that answer *When? Where?* and *How?* Draw a line under each group.

Using Adverbs
That Compare

> **An adverb can be used to compare actions. For two actions, use *-er* or *more*. For three or more actions, use *-est* or *most*.**
>
> My cat gets up <u>earlier</u> than I do.
> My bird is awake <u>earliest</u> of all.

Adverbs are used to compare actions. When you compare two actions, add *-er* to most adverbs that do not end in *ly*. Use *more* with many adverbs that end in *ly*.

See how these adverbs are used.

A horse runs **faster** than a person runs.

A cheetah runs **more quickly** than a horse.

The word *than* is used when two actions are compared.

When you compare three or more actions, add *-est* to adverbs that do not end in *ly*. Use *most* with many adverbs that end in *-ly*. Look at these adverbs.

Of all birds, the duck hawk flies **fastest.**

The snail moves **most slowly** of all animals.

Forming Adverbs

For some adverbs, change the *y* to *i* and add *-er* or *-est*.	early earlier earliest
For some adverbs, drop the final *e* and add *-er* or *-est*.	late later latest

PRACTICE

A. (Oral) Give the forms of these adverbs that are used to compare actions.

Example: high   quickly
higher   highest   **more quickly   most quickly**

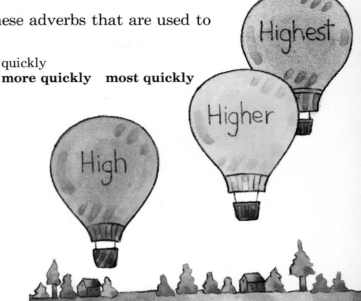

1. fast	**10.** slowly
2. closely	**11.** happily
3. softly	**12.** lamely
4. early	**13.** sharply
5. quietly	**14.** soon
6. late	**15.** sneakily
7. easily	**16.** crisply
8. low	**17.** sadly
9. near	**18.** friendly

B. (Written) Choose the adverb that best completes each sentence. Write the sentence.

1. The cheetah runs (faster/fastest) than other animals.
2. Barracudas swim (more/most) swiftly than sharks.
3. At high speed, some pigeons fly (longer/longest) of all birds.
4. A pigeon can fly (farther/farthest) than a parakeet.
5. A duck hawk flies (faster/fastest) than a sparrow.
6. Whales swim (farther/farthest) of all mammals.
7. Giraffes can reach (higher/highest) of all animals.
8. Hawks can see (more/most) sharply than people.

APPLY

Write three sentences about a racing car, a dump truck, and a bicycle. Use the same adverb in different forms to compare the vehicles.

Building Sentences by Adding Details

> **A short sentence may have one noun and one verb. It may have two nouns and one verb. Adding details builds sentences.**
>
> Dogs bark. Cooks bake bread.
> Small dogs often bark fiercely.
> Skillful cooks bake crusty bread in hot ovens.

A noun and a verb can form a sentence. They are the complete subject and predicate. Other sentences have a noun in the predicate, too. Look at these sentences.

Children run.   Children run races.

Details may be added to these short sentences. To build a sentence, ask the questions that adjectives and adverbs answer. Add the answers to the sentence.

See how each sentence is built.

How many?	**Six** children run races.
Where?	Six children run races **in the park.**
When?	**Now** six children run races in the park.
What kind?	Now six children run **sack** races in the park.
How?	Now six children **slowly** run sack races in the park.
Which one?	Now six children slowly run sack races in **that** park.

PRACTICE

A. (Oral) Add a detail to each sentence. Answer the question that follows the sentence.

> **Example:** Children study. (Where?)
> **Children study at their desks.**

1. Rain fell. (When?)
2. People play ball. (Where?)
3. Acrobats tumbled. (How?)
4. Spacecraft explore. (What kind?)
5. Clowns dance. (How many?)
6. Mice scampered. (Which ones?)
7. Flags fly. (What kind?)
8. Adults give gifts. (How many?)

B. (Written) Add details to each sentence. Write each new sentence you build.

> **Example:** Fish swim.
> **Small green fish swim down and up.**

1. Carpenters cut wood.
2. Bees buzz.
3. Engines roared.
4. Children jump rope.
5. Gardeners plant seeds.
6. Keys rattle.
7. Music plays.
8. Flowers grow.
9. Cows give milk.

Children study at their desks.

APPLY

Choose three sentences from Practice A. Change the details. Write each new sentence.

Review the Basics II

A. Adverbs
Write the adverb from each sentence. Write the question it answers: *When? Where?* or *How? (pages 162–163)*

1. Yesterday, Ken lost his glasses.
2. He looked everywhere.
3. Ken was very worried.
4. He needed the glasses then.
5. Ken's friends searched carefully.
6. The glasses could not be found anywhere.
7. "I see them there," announced Ken's mother.
8. "You're wearing them!" she said laughingly.
9. Now Ken remembers.
10. He slowly smiles.

B. Adverbs for *When, Where,* and *How*
Write the group of words from each sentence that acts as an adverb. Write the question each group answers.
(pages 164–165)

1. We play ice hockey after school.
2. The game is played on an ice rink.
3. Our games take place in the winter.
4. A game lasts for three twenty-minute periods.
5. Each team puts six players on the ice.
6. Players hit a puck toward a goal cage.
7. Players chase after the puck.
8. They hit the puck with their sticks.
9. The puck may hit against the boards.
10. The players skate in a hurry.
11. They move to the side.

C. Using Adverbs That Compare

Write the forms of these adverbs that are used to compare actions. *(pages 166–167)*

1. close
2. rapidly
3. distantly
4. friendly
5. sadly
6. swiftly
7. fast
8. high
9. near
10. happily
11. soon
12. late
13. loudly
14. quickly
15. mildly
16. carefully
17. hard
18. quietly
19. tightly
20. gladly

D. Building Sentences by Adding Details

Add a detail to each sentence. Answer the question that follows the sentence. Write the sentence. *(pages 168–169)*

1. Authors write quickly. (How many?)
2. Shadows moved. (When?)
3. Rivers flow. (How?)
4. Beavers build dams. (Where?)
5. Wolves howled. (How?)
6. People sing songs. (What kind?)
7. Mail carriers deliver mail. (Which ones?)
8. Neighbors chatted. (Where?)
9. The baby slept. (When?)
10. Trains arrived. (How many?)
11. Children ran races. (How?)
12. Students answer questions. (Which ones?)

13 COMMUNICATING

Stories

A story has several parts. Most stories have a *title*, *characters*, a *setting*, and a *plot*.

The *title* is the name of the story. It should make you want to read the story.

> Alex and the Big Race Day

The *characters* may be people, animals, or things. They are the actors in the story.

> Alex, Marta, and several other
> children and adults

The *setting* is when and where the story takes place. It tells you what you would see or hear if you could be in the story. The setting may be real or imagined.

> an imaginary bike shop in France, not long ago

The *plot* is the idea of the story. The plot tells what happens. It may tell a problem the characters have. It is what the characters do and what happens in the story.

> Alex and some other children want to ride in the
> Great Bicycle Race through France. They visit
> Marta's Bike Shop. Some of the children do not have
> racing bikes. Others do not own bikes. Marta and
> Alex think of a way for all the children to take part
> in the race. They form a team and win the race.

PRACTICE

(**Written**) Write what each item describes: *title, characters, setting,* or *plot.*

Example: "The Wizard of Oz"
> **title**

1. Dorothy, a scarecrow, a tin woodsman, a cowardly lion
2. The land of Oz
3. A storm carries a girl to a strange land. She has many adventures. She tries to get back home.
4. "The Nightingale"
5. Long ago, in China
6. An emperor likes a mechanical nightingale better than a real one. The real one goes away. The other one breaks and the emperor falls sick. The real bird returns and the emperor gets well.
7. An emperor, a nightingale
8. A Swiss family is shipwrecked. They live on an island for ten years. At last, they are rescued.
9. Mother, father, three sons
10. Island near Australia, 200 years ago
11. *The Swiss Family Robinson*

APPLY

Think of a story you like. Use four or five sentences to describe it. Give the title, characters, setting, and plot.

Writing about Story Characters and Setting

A story may start with a description of the characters. Or, the setting may be described first. Sometimes the first paragraph tells about a problem the characters must solve.

Stories are often built on one small idea. The chart below gives some examples. After you have studied them, choose one. Later you will write a paragraph about it.

Think about these ideas.

Ideas for Stories

People are waiting for a bus. Full buses are going by without stopping.	A doorbell is ringing. The mail carrier is delivering a package.
A person is in a crowded store, in a hurry to buy something. No clerks are there to wait on people.	It is the first day in a new class at a new school.
A waiter in a restaurant has served the wrong meals to people.	Someone wants to buy your latest invention.

Which idea for a story did you choose? Think about the setting. Is it indoors or outdoors? If it is outdoors, what is the weather like? What is the time of day? Make a list of the answers to these questions.

Think about your senses and what they tell you. What would a person in the setting see and hear? What would they smell, taste, or touch?

List some words or phrases about where the story takes place. Use adjectives and adverbs. Answer *When? Where? How? What kind? How many?* and *Which ones?*

Now think of two characters. Give each one a name. What do they look like? How old are they? How do they feel and act?

Imagine that you are in the same setting. What would your feelings be? How would you act? Make a new list to describe each character.

Think about a problem that must be solved. Write a sentence telling what the problem is.

PRACTICE

(Written) Look at what you wrote. Did you tell enough about the setting and the characters? Change your lists of words into sentences. Write about the characters or the setting. Write your sentences in the form of a paragraph. Change words if you need to. Make each sentence go smoothly from one thought to the next. Your paragraph will be the first part of a story.

APPLY

If your Practice sentences tell about the characters, write four sentences to tell about the setting. If you wrote about the setting, now tell about the two characters.

A Story: Plan, Write, Edit

You have written about the characters and setting for a story. In this lesson, you will tell the plot of the story. The plot is what the characters do in the setting. What problem do the characters have? The plot of your story will tell what your characters do about their problem.

PLAN

A story plot has three parts. The *beginning* tells about the problem to be solved. In the *middle,* the characters try to solve the problem. The *end* of the plot tells how the problem is solved.

Reread what you wrote for Lesson 14. Think about your characters, the setting, and the problem. Then look at these pictures for more ideas.

Think of what will happen to the characters. What will happen first? Will one or both characters be involved? Answer each question. Write one or two sentences for each.

Think of how the characters will deal with the problem. What will happen second? You may think of dialogue. Tell what one character says to the other. Write sentences for the middle part.

Think of how the problem will be solved. What will happen? How will the story end? Add these answers to your sentences.

WRITE

In Lesson 14 you began your story. The first part introduced the characters and setting. Now you will write a paragraph about what happens to the characters.

Use the sentences you wrote for the Plan. Change them if you wish. Write them as a paragraph. Before you write, study the Guidelines on page 178.

Give your story a title. The title should give people an idea about what is in the story. The title should make people want to read the story.

EDIT

Now you are ready to edit your story. Pretend that you are reading it for the first time. Ask each of these questions. Mark any changes you need to make.

✔ Do the characters seem to fit the story?
✔ Is it clear where the story takes place?
✔ Does the plot have a beginning, middle, and end?
✔ Are any words missing?
✔ Are all sentences in order?

Now read your story again. Check its form.

✔ Is the first line of each paragraph indented?
✔ Is the first line of each quotation indented?
✔ Are all quotation marks in the right place?
✔ Does each quotation start with a capital letter and end with the right punctuation mark?
✔ Are all words spelled correctly?

Now copy the story in your best handwriting.

16 COMMUNICATING

Telling Stories

Telling a story can be fun. Before you speak, think about what you will tell. That way, you will not forget any details. Tell things in the order they happen. Make sure everyone hears you.

GUIDELINES

1. Choose a story to tell.
2. Think about the story. Make notes.
   The plot needs a beginning, middle, and end.
   Make notes about the characters and setting.
3. Practice telling the story out loud.
4. Tell your story to the class. Speak clearly and loudly.
   Include details of who, what, when, where,
      why, and how.
   Use your voice. Show how the characters feel.

PRACTICE/APPLY

(Oral) Choose one of your favorite stories. Think about telling the story. Then tell the story to a friend or to the class.

Unit 4 Test

A. Adjectives

For each sentence, write the adjective and the noun it describes. Then write the question each adjective answers: *Which ones? How many? What kind? (pages 144–145)*

1. The clanging alarm woke me up.
2. Trish squeezed out the wet sponge.
3. Six acrobats tumbled across the stage.
4. I want to have a gray kitten.
5. Jeff bit into a crunchy piece of celery.
6. Brenda breathed in the sweet scent of the rose.
7. A camel crossed the empty desert.
8. I had a sour pickle for lunch.
9. Many clowns work in parades.
10. I drank a glass of cool water.
11. Friends gave me a striped shirt.

B. Using Adjectives That Compare

Choose the correct word to complete each sentence. Write the sentence. *(pages 146–147)*

1. The (more/most) famous tree of all is a sequoia.
2. This 4000-year-old tree is the (largest/larger) in the world.
3. Some pines are (oldest/older) than sequoias.
4. Bristlecones are the (oldest/older) living trees.
5. The (more/most) ancient of all pines is 4800 years old.
6. The (taller/tallest) tree is a redwood.
7. The (wider/widest) plant of all is a 113 foot cypress.
8. Red oaks are (wider/widest) at the top than a cypress.
9. Apple trees are (easier/easiest) to climb than pine trees.
10. Some birch trees have (whiter/whitest) bark than others.

C. Adverbs

Write the adverb from each sentence. Write the question it answers: *When? Where?* or *How? (pages 162–163)*

1. A hill is now being made in my backyard.
2. Two machines are slowly moving the earth.
3. An eight-foot deep hole is quickly growing.
4. Soon the workers will leave for the day.
5. They will finish the job tomorrow.
6. The hill will be taken away.
7. Someday the pool will be ready.
8. We will spend summer here in our own pool.

D. Using Adverbs That Compare

Choose the adverb that best completes each sentence. Write the sentence. *(pages 166–167)*

1. Kathy ran (faster/fastest) than Jake.
2. A long jumper has to jump (longer/longest) of all.
3. Bud must vault (higher/highest) than Pete to win.
4. A high jumper tries to jump (higher/highest) of all.
5. Tara must score (more/most) points than Carol.
6. A shot-putter has to throw (farther/farthest) to win.
7. Lynn made the (more/most) difficult dive of all.
8. Carl threw a pass (longer/longest) than Bob.

E. Writing

Look at the pictures on page 176 and 177. Choose one you did not use. Invent a problem. Write a paragraph for the plot of a story. Be sure to write a beginning, middle, and end. Show a title. *(pages 176–178)*

Keep Practicing

A. Subject-Verb Agreement

Use the correct form of the verb to fill each blank. Use the plain form if the subject is plural. Use the *s*-form if the subject is singular. Write each sentence. *(Unit 3, Lesson 3)*

1. Ramon's family _____ to conserve energy. (try)
2. They _____ bottles, cans, and newspapers. (save)
3. They _____ these to the recycling center. (take)
4. No one in the family _____ water or heat. (waste)
5. The family _____ its clothes in cold water. (wash)
6. Ramon's father _____ a bike to work. (ride)
7. Ramon's mother _____ the subway to get to work. (use)
8. They _____ the car as little as possible. (drive)

B. Verb Tenses

Write the verb from each sentence. Name its tense. Write *present, past, or future. (Unit 3, Lesson 4)*

1. Today people clean their teeth with brushes.
2. Some people use electric toothbrushes.
3. Once people cleaned their teeth with twigs or rags.
4. Around 1770 William Addis invented the toothbrush.
5. Addis drilled tiny holes in a small bone.
6. Then he pushed bristles into the holes.
7. Today's brushes are like that first one.

C. Helping Verbs

Write the complete verb from each sentence. Circle each helping verb. *(Unit 3, Lesson 5)*

1. Silhouettes are made with scissors and paper.
2. An artist has cut paper into a picture.

3. Few people can buy an oil painting.
4. A person may own a silhouette instead.
5. The subject should sit sideways in front of a light.
6. A shadow is shaped on a sheet of paper.
7. The artist will trace around the shadow.
8. Then the shape is cut out.

D. Contractions with *Not*
Write the two words that form each of these contractions. *(Unit 3, Lesson 9)*

1. hadn't	5. won't	9. can't
2. couldn't	6. isn't	10. don't
3. haven't	7. shouldn't	11. wasn't
4. didn't	8. weren't	12. aren't

E. The Verb *Have*
Write each statement as a question. Write each question as a statement. *(Unit 3, Lesson 10)*

1. Smog has become a problem in many cities.
2. Car exhaust fumes have polluted the air.
3. Has factory smoke also dirtied the air?
4. People have tried to solve this problem.
5. Had laws been passed to reduce pollution?
6. Have factory owners started cleaning the smoke?
7. Car makers have reduced exhaust fumes in new cars.
8. Has a beginning been made to end air pollution?
9. We have other pollution to take care of.
10. Have you done your part?

F. Irregular Verbs

Write each sentence using the correct form of the verb.
(Unit 3, Lesson 12)

1. The day of the All-City Races had _____ . (come)
2. Everyone in the school had _____ to watch. (go)
3. Marta _____ in the race for fourth graders. (run)
4. The time for that race _____ . (come)
5. "I have just _____ Marta!" shouted Kim. (see)
6. "She is _____ in front of the others!" (run)
7. Marta _____ past her friends. (run)
8. Everyone _____ her win the race. (see)
9. Now Marta is _____ to the awards table. (come)
10. Her teacher _____ with her. (go)
11. The principal _____ them. (see)
12. He is _____ to give Marta a ribbon. (go)

G. The Verb *Do*

Choose the form of the verb that best completes each sentence. Write the sentence. *(Unit 3, Lesson 13)*

1. Andy (do/does) his homework right after school.
2. The team members are (done/doing) their exercises.
3. The moon (did/do) not shine last night.
4. We have (done/did) all our chores.
5. (Does/Did) you have a good day in school?
6. Sally (does/done) have two brothers.
7. (Do/Does) all dogs have fleas?
8. Our class is (done/doing) a project on pollution.
9. Have you (does/done) the dishes?

H. The Dictionary
Write these three headings on your paper.

Before   **Guide Words**   **After**
              lap–look

Then list these entry words in the correct column on your paper. *(Unit 3, Lesson 7)*

Entry Words
laugh   leek   lean   lone   lad   lose   lock   lion
lore   long   lead   load   lend   line   list   lost

I. Time Order and Space Order
Read these events. Tell which is important, space order or time order. *(Unit 3, Lesson 8)*

1. The diver's air tank was running low. She had to rise slowly to the surface.
2. Our team needs one goal to win. The ball is sailing over the goalpost.
3. The pilot knows that the field is short. He has to land at the beginning of the runway.
4. The teacher will call "Time" in a few minutes. Tom still has five problems to solve.
5. Ms. Gomez's train is leaving at 8:15. Her cab is stuck in traffic six miles from the station.
6. Carrie threw the ball too high. Ron leaped as high as he could to try to catch it.
7. Angie waited by the window. The clock rang four times. Her friends would arrive in ten minutes.

Something Extra

Alike and Different

The picture shows two boys playing catch. In some ways the boys look alike. In some ways they look different from each other.

Both boys are using fielder's gloves. Both are wearing jeans, sneakers, and a tan shirt.

The boys are dressed the same way, but they do not look very much alike. Dave is taller and thinner than Mike. Dave's hair is red and straight. Mike's hair is black and curly.

Imagine that there was no picture on page 186. You probably could read the description and then draw the picture.

In a way, the writer drew a picture with words. The description tells you where the action takes place. Then the writer compared and contrasted the boys. When you *compare,* you tell about details that are the same. When you *contrast,* you tell about details that are different.

Write Away!

Look at the picture of the girls playing basketball. Write two paragraphs that compare and contrast the girls. In the first paragraph tell how the girls are alike. In the next paragraph, tell how they are different. Use some of these words.

underhand
both
shorter
each one
red T-shirt
neither one
different from
also

Arithmetic

Arithmetic is where numbers fly like pigeons
   in and out of your head.
Arithmetic tells you how many you lose or
   win if you know how many you had
   before you lost or won.

Arithmetic is where the answer is right and
   everything is nice and you can look out
   the window and see the blue sky—or the
   answer is wrong and you have to start all
   over and try again and see how it comes
   out this time.

Arithmetic is where you have to multiply—
   and you carry the multiplication table in
   your head and hope you won't lose it.

If you ask your mother for one fried egg for
   breakfast and she gives you two fried
   eggs and you eat both of them, who is
   better in arithmetic, you or your mother?

—*Carl Sandburg*

5

Giving
a Report

SKILLS TO BUILD ON

Pronouns
Pronoun-Verb Agreement
Possessive Pronouns
Facts in an Encyclopedia

PRACTICAL APPLICATIONS

Writing a Report
Giving an Oral Report

MULTIPLICATION
TABLE

Pronouns

> A *pronoun* stands for one or more nouns. The pronouns *I, you, he, she, it, we,* and *they* are used in the subject.
>
> Lois|fed Spot and Rover. <u>She</u>|fed Spot and Rover.

A *pronoun* can take the place of one or more nouns. A pronoun may be the subject of a sentence.

Look at the subject of each sentence.

> **The officer**|held up a hand.
> **She**|held up a hand.
> **Raul and Gina**|stopped.
> **They**|stopped.

The pronoun *she* takes the place of *the officer. She* is the subject. The pronoun *they* takes the place of three words. *They* is the subject. What nouns does it replace?

Sometimes a pronoun is used with a noun in a compound subject. Put the pronoun last.

Where are the pronouns in these subjects?

> **Rico and I**|are walking home.
> **Laura and he**|are riding.
> **Noel and they**|are friends.

In the Word Bank, one of the pronouns is in both lists. Which one is it? The pronoun *you* can take the place of a singular noun or a plural noun. Remember, always write the pronoun *I* as a capital letter.

WORD BANK

Singular

I
you
he/she
it

Plural

we
you
they

PRACTICE

A. (Oral) Name the pronoun in each sentence.

Example: I asked Mom for a book.
I

1. She bought the book.
2. It cost $4.65.
3. "You pay the clerk," said Mom.
4. I gave the clerk a five-dollar bill.
5. He gave seventeen cents change.
6. "You did not give the right change," Mom said.
7. We should be given thirty-five cents.
8. He said that there was a tax on the book.
9. They figured the tax was eighteen cents.

B. (Written) Write each sentence. Replace the underlined word or words with a pronoun from the Word Bank.

Example: My friend and I went walking.
We went walking.

1. Janine's cat does funny things.
2. Jon can get Janine's cat to chase a ball.
3. Jon's dog, Reggie, chases a ball, too.
4. The cat and dog like to play together.
5. Janine plays with the cat.
6. A soup bone is a treat for the dog .
7. Janine and Jon watch the dog eat.

APPLY

Think of a cartoon character. Write three sentences about the character. Use nouns in one sentence. Use pronouns in two sentences. Circle the pronouns.

Pronouns after Verbs

> **Some pronouns may be used after an action verb.
> The pronouns *me, you, him, her, it, us,* and *them* are
> used after verbs.**
>
> Lou|saw the boys. Lou|saw them.

You know that a pronoun may replace a noun in the
subject. Some pronouns take the place of nouns in the
predicate. *Me, you, him, her, it, us,* and *them* are
used after a verb.

What nouns do the pronouns replace?

The officer|gave the children a signal.
The officer|gave **them** a signal.
The children|obeyed the officer.
The children|obeyed **her.**

WORD BANK

Singular

me
you
him/her
it

Plural

us
you
them

Sometimes a pronoun is used with a noun after the verb.
Put the pronoun last.

Look at these examples.

Mr. Perez|took his **son and us** to the museum.
The guide|gave **Luis and me** a tour.

In the Word Bank, one word is in both lists. Which word
is it? Notice that *you* can take the place of both a singular
and a plural noun.

PRACTICE

A. (Oral) Name the pronoun in each sentence.

> **Example:** The bus took us to the museum.
> **us**

1. The teacher showed me an old bone.
2. Carol asked, "Who found it?"
3. A guide told us these animals lived long ago.
4. The world was full of them.
5. What killed them?
6. The class asked her many questions.
7. The teacher told her that no one knew.

B. (Written) Write each sentence. Replace the underlined word or words with a pronoun. Look at the Word Bank for help.

> **Example:** Our teacher gave the class a project.
> **Our teacher gave us a project.**

1. Our teacher helped the class.
2. Ann and I worked on our science projects.
3. The library has books on horses.
4. We studied one horse.
5. The teacher asked Ann and me to give a report.
6. Our class enjoyed our report.
7. We let the students ask questions.
8. Ann and I enjoyed answering the questions.

APPLY

Pretend that you and a friend found an old bone. Write three sentences telling about your discovery. Tell what the two of you did. Use pronouns.

Using *I* or *Me*, *We* or *Us*

> **Use *I* and *we* in the subject. Use *me* and *us* after a verb.**
>
> **I|called Lou yesterday. Lou|will call <u>me</u> today.**

Use *I* and *we* only to replace a noun in the subject. Remember to capitalize *I*. Use *me* and *us* after a verb.

Look at these examples.

> **We**|turn on lights after dark.
> **I**|like to read before bedtime.
> The teacher|told **us** about electricity.
> The teacher|asked **me** a question.

When you talk about yourself and someone else, put the other person's name first. *I* and *we* are last in a compound subject. *Me* and *us* are also placed last.

> **Lupe and I** knew the answer.
> The teacher gave **Lupe and me** a chance.

At times you must decide which pronoun to use. First separate the two parts of the compound. Do this to decide if the noun to be replaced is in the subject or the predicate.

> Mrs. Diaz and **the class** went.
> Mrs. Diaz went. **The class** went.

The class is part of the subject. Replace *the class* with *we*.

See how the noun is replaced.

> The class went. **We** went.
> Mrs. Diaz and **we** went.

PRACTICE

A. (Oral) Use *we* or *us* to replace each group of underlined words.

> **Example:** Mrs. Diaz showed <u>the students</u> some pictures.
> **us**

1. Mrs. Diaz and <u>the students</u> studied the past.
2. She asked <u>the students</u> to think about 1880.
3. <u>People</u> had no electricity.
4. <u>My friends and I</u> would have read by candlelight.
5. <u>People</u> had no TV or radio.
6. There was no air conditioning to cool <u>people</u>.
7. Animals and <u>people</u> did the work of our machines.

B. (Written) Choose *I, me, we,* or *us* to complete each sentence. Write the sentence.

> **Example:** Grandpa tells Sandy and _____ stories.
> Grandpa tells Sandy and **me** stories.

1. _____ both like to hear his stories.
2. _____ both ask him to tell us more.
3. Once, he told _____ about a horse that raced a train.
4. Sandy and _____ disagreed about which would win.
5. _____ thought the train would win.
6. Grandpa told Sandy and _____ that the horse won!
7. Of course, that was in 1830, he told _____ .

APPLY

Think about life without electricity. Write four sentences telling what you and your family might do differently. Use *I, me, we,* and *us.*

Pronoun-Verb Agreement

> **A pronoun must agree with the noun it replaces.**
> **The verb must agree with the subject pronoun.**
>
> She grows daisies. They grow quickly.

A noun can be singular or plural. Pronouns are also singular or plural. Replace a singular noun with a singular pronoun. Replace a plural noun with a plural pronoun.

Look at these examples.

> **The girl** picked roses. **She** picked roses.
> **The bunch** was pretty. **It** was pretty.
> **Eva** smelled **the roses. She** smelled **them.**
> **Eva** gave one to **Dad. She** gave one to **him.**

Which pronouns are singular? Which one is plural?

A verb must agree with the subject of a sentence. If the subject is a singular pronoun, use the *s*-form of the verb. If the subject is plural, use the plain form of the verb.

Find the subject and verb in each sentence.

> Dolores likes movies.
> She sees a new movie each week.
> She and I meet friends there.
> They walk home with us.

PRACTICE

A. (Oral) Replace the underlined word or words in each sentence with a pronoun.

> **Example:** Dad took a first-aid course that helped <u>his daughter</u>.
> **her**

1. He saved his daughter from choking on <u>a bone</u>.
2. First <u>his daughter</u> tried to cough the bone out.
3. <u>The bone</u> did not come out.
4. Next Dad put his arms around <u>his daughter</u>.
5. He clenched his hands just under <u>his daughter's ribs</u>.
6. Then he pulled <u>his hands</u> sharply against her.
7. <u>The bone</u> popped right out.

B. (Written) For each sentence, choose the verb that agrees with the subject. Write the sentence.

> **Example:** My friend and I (<u>study</u>/studies) after school.
> **My friend and I study after school.**

1. Ruth and I (<u>go</u>/goes) to the same school.
2. After school, she and I (<u>attend</u>/attends) special classes.
3. Ruth (go/<u>goes</u>) to Hebrew school.
4. She (study/<u>studies</u>) the Hebrew language.
5. It (<u>has</u>/have) a different alphabet from English.
6. I (<u>go</u>/goes) to Chinese school.
7. I (<u>learn</u>/learns) to read and write in Chinese.
8. Chinese writing (use/<u>uses</u>) symbols, not letters.

APPLY

A friend sends you a message. It is written in a secret code. In three sentences, tell how you would read the message. Use pronouns.

Review the Basics I

A. Pronouns

Write each sentence. Replace the underlined word or words with a pronoun. Use one of these pronouns: *I, you, he, she, it, we,* or *they. (pages 190–191)*

1. <u>Kevin</u> read about a cure for bee stings.
2. <u>Everyone</u> should keep baking soda handy.
3. <u>Baking soda</u> acts against the poison.
4. <u>The soda paste</u> is put on the sting.
5. <u>Kevin's sister</u> heard about this cure.
6. Later <u>a bee</u> stung her twice.
7. <u>Kevin and I</u> put a soda paste on the stings.
8. <u>The stings and pain</u> went right away.
9. <u>Kerry's arm</u> felt better.

B. Pronouns after Verbs

Write each sentence. Replace the underlined word or words with *me, you, him, her, it, us,* or *them.*
(pages 192–193)

1. Lee jumps rope with <u>Pam</u>.
2. Ralph taught <u>his friends</u> to play checkers.
3. I delivered <u>a package</u> to Carol and Red.
4. We are going bowling with <u>my friends</u>.
5. Alice is moving with <u>her brother</u>.
6. The class watched <u>the walk on the moon</u>.
7. Aunt Liz wrote to <u>my sister</u>.
8. I went hiking with John and <u>the scouts</u>.
9. Adam and Gail painted <u>that fence</u>.
10. Please come to the library with <u>my class</u>.

C. Using *I* or *Me, We* or *Us*

Choose *I, me, we,* or *us* to complete each sentence. Write the sentence. *(pages 194–195)*

1. Dad took Sue and _____ to the fair.
2. _____ both wanted to ride on the big wheel.
3. Dad took _____ both on the wheel first.
4. _____ wanted to ride the looper, but Sue and Dad did not.
5. Sue said, "That scares _____ ."
6. _____ went on the looper alone.
7. Then _____ all wanted something to eat.
8. Dad bought _____ some food and drinks.
9. Dad and _____ sat down on a bench.
10. Dad asked _____ what we wanted to do next.
11. Dad gave _____ the choice.
12. We told _____ to decide.

D. Pronoun-Verb Agreement

For each sentence, choose the verb that agrees with the subject. Write the sentence. *(pages 196–197)*

1. Hector and Laura (like/likes) animals.
2. He (has/have) a parrot.
3. It (say/says), "Pretty bird."
4. She (own/owns) two hamsters.
5. Hector and she (help/helps) each other.
6. Sometimes, she (feed/feeds) Hector's parrot.
7. Sometimes, he (clean/cleans) her hamsters' cage.
8. Laura and he (save/saves) their money.
9. They (hope/hopes) to get some new pets.

Pronouns in a Paragraph

Pronouns can improve a paragraph. They make it easier to read. It can become more interesting, too.

Read this paragraph. Notice the pronouns.

Gutzon Borglum wanted to honor great people. **He** chose four past presidents. **They** were Washington, Jefferson, Lincoln, and Roosevelt. The face of each man is sixty feet tall. Borglum began work on the sculpture in 1925. **He** was still working when **he** died in 1941. **You** can see each face today. All four were carved in Mount Rushmore. **They** will be there forever.

REMINDERS

1. Replace a subject with *I, you, he, she, it, we,* or *they.*
2. Replace other nouns with *me, you, him, her, us,* or *them.*
3. A pronoun must agree with the noun it replaces.
4. A verb must agree with the subject.

No pronouns are used in the next paragraph. The nouns are repeated. All the sentences sound the same. Using pronouns will improve the paragraph.

Which nouns would you replace?

Gutzon Borglum turned a mountain into a monument. Borglum was a sculptor. Borglum wanted to make the biggest sculpture of all time. Borglum had seen Mount Rushmore in South Dakota. Mount Rushmore had high towers of bare rock. Borglum wanted to turn Mount Rushmore into a great carving.

PRACTICE/APPLY

A. **(Written)** Replace the underlined words with pronouns. Rewrite the paragraph.

The Colorado River is a strong river. In 1904 the Colorado River flooded a great valley. Many people lived there. The people had to flee. Arthur Davis wanted to dam the river. Davis planned to build a giant dam. The dam would control the river. The dam would end floods.

B. **(Written)** Now replace the repeated words in this paragraph. Use pronouns. Rewrite the paragraph.

People said that the dam could not be built. People said the dam was too big. People said the dam would cause earthquakes. Other people wanted to try. Other people built the great dam. In 1936, Hoover Dam was finished. Hoover Dam still tames the wild Colorado River today.

Books in the Library

A library is a place where books are kept. There are many kinds of books. A library also contains more than books. You should know what to look for in a library.

Look at these library terms.

reference books	dictionary	almanac
encyclopedia	thesaurus	atlas

An encyclopedia, an atlas, a dictionary, a thesaurus, and an almanac are **reference books.**

Encyclopedia	An **encyclopedia** is a set of books. The set has facts on many things. You do not have to read the whole book to find out about a subject.
Atlas	An **atlas** is a book of maps. Some atlases have special maps. Some maps show a country's products. Others show plant life or rainfall.
Dictionary	A **dictionary** is a book of words. The words are in alphabetical order. You can find the meaning of a word, and how to spell or say a word.
Thesaurus	A **thesaurus** is like a dictionary in some ways. The words are in **alphabetical order.** It shows words that mean almost the same as another word.
Almanac	An **almanac** has information on many subjects. The facts may be in lists, tables, charts, or graphs. A new almanac comes out each year.

PRACTICE

(Written) Write the sources you would use to find the answers to these questions. Some information may be found in more than one place.

Example: When was George Washington born?
   encyclopedia

1. How do you say *fierce*?
2. Who won the Super Bowl in 1981?
3. Who won last year's election?
4. Where can I find a book about elephants?
5. What river flows through Memphis, Tennessee?
6. What words have the same meaning as *walk*?
7. Which state has the most people?
8. How is peanut butter made?
9. Who invented spaghetti?
10. What mountains are in Japan?
11. Who was the fourteenth president?
12. Who played in the 1917 World Series?
13. What words have the same meaning as *peace*?
14. How many meanings are there for *row*?
15. How much rain fell in Texas last year?
16. Does Washington, D.C. have a city hall?
17. When did Babe Ruth hit his last home run?
18. Do sea lions roar?
19. Why do falling stars fall?

APPLY

What interests you? Which reference books could tell you about your interest. Write three questions about something that interests you. Then tell where you will look for the answers.

Information in Encyclopedias

Where can you find the answer to a question no one can answer for you? The encyclopedia is a resource to use. It contains facts about many topics. To use an encyclopedia, you must know how it is organized.

The facts in each book are arranged in alphabetical order. The letters on a book's *spine* tell which facts are in that book. Each book is called a *volume.* To find out about Kit Carson, for example, look in volume 2 under C.

Look at this set.

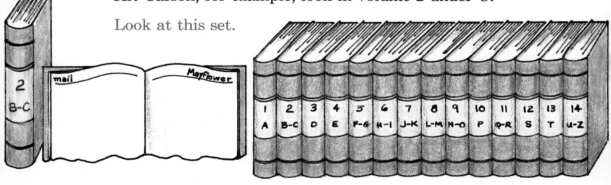

The numbers on the books help keep them in order. In this set, volume 1 has topics that start with A. Which volume has topics that start with J? Which one will have facts about tunnels?

The *guide words* at the top of each page help you find a topic. Facts about the guide words are on these pages. Facts about other topics are also there.

Think of the topics *maze, maid, match,* and *market.* Which are on these pages? Check the third letter of each word. Will *medicine* come before or after these pages? What about *machine?*

PRACTICE

A. (Oral) Look at the set of encyclopedias on page 204. Give the number of the volume where facts on each of these topics are found.

    Example: Labrador
             volume 8

1. platypus
2. Florida
3. calendar
4. Marian Anderson
5. Franklin D. Roosevelt
6. automobile
7. baseball
8. violin
9. money
10. cork
11. juniper
12. Germany
13. Philadelphia
14. liver

B. (Written) Look at the guide words pictured on page 204. On your paper, make three columns. Label them *Before, On These Pages,* and *After.* List each topic according to where it would come.

1. magazines
2. manufacturing
3. migration
4. James Madison
5. Mary Mitchell
6. Maryland
7. maps
8. marathon
9. margarine
10. mail
11. maximum
12. marigolds

APPLY

Choose a topic from Practice B or think of one of your own. Find the topic in an encyclopedia. Write three sentences. Tell what the topic is. Tell the volume you found it in. Tell the guide words on that page.

Notetaking

When you read something you want to remember, take notes. Notes are just reminders. They do not have to be whole sentences. Do not copy what you read. Put the facts in your own words.

As you take notes, keep in mind the WH-questions. Write notes that answer *Who? What? Where? When? Why?* and *How?* Your notes should be the answers. Look for key words in what you read. They can help you answer the WH-questions.

Study this article and the notes.

The Grand Canyon in Arizona is a deep gorge. It was carved by a river over millions of years. It is 277 miles long and a mile deep. The river carved the canyon's rock walls into strange shapes. The rocks seem to be many colors—red, pink, orange, gold, and purple.

The first Europeans to see the canyon were Spanish soldiers. They reached it in 1540. Later, the Spanish found a group of people living at the bottom of the canyon. This tribe still lives there.

Gorge carved by river
Made over millions of years
277 miles long, mile deep
Rocks in strange shapes,
   many colors

Spanish soldiers first
   Europeans
Arrived in 1540
Tribe lived in canyon—
   then and now

If you take notes from a book, write the title of the book. Write it exactly as it appears on the book. Draw a line under the title. Write the name of the author, too.

REMINDERS

1. Notes do not have to be whole sentences.
2. Notes should give facts that answer WH-questions.
3. Do not copy a fact. Put it in your own words.
4. Write your notes as a list.

PRACTICE

(**Written**) Read this article. Think of WH-questions. Take notes that answer your WH-questions.

In 1932, Laura Ingalls Wilder wrote a book titled *Little House in the Big Woods.* The story is from Wilder's own life. *Little House in the Big Woods* is the first in a series of books. It tells of when the Ingalls family lived in Wisconsin. Laura was a young child at that time. That book was followed in 1935 by *Little House on the Prairie.* Her story about life in Kansas became a television show. There are six other books in the series. A ninth book, *The First Four Years,* is dated 1971. That story is the last. It tells about Ms. Wilder's life as an adult.

APPLY

Reread the paragraphs about the Gutzon Borglum in Lesson 5. Take notes in your own words.

Organizing Notes by Outlining

Notes are often quickly written. As you read, you may write a word or two. You may write more. The notes you take may not be in order. You may need to organize them. They will be more useful in this way. Making an outline is one way to put your notes in order.

Look at these notes from Lesson 8.

Gorge carved by river
Made over millions of years
277 miles long, mile deep
Rocks in strange shapes,
many colors

Spanish soldiers first
Europeans
Arrived in 1540
Tribe lived in canyon—
then and now

Study the outline made from the notes.

The Grand Canyon

I. What does the Grand Canyon look like?
   A. Trench carved by a river over millions of years
   B. 277 miles long, mile deep, with rocks in strange shapes and colors
II. Who has lived in the canyon?
   A. Spanish soldiers first Europeans in 1540
   B. A tribe lived in canyon—then and now

Look at the title. Each important word plus the first word starts with a capital letter. The title tells the subject of the outline. It does not give details. The subject is very general. What is the title?

There are two *main topics* in the outline. Each main topic is a WH-question. The questions are complete sentences. They are written next to Roman numerals (I, II). What are the main topics?

Each group of ideas is put under a main topic. The *ideas* are put below the WH-question they answer. They come from the notes. In an outline, each idea is marked with a capital letter (A, B). The ideas are not complete sentences.

PRACTICE

(Written) Write these two WH-questions and notes in outline form. Use the two WH-questions as main topics.

Who was Martin Luther King?
What did Martin Luther King do?
Organized march on Washington, 1963
Leader of U. S. civil rights movement
Minister
Given Nobel Peace Prize, 1964

APPLY

Use the notes you wrote in Lesson 8. Decide on two WH-questions to ask. Put your notes in outline form. Use the two WH-questions as main topics.

Possessive Pronouns

> A *possessive pronoun* takes the place of a possessive noun. A possessive pronoun does not use an apostrophe.
>
> <u>Nick's</u> aunt lives in Iowa. <u>His</u> aunt is named Hattie.

A *possessive pronoun* is like a possessive noun. Each shows that someone or something owns or has something.

Look at these sentences.

> **Grandma's** canary sings. **Her** canary sings.
> Where is the **cat's** ball? Where is **its** ball?

The possessive pronoun *her* stands for the possessive noun *Grandma's.* What pronoun takes the place of *cat's?*

Most possessive pronouns have two forms. See how the forms are used.

> The dog belonging to me is **mine.** It is **my** dog.
> The tools are **hers.** They are **her** tools.
> The house belonging to us is **ours.** It is **our** house.

WORD BANK

Possessive Pronouns

for me—my, mine
for you—your, yours
for her—her, hers
for him—his

for it—its
for us—our, ours
for them—their, theirs

PRACTICE

A. (Oral) Name the possessive pronoun that correctly completes each sentence.

> **Example:** This is her elephant. It is _____ .
> **hers**

1. That truck belongs to them. It is _____ .
2. This skunk is _____ . It is your skunk.
3. These sheep belong to him. They are _____ .
4. The pumpkin is _____ . It is our pumpkin.
5. This shawl belongs to her. It is _____ .
6. That is _____ comb. It is mine.
7. Those boxes belong to you. They are _____ .

B. (Written) Choose the form of the pronoun that correctly completes the second sentence in each pair. Write the sentence.

> **Example:** All of us had fun. (Our/Ours) pets had fun, too.
> **Our pets had fun, too.**

1. Jay had a party. (Him/His) party was for pets.
2. His friends came. They brought (they/their) pets.
3. Liz owns a snake. (Her/Hers) snake is striped.
4. I brought my dog. That poodle is (my/mine).
5. Bruce has a mouse. (It/Its) tail is long.
6. Ana has a cat. The white one is (her/hers).
7. You have a nice pet. Is the skunk (yours/your)?

APPLY

Pretend your friends have a pet from outer space. Write four sentences that tell about their pet. Use possessive pronouns in your sentences.

Clear Pronoun References

> **Be sure each pronoun makes clear whom or what you mean.**
>
> **Confusing:** Mike told Pete that <u>he</u> was late. Who was late, Pete or Mike?

Pronouns can be confusing. A pronoun must make clear whom or what you mean.

These sentences have confusing pronouns.

> Alice wore a brown shoe and a black shoe, so she changed **it.**
> Alice told Sara that **she** was the winner.

Who is the winner, Alice or Sara? The meaning is not clear. You would have to ask Alice to find out who won. What would you ask Alice to make the meaning clear in the first example?

An unclear sentence should be changed. How could you change the sentences to make their meanings clear?

Here is one way. What is another way?

> Alice had on one brown shoe and one black shoe, so she changed the brown one.

When you use pronouns, check that the meaning is clear. Make sure that others understand what you mean to say.

Is each pronoun clear? Why?

> Alice and Phil were skating, but **he** fell down.
> Alice petted her cat, and **it** purred.

PRACTICE

A. (Oral) Choose the word that best completes each sentence. Choose the pronoun if the meaning is clear. Say the sentence.

Example: Roger and Ken study. (He/Ken) helps him.
Ken helps him.

1. Hector helps Fred. (He/Fred) is happy.
2. Sally races Paul. (She/Sally) wins.
3. Mitch tells Betty a joke. (She/Betty) laughs.
4. Joy picks up April. (She/Joy) is very strong.
5. Rufus and Jim play ball. (He/Jim) pitches.
6. Lila and Lou make bread. (She/Lila) kneads the dough.
7. Paul talks with Maria. (He/Paul) knows a secret.
8. Alex and Pete fly kites. (His/Pete's) kite falls.
9. Mimi and Jack write letters. (Jack's/His) was mailed.

B. (Written) Write the pronouns and the words to which they refer.

Example: 1. They—families

Today, most families have a television set. (**1.** They) gather around the set to watch TV shows. Dad said that (**2.** he) used to listen to radio shows. (**3.** They) were like TV but without pictures. Dad and Aunt Reba each had a favorite show. (**4.** He) liked "The Green Hornet." (**5.** She) preferred "Baby Snooks."

APPLY

Pretend that two of your friends are putting on a radio show. Write four sentences telling about the show. Use clear pronouns in two of the sentences.

-*Self* Pronouns

> **Some pronouns end in -*self* or -*selves*. Such a pronoun is used as a partner with another pronoun or a noun in the sentence.**
>
> Lara|surprised <u>herself</u> by winning the prize.

Some pronouns end in -*self* or -*selves.* Often the pronouns are used with the subject of a sentence. The subject may be a noun or another pronoun.

Look at each example.

John|cut **himself** on the thumb.

A skunk|can protect **itself.**

I|gave **myself** a treat.

Mrs. Adams|sent the card to **herself.**

We|helped **ourselves** win the prize.

The chart of pronouns shows which words act as partners with -*self* pronouns.

Study the chart.

Pronoun Partners

(*I*) myself	(*we*) ourselves
(*she*) herself	(*you*) yourself (*one person—you*)
(*he*) himself	(*you*) yourselves (*you and others*)
(*it*) itself	(*they*) themselves

PRACTICE

A. (Oral) Name the *-self* pronoun that matches the underlined word or words.

Example: Our club found (itself/themselves) a job.
    itself

1. We plan to do it (yourselves/ourselves).
2. Our parents thought about (ourselves/themselves).
3. Dad told us about his friends and (himself/herself).
4. Mom told us about her friends and (himself/herself).
5. Our aunts spoke about (herself/themselves).
6. I may learn a lot about (yourself/myself).
7. You can learn about (yourself/ourselves), too.

B. (Written) Use the right *-self* pronoun to complete each sentence. The pronoun partner is underlined. Write the sentence.

Example: We saw the flying saucer _____ .
    We saw the flying saucer ourselves.

1. All of you must work by _____ .
2. James will serve _____ some spinach.
3. I told _____ I would get an A in math.
4. Aunt Sara bought _____ a new dress.
5. You should not talk to _____ , Max.
6. The snakes twisted _____ into knots.
7. A hedgehog can curl _____ into a ball.

APPLY

Think of three famous people. Write a sentence telling what each can do. Use *-self* pronouns in your sentences.

Too Many Pronouns

> **A pronoun should not follow and repeat a noun in the same sentence part.**
>
> <u>Incorrect:</u> Milk it tastes sweet.
> <u>Correct:</u> Milk tastes sweet. <u>Or:</u> It tastes sweet.

You have studied pronouns. You know that using the same noun too often can be a mistake. Too many pronouns is also a mistake.

Each example has an error.

> **Amerigo Vespucci he** explored America in 1497.
> **America it** was named for him.

The pronouns should *not* follow and repeat the subjects. Pronouns should not be used with the nouns. Use either a noun or a pronoun as the subject. Do not use both.

These examples are correct.

> **Amerigo Vespucci** explored America in 1497.
> **It** was named for him.

When you use a pronoun, be sure that it makes clear whom or what you mean. In the next paragraph, there are eight errors. Find them.

> Columbus and Vespucci they both found the New World. He did not know this was a new land. He died thinking he had reached Asia. Vespucci he was the first to realize it was a new land. It was named for Vespucci, not him.

In this paragraph, the pronoun meanings are clear.

Columbus and Vespucci both found the New World. Columbus did not know this was a new land. Columbus died thinking he had reached Asia. Vespucci was the first to realize America was a new land. America was named after him, not Columbus.

Look at both paragraphs. How was each error fixed?

PRACTICE

A. (Oral) Each pair of sentences contains pronoun errors. Say each pair correctly. There are five errors to correct.

1. The Statue of Liberty it stands in New York Harbor. It was given to the United States by France.
2. The statue it is on Liberty Island. It was first named Bedloe's Island.
3. The statue it came in pieces. It took more than a year to put them together.

B. (Written) This paragraph has too many pronouns. Rewrite the paragraph. Correct the four errors.

In 1783 a duck, a sheep, and a goat they were the first group to go up in a balloon. It was in the air for eight minutes. The king and queen of France they watched them fly. They landed safely.

APPLY

Write four sentences about what you think a hot-air balloon ride feels like. Use pronouns correctly.

Review the Basics II

A. Possessive Pronouns
Choose the form of the pronoun that correctly completes the second sentence in each pair. Write the sentence. *(pages 210–211)*

1. The class held a show. (It/Its) theme was hobbies.
2. We all took part. We showed (our/ours) hobbies.
3. Meg has a good hobby. (Hers/Her) hobby is drawing.
4. Juan collects stamps. Those stamps are (his/hers).
5. I collect coins. This coin is (my/mine).
6. Ellen raises hamsters. Those are all (her/hers)!
7. Other students came. We will go to (their/theirs) show.
8. Do you have a hobby? What is (yours/your)?
9. You can come to the next show. Bring (your/yours) hobby.
10. My dog has a hobby. (Its/It) hobby is burying bones.

B. Clear Pronoun References
Choose the word that best completes each sentence. Choose the pronoun if the meaning is clear. Write the sentence. *(pages 212–213)*

1. Jane and Theresa swim. (She/Jane) is fast.
2. Mark skates with Sam. (He/Sam) falls.
3. Nan helps Raul. (He/Raul) says, "Thank you."
4. Derek is Ann's brother. (He/Derek) is older than Ann.
5. Roz runs after Peg. (She/Roz) trips.
6. Rita and Ron paint the fence. (He/Ron) is neat.
7. Joan helps Dad. (She/Joan) washes the car.
8. Cindy and Karen make music. (She/Karen) plays drums.
9. Al and Mark race to school. (Al/He) wins.

C. -*Self* Pronouns

Write the -*self* pronoun that matches the underlined word or words. *(pages 214–215)*

1. The <u>dog</u> pulled the sled by (itself/himself).
2. <u>We</u> walk to school by (yourselves/ourselves).
3. <u>The new girl</u> told us about (herself/himself).
4. <u>Gary</u> fell and hurt (herself/himself).
5. <u>Gina</u>, did you write that story (yourselves/yourself)?
6. <u>I</u> make (itself/myself) get up early.
7. <u>Those people</u> built their house (ourselves/themselves).
8. <u>All of you</u> may stay here by (yourselves/yourself).

D. Too Many Pronouns

Each pair of sentences contains pronoun errors. Write each pair correctly. *(pages 216–217)*

1. Clouds they are made of water droplets. They tell what the weather will be.
2. Clouds they are named after their shapes. Clouds they have Latin names.
3. Cirrus clouds they look like soft feathers. They are signs of fair weather.
4. A thunderhead it is in storms. It has a high, flat top.
5. Stratocumulus clouds have rolls or folds. They often mean that it will rain.
6. Ground fog it is like a cloud lying on the ground. It rises in the morning.
7. Weather is fun to watch. Weather science it is part of our school science book.

The Parts of a Report

At times you may read or hear something that you want to know more about. When you find out more, you may want to tell others. Reports are written to tell others about something. You should know the parts of a report and the purpose of each part. A report is more interesting and useful when it is complete.

Read this model report.

Worker Bees

Worker bees are the busiest in a hive. They are female bees. They do almost all the work.

The workers keep the queen bee safe. They feed her and the young bees. In the winter, the workers keep them warm. They beat their wings over the queen to make heat.

Worker bees do most of the chores in a hive. They build honeycomb cells. The new cells are made for eggs. The workers clean the cells, too.

This report tells facts about worker bees. The topic of the report is worker bees. Every report has a topic. The *topic* tells what the report is about. In this report the title tells the topic.

A report has paragraphs. Each one tells about the topic. Each one tells about one main idea. The *main idea* is what the whole paragraph is about. It is in the *topic sentence* of the paragraph. It is often in the first sentence.

Each paragraph has *details,* too. They tell more about the main idea. They are in the other sentences in the paragraph.

PRACTICE

(Oral) Read these short reports. For each one, answer the questions.

1. What is the title?
2. Which part tells the topic?
3. What is the topic?
4. Which sentence tells the main idea in each paragraph?
5. How many sentences tell details about each main idea?

A. Queen Bees

The queen bee is the most important member of the hive. She is the ruler of the hive. Her job is to lay the eggs. There are thousands of other bees in the nest. There is only one queen.

When the queen dies, the worker bees can make another queen. A bee that will become a queen is given special food. It is the food that turns a bee into a queen or into a worker.

B. Sandwich

Not many of us know that the sandwich was named after an English nobleman. John Montagu, 4th Earl of Sandwich, lived in London in the 1700s.

One day, the Earl was playing a game with his friends. Even though he was hungry, he refused to leave the game. So, meat was brought to him wrapped in bread. From that day on, food served this way was called a sandwich.

APPLY

Reread the report on worker bees. Write the answers to questions 2 and 3 listed with the Practice.

15

Writing a Paragraph in a Report

Sara took notes for her report on skunks. She organized her notes. She put her facts with the main idea they told about. Then she wrote topic sentences that answered her questions. Sara was ready to write the rest of her report.

Sara needed a separate paragraph for each question. She had two questions, so she needed two paragraphs.

Read Sara's notes.

What do skunks look like?
easily known by the way they look
are small
are furry with a bushy tail
black with white stripes

How do skunks protect themselves?
special form of protection
spray a liquid that smells awful
can aim the spray for twelve feet
stamp and growl before they spray

This is the first paragraph she wrote.

> Skunks
> Skunks are easily known by the way they look. They are small animals. Their bodies are furry with a bushy tail. Skunks are black with white stripes.

You have read Sara's notes and report. The questions below are about Sara's work. Try to answer each one.

1. What is the topic of the report?
2. What is the topic sentence of the paragraph?
3. Which sentences tell details?

What will the second paragraph of Sara's report be like? Think of a topic sentence for her paragraph. Use her notes. Think of the detail sentences. What will they tell?

PRACTICE

(Written) Read the notes about trees. The title and first paragraph are complete. Write the second paragraph of the report.

What kinds of trees are there?
    endless kinds of trees
    pine and fir trees in cold north
    palm trees in warm places
    cypress trees live in water

What are trees used for?
    have many different uses
    fruits and nuts eaten as food
    furniture and houses made from wood
    wood pulp turned into paper

Trees

There are endless kinds of trees in the world. Pine and fir trees grow in the cold north. Palm trees grow in warm places. Cypress trees live in water.

APPLY

Use Sara's notes. Write a second paragraph for her report.

A Report: Plan, Write, Edit

In this lesson, you will write your own report. As with other kinds of writing, you will first plan, then write, and finally edit your work.

Before you start to plan your report, you must choose a topic. Choose something that interests you. Try to choose a topic that others will want to learn about. In a short report, you will want to tell interesting facts. You might report on a hobby, a sport, or a special place you like.

PLAN

Once you have picked a topic you can start to plan. The first step is to make a long list of questions about the topic. Ask WH-questions. Write as many as you can. Then choose two questions to answer.

Look up the topic. Use library books. You may find books at home. Use an encyclopedia. Look at more than one source.

Take notes. Write the important facts. Write the name and author of each book you use. Leave out facts that do not fit your questions. Do not copy facts. Write them in your own words. Keep each note separate. Use note cards or make a line on your paper to keep the notes apart.

The last planning step is to organize your notes. Look them over. Put each fact under the question it answers. Leave out any fact that does not belong. Arrange the notes in an order that makes sense.

WRITE

You have a plan. Your notes are organized. You are ready to write your report. Look at the WH-questions. Decide which one to write about first. You will write a separate paragraph for each question.

Think about each paragraph. You know that a paragraph is a group of sentences. The sentences all tell facts about one main idea. One sentence tells the main idea. The others tell details.

Indent the first line of each paragraph. The topic sentence should be first. Then write the detail sentences that will follow.

The topic sentence should answer the WH-question. It should tell what the paragraph is about. Look at Lesson 15 if you need help. See how each topic sentence answers a WH-question.

Write each detail in a complete sentence. Start each one with a capital letter. End each sentence with a punctuation mark.

The last step is to write a title. The title should tell what your topic is. It could be a whole sentence. Most often it is only a few words. Try to make it interesting.

EDIT

Your report is written. Your last step is to edit it. Read your report carefully. Mark any changes that are necessary. Try to make it better. You may want to look at Unit 1, page 43, for the special marks used in editing.

First look at the whole report. Pretend that you are seeing it for the first time. Is there a title? Does the report have two paragraphs? Is each one indented?

Look at each part carefully. There are many things to look for. Does the title tell the topic? Is it interesting? Is it spelled correctly? Now read the report.

✓ Is each paragraph about one main idea?
✓ Does each paragraph have a topic sentence?
✓ Are all the facts in the paragraph where they belong?
✓ Are the details in order? Do they make sense?

Now read each paragraph. Check each sentence.

✓ Is the same noun used too often? Would a pronoun fit instead?
✓ Are pronouns used correctly?
✓ Does each pronoun make clear who or what you mean?
✓ Does each sentence have a subject and predicate.
✓ Is each word spelled correctly?

The last step is to copy your edited report. Use your best handwriting.

17 COMMUNICATING

Giving an Oral Report

At some time, you may have to give a report aloud. When you report to others, you must speak clearly. You must remember to say all the important points.

Follow the Guidelines when giving an oral report.

GUIDELINES

1. Tell the topic. Say, "My topic is _____ ."
2. Tell the questions. Say, "I wanted to find answers to the questions _____ and _____ ."
3. Tell the facts you found. Say, "When I looked up the topic, I learned _____ . " Use your notes.

PRACTICE/APPLY

(Oral) Use the notes made for the report you wrote for Lesson 16. Or, you may think of questions about one of these topics: *Kansas, penguins, earthquakes, sports heroes.* Look up the answers. Take notes. Report to a group of classmates.

Unit 5 Test

A. Pronouns
Write each sentence. Replace the underlined word or words with a pronoun. *(pages 190–191)*

1. Marta and <u>Nicole</u> went to a special camp last summer.
2. <u>Marta and Nicole</u> went to Seacamp in Florida.
3. <u>Ocean shipwrecks</u> are studied at Seacamp.
4. <u>Diving gear</u> is worn by all divers.
5. <u>My class</u> has ten students.
6. <u>Mr. Jensen</u> gives the lessons.

Write each sentence. Replace the underlined word or words with a pronoun. *(pages 192–193)*

7. A new way to use old cans was found by <u>Michael Reynolds</u>.
8. He turns <u>the cans</u> into building blocks.
9. Eight cans wired together make <u>a block</u>.
10. Reynolds builds <u>houses</u> from the cans.
11. Did he live in <u>the house</u>?

B. Using *I* or *Me, We* or *Us*
Write *I, me, we,* or *us* to complete each sentence. Write the sentence. *(pages 194–195)*

1. _____ had a visitor in our classroom.
2. Officer May talked to _____ about bike safety.
3. _____ all had a lot of questions for her.
4. She showed _____ how to use my left hand to signal.
5. She told _____ to ride single file.
6. _____ should stay to the right of the road.
7. She told _____ to take good care of our bikes.
8. _____ went home and checked out my bike.

C. Possessive Pronouns

Complete the second sentence in each pair with the correct pronoun. Write the sentence. *(pages 210–211)*

1. We made sculptures. (Our/Ours) were made of sand.
2. I made a tall one. (Mine/My) was a skyscraper.
3. You made a sea monster. I liked (yours/your) sea monster.
4. Al and Beth worked together. The dragon was (their/theirs).
5. Mr. Levi worked, too. I liked (his/her) castle.
6. Jill made a long one. The snake was (her/hers).

D. Clear Pronoun References

Complete each sentence. Make the meaning clear. Write the sentence. *(pages 212–213)*

1. Eileen fixes Tina's bike. (She/Tina) smiles.
2. Ann beats Ed at checkers. (He/Ed) gets angry.
3. Dick and Len eat lunch. (He/Dick) eats more.
4. Laura writes to her Aunt Rosa. (She/Aunt Rosa) is happy.
5. Mom and Dad work outside. (She/Mom) mows the lawn.
6. Nancy asks Ralph a question. (He/Ralph) answers.

E. Writing

Write a one-paragraph report about old dolls. Use the question and notes listed. Write a topic sentence and three detail sentences. Write a title. *(pages 224–226)*

> What were the earliest dolls like?
>> dolls of different types
>> oldest made of wood or clay
>> clothes painted on simple dolls
>> some look like famous people

Keep Practicing

A. Adjectives
Add at least one adjective to each sentence. Write each new sentence. *(Unit 4, Lesson 1)*

1. Animals take baths.
2. Baths get rid of fleas and ticks.
3. Owners give baths to pets.
4. Birds splash in water.
5. Birds take dust baths, too.
6. Birds clean their feathers with their beaks.
7. Elephants use their trunks to clean themselves.
8. An elephant throws dust on his back.
9. A horse rolls in the dust.
10. Cats wash with their tongues.
11. Snakes do not need baths.
12. Snakes shed their skins.

B. Using Adjectives That Compare
Choose the correct word to complete each sentence. Write each sentence. *(Unit 4, Lesson 2)*

1. Jupiter is (bigger/biggest) of all the planets.
2. Saturn is a little (smaller/smallest) than Jupiter.
3. Earth is (larger/largest) than Mars.
4. Mercury is (smaller/smallest) of all.
5. Mercury is also (faster/fastest) of all.
6. Is Earth (rounder/roundest) than Pluto?
7. Pluto is the (slower/slowest) planet of all.
8. Saturn is the (more/most) beautiful of all planets.
9. Venus is (closer/closest) to the sun than Earth.

C. The Adjectives *Good, Bad, Many,* and *Much*

Write the adjective that correctly completes each sentence. *(Unit 4, Lesson 4)*

1. I had a (good/better) time making puppets.
2. My puppets were (better/good) than other's.
3. I made (more/most) puppets than Larry did.
4. My first puppet was the (worse/worst) of the three.
5. My second puppet was (better/best) than the first.
6. My third puppet was the (better/best) of the three.
7. Ken made the (many/most) puppets of all.
8. Shane's puppets were (worse/worst) than last year's.
9. Making puppets was (more/most) fun than drawing.
10. It was the (more/most) fun I ever had in school.

D. Adverbs

Write the adverb from each sentence. Write the question it answers. Use the words *When? Where?* or *How?* *(Unit 4, Lesson 9)*

1. Very hot volcanoes formed the Hawaiian Islands.
2. Once there were no Hawaiian Islands.
3. Then the ocean floor cracked.
4. Melted rock flowed up.
5. The rock quickly cooled.
6. Layers of rock slowly formed.
7. Finally the layers reached above the water.
8. There the first Hawaiian Island was born.
9. Recently scientists found a new volcano.
10. One day we may see a new island there.

E. Adverbs for *When, Where,* and *How*

Write the group of words from each sentence that acts as an adverb. Write the question each group of words answers. Use the words *When? Where?* or *How?* *(Unit 4, Lesson 10)*

1. Elephants have important jobs in Thailand.
2. They work in the logging industry.
3. They have helped people for many years.
4. Elephants can go into the deepest forest.
5. They push logs with their heads.
6. They pull logs with chains.
7. Elephants learn their jobs in a school.
8. The elephants are trained for seven years.
9. Their trainers give them treats after good work.
10. A trainer works with just one elephant.
11. The elephant stays with the trainer.
12. One elephant is used as a leader.

F. Using Adverbs That Compare

Write the forms of these adverbs that are used to compare actions. *(Unit 4, Lesson 11)*

1. slow	8. fast	15. wildly
2. high	9. soon	16. gently
3. clearly	10. smoothly	17. brightly
4. busily	11. swiftly	18. carefully
5. loud	12. quickly	19. often
6. slowly	13. loudly	20. badly
7. late	14. angrily	21. happily

G. Finding Books in the Library

The letters BAG-BAS are on a card catalog drawer. For each item, write *yes* if the topic can be found in the drawer. Write *before* or *after* to tell where other topics come. *(Unit 4, Lesson 7)*

1. baseball
2. backs
3. Baltimore
4. ballet
5. banana
6. Bahamas
7. badminton
8. bat
9. J. S. Bach
10. bathtubs
11. barrels
12. barter

H. Punctuating Dialogue

Write these sentences. Put in the correct punctuation.
(Unit 4, Lesson 8)

1. How does a dragon count to twenty? asked Sofia.
2. I don't know, answered Anita.
3. Sofia yelled It counts on its fingers!
4. Carmen asked What do you call a ten-foot-tall dragon with four arms and sharp teeth?
5. You tell me, said Barbara.
6. Sir! shouted Carmen.
7. What do you do with a green dragon? Fran asked.
8. Fran stated You wait until it gets ripe!

Something Extra

A Pro's Prose

Read the story on page 235. Darla knows that dragons are make-believe creatures. Stories that have make-believe creatures or events are called *fantasies.*

In this fantasy, the writer compares different things. The writer says, "The trees were twisted like corkscrews." This comparison helps you form a clear picture of the trees. The word *like* signals the comparison. A comparison that uses the words *like* or *as* is called a *simile.* Can you find other similes in "Darla and the Dragon"?

Write Away!

The story of "Darla and the Dragon" is not finished. What do you think will happen next? Write an ending. Use similes to help readers imagine the characters. Here are some ideas to help you start.

> Darla and the dragon become friends. They are as close as a squeak and a rusty hinge. Darla decides to help the dragon meet new friends. They . . .

> The dragon likes being kind. It stops breathing fire and smoke and becomes as gentle as a fat, sleepy cat. Then . . .

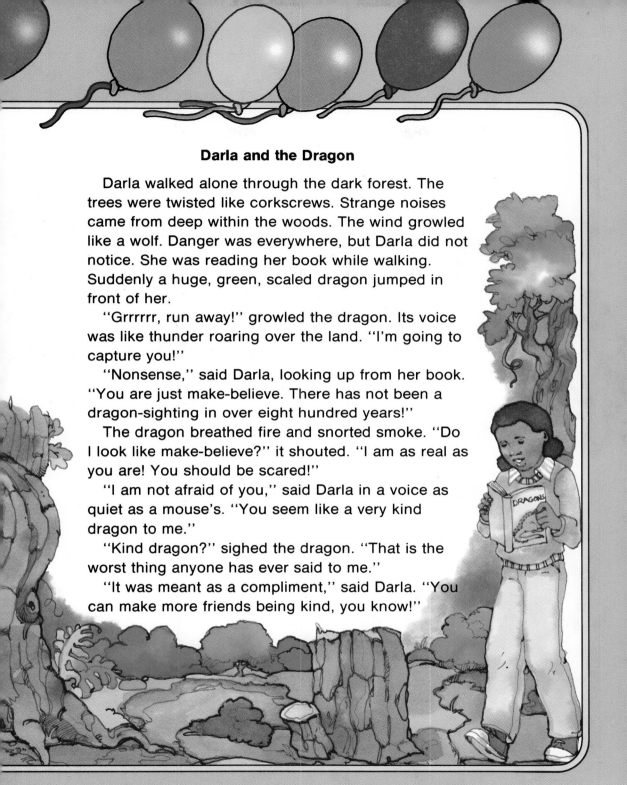

Darla and the Dragon

Darla walked alone through the dark forest. The trees were twisted like corkscrews. Strange noises came from deep within the woods. The wind growled like a wolf. Danger was everywhere, but Darla did not notice. She was reading her book while walking. Suddenly a huge, green, scaled dragon jumped in front of her.

"Grrrrrr, run away!" growled the dragon. Its voice was like thunder roaring over the land. "I'm going to capture you!"

"Nonsense," said Darla, looking up from her book. "You are just make-believe. There has not been a dragon-sighting in over eight hundred years!"

The dragon breathed fire and snorted smoke. "Do I look like make-believe?" it shouted. "I am as real as you are! You should be scared!"

"I am not afraid of you," said Darla in a voice as quiet as a mouse's. "You seem like a very kind dragon to me."

"Kind dragon?" sighed the dragon. "That is the worst thing anyone has ever said to me."

"It was meant as a compliment," said Darla. "You can make more friends being kind, you know!"

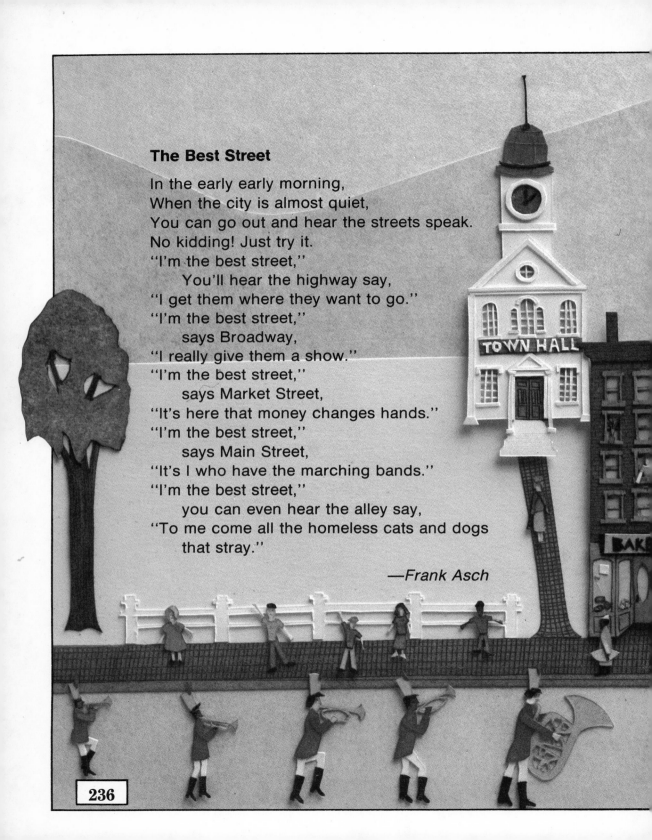

The Best Street

In the early early morning,
When the city is almost quiet,
You can go out and hear the streets speak.
No kidding! Just try it.
"I'm the best street,"
     You'll hear the highway say,
"I get them where they want to go."
"I'm the best street,"
     says Broadway,
"I really give them a show."
"I'm the best street,"
     says Market Street,
"It's here that money changes hands."
"I'm the best street,"
     says Main Street,
"It's I who have the marching bands."
"I'm the best street,"
     you can even hear the alley say,
"To me come all the homeless cats and dogs
     that stray."

—Frank Asch

TOWN HALL

BAKE

6

Persuading Others

SKILLS TO BUILD ON

Linking Verbs
Irregular Verbs
Pronoun-Verb Contractions
Reasons—Facts and Opinions

PRACTICAL APPLICATIONS

Writing a Persuasive Note
Speaking to Persuade

The Verb *Be*

> **The verb *be* has many forms. There are rules for using *be, being, been, am, is, are, was,* and *were.***
>
> I <u>am being</u> good. You <u>have been</u> noisy. We <u>will be</u> sorry.

If you have been using forms of *be* incorrectly, now is your chance to start being more careful.

Use *is* or *was* if the subject is one person, place, or thing. Use *are* or *were* if the subject is more than one.

Read these examples.

> Liz's hobby **is** acting. She **was** in the class play.
>
> My friends **are** hikers. They **were** on a hike.

Why is *was* used in one sentence and *were* in another?

Use *am* or *was* with the pronoun *I.* Use *are* or *were* with the pronoun *you.* Notice how *are* and *am* are used.

> I **am** a bird watcher.
>
> I **was** in a nature club once.
>
> You **are** a coin collector.
>
> You **were** a stamp collector.

You learned about helping verbs in Unit 3. Do you remember what they are? They are forms of *be* and *have.* Always use a helping verb before *be, being,* and *been.*

Find the helping verbs here.

> Miguel will be a good magician.
>
> Jan is being helpful today.
>
> Elaine has been a shell collector for two years.

PRACTICE

A. (Oral) Name the form of *be* that best completes each sentence.

> **Example:** Bobby (is/are) in a junkyard band.
> **is**

1. His friends Carmen and Dave (is/are) in the band.
2. They have (being/been) in the band for a year.
3. The band (was/were) fun for them.
4. Their instruments (are/is) homemade.
5. Drums (was/were) made from cans and boxes.
6. I (is/am) interested in joining the band.
7. You can (be/been) a member, too.
8. They will (be/been) happy.

B. (Written) Use a form of *be* to complete each sentence. Write the sentence.

> **Example:** Marsha's favorite hobby _____ puppet-making.
> **Marsha's favorite hobby is puppet-making.**

1. She has _____ making puppets for three years.
2. Marsha's puppets can _____ very real looking.
3. Some puppets _____ funny.
4. We _____ going to help her with a show.
5. Yesterday, we _____ practicing all day.
6. I _____ good at moving a puppet's arms.
7. You _____ good at making your puppet talk.

APPLY

What would you like to be when you grow up? Write three sentences telling what you might be. Use forms of the verb *be.*

Linking Verbs

> *Linking verbs* join words together. A linking verb shows that something *is, was,* or *will be.* Forms of *be* are linking verbs.
>
> John <u>is</u> tall. He <u>was</u> short last year.

You know that some verbs show action. An *action verb* tells what the subject of a sentence does or did, has or had.

Look at these examples.

> Amy **has** tap shoes.
> She **dances.**
> Joe **drives** a truck.
> He **paints** houses.

Linking verbs do not show action. A *linking verb* states that a subject *is, was,* or *will be* something. It links the subject with a word or words in the predicate.

Which words are linked in each sentence?

> My brother **is** a dancer.
> His dances **are** fun to watch.

Many action verbs can be used alone in the predicate of a sentence. For example, *Seth writes.* A linking verb is not often used alone. A linking verb links, or joins, the subject to a word or words in the predicate.

> **Incomplete:** Seth is.
> **Complete:** Seth is a poet.
> Seth is happy.

PRACTICE

A. (Oral) Name the subject and verb from each sentence.

> **Example:** I am an inventor.
> **I am**

WORD BANK

am
is
are
was
were
be
being
been

1. My inventions are useful.
2. My best invention was a room-cleaning robot.
3. It is possible to clean my room in record time.
4. My parents were happy with that invention.
5. Some other inventions were not as successful.
6. My dish-washing robot was a complete failure.
7. Our dishes are now just paper plates!
8. My dishwashing job is easier.

B. (Written) Write the verb from each sentence. Label the verb *linking* or *action*.

> **Example:** Jan's hobby is roller skating.
> **is—linking**

1. He practices for two hours every day.
2. Jan's skating is better than mine.
3. His tricks are too hard for me.
4. Fay and I were at the rink yesterday.
5. I watched Jan for a while.
6. He spun three times in the air.
7. That spin was very exciting.
8. Fay can spin like Jan.

APPLY

You are a world famous explorer. Write four sentences telling about your next trip. Use linking verbs. Tell what you will find. Circle each verb you write.

Words after Linking Verbs

> **A linking verb joins the subject to a word in the predicate. That word may be a noun or an adjective.**
>
> noun
> **Sherlock Holmes was a detective.**
>
> adjective
> **Holmes was famous.**

A linking verb joins the subject to a word in the predicate. The word in the predicate may be a noun.

Which words are joined by linking verbs?

Some books **are** novels. This book **is** a mystery.

Each linking verb joins the subject to a noun. The linking verb is almost like an equal sign: Some books = novels.

The word in the predicate may be an adjective. An adjective in the predicate describes the subject.

Which words are joined here?

That book **is** small. Those stories **are** funny.

The adjective *small* describes *that book.* What word describes *those stories*?

A compound subject may be linked to the predicate. More than one adjective may be joined to a subject.

What words are linked in these sentences?

Jake and Alice **are** good detectives.
He and she **are** very smart.
That story **is** long and sad.

PRACTICE

A. (Oral) For each sentence, name the subject, linking verb, and word or words in the predicate.

> **Example:** You are students.
> **subject—you; linking verb—are; word in the predicate—students**

1. The building is cold.
2. My favorite subject is English.
3. Last year science was easy.
4. My aunt and uncle are teachers.
5. My uncle is tall and bald.
6. All teachers were students.

B. (Written) Write each sentence. Underline the linking verb. Draw an arrow from an adjective in the predicate to the subject. Circle a noun in the predicate.

> **Example: The maps are colorful.**
> **An almanac is a (book.)**

1. Some pages are charts.
2. Most facts are interesting.
3. The atlas can be valuable.
4. Its maps are useful.
5. A dictionary is necessary.
6. Its information is helpful.

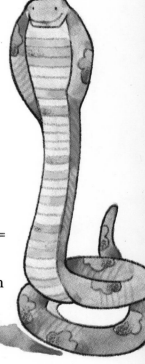

APPLY

Write three sentences about snakes. Use a linking verb in each sentence. Circle any noun after the verb. Draw an arrow from any adjective in the predicate to the subject.

Review the Basics I

A. The Verb *Be*
Write the form of *be* that best completes each sentence.
(*pages 238–239*)

1. A newspaper (is/are) a source of facts.
2. Its items (is/are) up-to-date and timely.
3. Newspaper reporters must (be/been) hard workers.
4. At times, getting the news has (been/being) a problem.
5. People may (been/be) unwilling to talk to reporters.
6. Nellie Bly (was/were) a good reporter.
7. She (was/were) good at getting the facts.
8. Her stories (was/were) often exciting.
9. She (was/were) famous.
10. We have (be/been) studying her life.
11. I (am/be) learning many things.
12. She (was/were) a daring woman.
13. Many men (was/were) amazed by her skill.
14. Today, women (is/are) reporters, too.
15. They (be/are) daring, too.

B. Linking Verbs
Write the verb from each sentence. Label the verb
linking or *action*. (*pages 240–241*)

1. The world's fastest train is French.
2. The train runs at 236 miles per hour.
3. It moves on special tracks.
4. Electricity is its power source.
5. The train's first run was in 1981.
6. The passengers were ready.
7. The ride was smooth and quiet.

8. The trip was much faster than normal.
9. The land was a blur.
10. The speed fooled us.
11. We raced along.
12. At once, it was quiet.
13. Our ride ended too soon.
14. Each of us wanted to go on.
15. Our next ride will be in a month.

C. Words after Linking Verbs

Write each sentence. Underline the linking verb. Draw an arrow from an adjective in the predicate to the subject. Circle a noun in the predicate. (*pages 242–243*)

1. Apples are fruit.
2. Lettuce is green.
3. Lettuce is a vegetable.
4. Nuts are fruits.
5. Peanuts are crunchy.
6. Those peanuts are toasted.
7. Peas and beans are tasty.
8. Carrots were roots.
9. Wheat is a grain.
10. Broccoli is a flower.
11. That vegetable is squash.
12. Beans are long and thin.
13. Eggplant is purple.
14. Scallions are onions.
15. I am a gardener.

Verbs in a Paragraph

You know that forms of *be* are used as main verbs and as helping verbs. The verb *be* and the forms of *be* are not action verbs, so they are easy to overlook.

Look for *be* as a main verb in these examples.

I am a model builder. My models are rockets.

Look for *be* as a helping verb in these examples.

Ellen is collecting keys for a hobby.
Lee was saving ribbons.

What are the complete verbs?

You have also learned that forms of *be* can link subjects to words in the predicate. Look for this as you read the next paragraph. Also look for forms of *be* as main verbs and as helping verbs.

Now read the paragraph.

Eddie is a collector. His hobby is saving baseball cards. Eddie has been collecting cards for three years. His collection is huge and growing. Eddie's room is full of baseball cards. Boxes and bags are under his bed. They are filled with cards. There are no clothes in his closet. There is no room for anything but cards.

PRACTICE/APPLY

A. (Written) Read this paragraph. Find and write the full verb in each sentence. Underline the form of *be*. Label it as a helping verb or main verb.

Example: 1. <u>is</u>—main verb

(1) Keiko's hobby is coin collecting. (2) Keiko's coins are from different countries. (3) Some of her coins are very old. (4) Keiko's favorite coin is an Indian head penny. (5) This penny was made a hundred years ago. (6) Some old coins were made of gold. (7) Keiko is saving her money for a gold coin.

B. (Written) Choose the correct form of *be* to complete each sentence. Write the paragraph.

I have (been/being) collecting postcards. My cards (is/are) from all over the world. The pictures (is/are) of scenes in other countries. A card from Japan (was/were) my favorite. My new favorite (is/are) from Brazil. I (am/are) trying to get one card from each country!

Prefixes

When you studied adjectives in Unit 4, you learned to make new words by adding suffixes to base words. You can also make new words by adding prefixes to base words. A *prefix* is a word part. It is added to the beginning of a word. The new word has a different meaning from the base word.

Each prefix has its own meaning. Each changes a base word in a certain way. One common prefix is *in-*. It means "within" or "not."

How does the prefix *in-* change these words?

side—inside   active—inactive   visible—invisible

Other prefixes have different meanings. The chart shows *in-* and three other prefixes.

Study the chart.

Prefixes and Their Meanings

Prefix	Meaning	Example
in- **un-** **re-** **mis-**	within, not not, do the opposite of again, back wrong, wrongly	**in**doors, **in**formal **un**happy, **un**tie **re**fill, **re**turn **mis**treat, **mis**spell

In each example, how does the word with a prefix compare in meaning to the base word?

Look carefully when you try to learn the meaning of a word. Some words begin with a prefix. Try to learn the meaning of the base word first. Take away the prefix letters. Look at what is left. Is it a word?

Some words that begin with prefix letters do not really have a prefix. In the next examples, which two words begin with a prefix?

missile   uncover   reason   incorrect

PRACTICE

A. (Oral) Give a meaning for each word. Use the chart if you need help.

    Example: repaint
            paint again

1. misplace
2. retie
3. unmade
4. refill

5. misread
6. unwrap
7. redo
8. incomplete

9. misprint
10. undo
11. redraw
12. invisible

B. (Written) Write a word for each meaning. Use the chart if you need help.

    Example: do the opposite of dress
            undress

1. answer again
2. not block
3. born within
4. not changed
5. wrongly called

6. close again
7. not covered
8. grow back
9. not ironed
10. light again

11. not direct
12. not fresh
13. folded again
14. not matched
15. turn back

APPLY

Write two pairs of sentences about a task you do each morning. Use a base word in one sentence. Use the base word with a prefix in the other sentence.

Building Sentences Using Exact Verbs

When you write, you use many verbs. The verbs you choose are important. Some verbs do not tell much. Other verbs give a better picture of the action. Compare the next two examples.

Which verb tells more about the action?

The acrobat **went** through the air.
The acrobat **flew** through the air.

Choosing exact verbs is important to good sentence writing. Make sure your words say what you mean. Even a simple sentence can be better if the verb is chosen carefully.

WORD BANK

raced
darted
dashed
galloped
sped
hurried
scowled
flew
hurtled
glanced
peeped
stared
gaped
glared

Which sentence in each pair tells more action?

Thunder **came.** Thunder **rumbled.**
Wind **blew.** Wind **whipped.**
Lightning **appeared.** Lightning **flashed.**
Rain **fell.** Rain **poured.**

If you use exact verbs, people will more easily understand what you are writing about. The Word Bank lists words that can be used to replace inexact verbs. Try replacing the less exact verbs in these sentences with more exact verbs from the Word Bank.

Does the picture change?

We ran past the empty old house. I looked at it.

PRACTICE

A. (Oral) Name the verb in each pair that best fits the meaning of the sentence.

Example: The bat (smacked/hit) the ball.
smacked

1. The ball (went/hurtled) through the air.
2. The runner (went/dashed) around the bases.
3. A fielder (stretched/reached) for the ball.
4. The ball (went/bounced) on the ground.
5. The fielder (grabbed/took) the ball.
6. The batter (went/slid) into third base.
7. "Safe!" the umpire (said/yelled).

B. (Written) Find the verb in each sentence. Replace the verb with a more lively, exact verb. Write the sentence.

Example: Fire went up a hillside.
Fire raced up a hillside.

1. The fire touched a tree trunk.
2. Flames went up the tree.
3. Fire went from tree to tree.
4. Animals ran from the fire.
5. A firefighting plane came low over the fire.
6. Water fell from the plane.
7. The fire stopped.

APPLY

Recall the last rainstorm you saw. Write three sentences describing that storm. Use lively, exact verbs in your sentences.

Synonyms and Antonyms

In our language, there are a large number of words. Some of these words have almost the same meaning. Words that have almost the same meaning are *synonyms.*

Kate ate a **large** meal. I ate a **huge** meal, too.
Kate had a **small** glass of milk. My glass of milk
was **tiny,** too.

The words *large* and *huge* are synonyms. Their meanings are almost the same. The words *small* and *tiny* are synonyms, too. You can use one instead of the other.

There is one sure way to remember which kinds of words are synonyms. The letter **s** is a clue. **S**ynonyms mean almost the **s**ame.

Some words have meanings that are the opposite of others. For example, *small* is the opposite of *large*. These words are *antonyms.* Name another antonym of *small.*

Find the antonyms in these sentences.

We drank the cold milk after eating the hot soup.
From the first to last bite, our meal was good.

PRACTICE

A. (Oral) Read each pair of words. Tell whether they are synonyms or antonyms.

Example: strange/unusual
synonyms

1. wet/dry
2. scream/yell
3. lift/raise
4. autumn/fall
5. laugh/cry
6. noisy/loud
7. live/die
8. long/short
9. straight/crooked
10. fat/thin
11. error/mistake
12. lumpy/smooth
13. damp/wet
14. summer/winter
15. empty/full
16. frighten/scare

B. (Written) Write an antonym or a synonym for each word. Label the word you write with an **A** or an **S**.

Example: loud
soft—A

1. rise
2. clean
3. walk
4. cook
5. hide
6. mean
7. last
8. better
9. throw
10. loose
11. foot
12. up
13. different
14. end
15. lost
16. inside
17. early
18. short
19. sunny
20. stop
21. add
22. quick
23. shout
24. win

APPLY

Write four sentences about your town. Use two synonyms and two antonyms. Circle each synonym. Draw a line under each antonym.

Reasons—Facts and Opinions

A *fact* is known to be true. A fact can stand by itself. An *opinion* is a belief. An opinion comes from a person.

Read these sentences.

I think living in a tall building is fun.

Many apartments are in tall buildings.

Which sentence tells what a person thinks? Which one tells a fact?

A *reason* is an explanation. Reasons often are given to answer the question *Why?* The question may be answered with both opinions and facts. Look at this question.

Why do some people live in apartments?

This question can be answered with opinions and facts.

Good reasons are made up of both facts and opinions. The facts are used to support the opinions. Without facts, opinions make poor reasons.

Sometimes people give no opinions and no facts. They answer a question with "Just because." They give no reasons at all.

Which person gives the best reasons to this question: Why do you want to go home early?

Sue: Because I do!

Eric: I want to go home early because I want to.

Karen: I want to go home early because I need to. My family is waiting for me. We have an appointment. We are going to look at a new apartment in town.

PRACTICE

(Written) Read each question and the answers given.
Write *good reason* or *poor reason* for each.

Example: Why did you eat my lunch? Because I wanted to!
       poor reason

1. Why do dogs bark? I think that dogs bark for good reasons. They bark to get our attention. They bark when they are hungry. They bark to warn us.

2. Why is an orange round and not square? I think round things bounce better.

3. Why are walnuts different from peanuts? Just because they are.

4. Why do I have to go to bed early? I think it is best for you to go to bed early on a school night. Tonight is a school night. You will get a full night's sleep.

5. Why do some people have brown eyes? Some people have brown eyes because their eyes are brown.

6. Why does it snow near the North Pole and not near the equator? Earth is tilted. Earth spins. The North Pole is colder. The equator is warmer. It is closer to the sun.

APPLY

The answer to the question below needs more facts.
Write three sentences to finish the answer. Use facts.
Question: Why can't I collect bathtubs?
Answer: I think bathtub collecting is not a good hobby.

Irregular Verbs

> **The spelling of an *irregular verb* changes. The basic part of an irregular verb does not end in *ed*.**
>
> We <u>grow</u> tulips. The tulips <u>grew</u> well. We have <u>grown</u> roses, too.

The verbs *fall, eat, find, grow,* and *take* are irregular. Do not add *-ed* to the present parts of these irregular verbs.

Basic Parts of Irregular Verbs

Present	Present + ing with helping verb am/was	Past	Past with helping verb have/had
fall	falling	fell	fallen
eat	eating	ate	eaten
find	finding	found	found
grow	growing	grew	grown
take	taking	took	taken

Irregular verbs are like regular verbs. They need helping verbs. Use *am, is, are, was,* or *were* with the *-ing* form. Use *have, has,* or *had* with *fallen, eaten, found, grown,* and *taken.*

How are the forms of *be* and *have* used here?

We **were** taking turns.

You **have** taken your share.

An irregular verb, like all verbs, must agree with the subject of a sentence. To match *fall, eat, find, grow,* or *take* with a singular subject, just add *-s.*

PRACTICE

A. (Oral) Name the form of the verb that best completes each sentence.

> **Example:** A magic tree (grew/growed) in the jungle.
> **grew**

1. Strange fruits were (growing/grow) on the tree.
2. One day, a fruit (fallen/fell) to the ground.
3. An elephant (founded/found) the fruit.
4. He (took/taken) the fruit in his trunk.
5. Then he (eaten/ate) the fruit.
6. After he had (ate/eaten) it, he felt strange.
7. He (found/find) himself floating in the air!

B. (Written) Write each sentence. Use the correct verb form to fill the blank.

> **Example:** People have _____ out about good food. (find)
> **People have found out about good food.**

1. Have we always _____ the right foods? (eat)
2. We have _____ strong and healthy. (grow)
3. Long ago, people _____ care of themselves, too. (take)
4. They _____ the right foods in the past. (eat)
5. Today we _____ strong, too. (grow)
6. The number of unhealthy people has _____ . (fall)
7. People today are _____ more natural foods. (eat)
8. Each day we _____ better foods to eat. (find)

APPLY

Pretend that you found a magic seed and planted it. Write four sentences telling how the seed grew. Use some forms of the verbs *fall, eat, find, grow,* or *take.*

10 MORE BASIC SKILLS

Avoiding Double Negatives

> **Avoid using two negatives in one sentence.**
> **Examples of negative words are *no, not, nobody,***
> ***nowhere, no one, none,* and *never.***
>
> <u>Wrong:</u> No one had no problems. None of us made no mistakes.
> <u>Correct:</u> No one had any problem. None of us made a mistake.

Two negative words in the same sentence are called a *double negative.* They say the same thing twice. One of those words is not needed.

Look at this example.

> I did not have none.

The example is confusing. If you did *not* have *none,* did you have *some?* To say what you mean, avoid using a double negative. The example could be corrected in one of these two ways. Each one is correct.

> I had none.   I did not have any.

Remember, *n't* stands for the word *not.* A verb plus *n't* and the word *no, nobody, nothing, nowhere, no one, none,* or *never* form a double negative. Avoid using a verb plus *n't* and a negative word in one sentence.

Look at these examples.

> **Incorrect:** We won't never tell a lie.
> **Correct:** We won't ever tell a lie.
>   We will never tell a lie.

PRACTICE

A. (Oral) Name the best word to complete each sentence.

> **Example:** She didn't get (<u>any</u>/none) of the pie.
> **any**

1. You will get (<u>any</u>/none) if you are late.
2. I can't go (<u>anywhere</u>/nowhere) after supper.
3. They said they didn't do (nothing/<u>anything</u>) wrong.
4. Paul didn't have (<u>any</u>/no) money for the movies.
5. We didn't see (<u>anybody</u>/nobody) we knew at the park.
6. Nan has (never/<u>ever</u>) missed a day of school.
7. Elephants don't (<u>ever</u>/never) forget.
8. I didn't get (nothing/<u>anything</u>) wrong on the test.

B. (Written) Read each sentence. Decide whether it is correct or incorrect. Fix each incorrect sentence.

> **Example:** They hadn't seen anyone.   I hadn't been given none.
> **correct**   **I hadn't been given any.**

1. We had nowhere to go today.
2. We couldn't think of nothing to do.
3. None of our friends weren't home.
4. We didn't see anybody around.
5. We didn't get no phone calls.
6. Nobody dropped by our house.
7. We haven't never had such a boring day!
8. I hope we won't never have another one like that.

APPLY

Write three sentences. Tell about something you will not do, somewhere you will not go, and something you do not like. Do not use double negatives.

Pronoun-Verb Contractions

> A *contraction* is made from two other words. Some contractions join pronouns and verbs. An *apostrophe* (') replaces the missing letters.
>
> <u>You are</u> here, and <u>you're</u> ready to go.

A *contraction* is a short way of writing two words. When the two words are joined to form a contraction, one or more letters are left out. An *apostrophe* (') takes the place of the missing letters. A pronoun and a verb can be joined to make a contraction.

Pronoun and Verb Contractions

I am→I'm	you are→you're	he is→he's
I will→I'll	you will→you'll	he has→he's
I had→I'd	you had→you'd	he will→he'll
I have→I've	you have→you've	he had→he'd
she is→she's	it is→it's	we are→we're
she has→she's	it has→it's	we will→we'll
she will→she'll	it will→it'll	we had→we'd
she had→she'd	it had→it'd	we have→we've
	they are→they're	
	they will→they'll	
	they have→they've	
	they had→they'd	

What letter or letters are left out in each contraction?

PRACTICE

A. (Oral) Give the two words that make up each contraction.

Example: we'll
we will

1. she's
2. I'll
3. they've
4. we're
5. I'm
6. they'll

7. he'd
8. they're
9. you'll
10. I'd
11. he'll
12. you've

13. we've
14. it's
15. she'd
16. it'll
17. you're
18. he's

B. (Written) Change the underlined words in each sentence into a contraction.

Example: I have a luna moth in my insect collection.
I've

1. <u>She is</u> the school chess champ.
2. <u>They have</u> a collection of old bottles.
3. I know <u>you will</u> like the horse show.
4. <u>I am</u> learning about cameras.
5. <u>He is</u> interested in cars.
6. <u>We have</u> started a hiking club in school.
7. <u>It is</u> a good day for a hike.
8. <u>We will</u> show you our autograph book.
9. <u>He has</u> won a prize in the baking contest.

APPLY

Imagine that you have made a new electronic game. Write three sentences to describe your game. Use contractions with pronouns.

12 MORE BASIC SKILLS

Using *They're, Their,* and *There*

> ***They're, their,*** and ***there*** **sound alike but have different meanings.**
>
> **They're** here, yet <u>their</u> voices echo over <u>there</u>.

The words *they're, their,* and *there* sound alike. They are not spelled alike. They have different meanings. *They're* is a contraction. What two words make up *they're?*

These two sentences have the same meaning.

> **They are** raising tropical fish.
> **They're** raising tropical fish.

If you are not sure when to use *they're,* replace the word with *they are.* If *they are* does not fit in the sentence, *they're* is incorrect.

Their is a possessive pronoun. *Their* means "belonging to them."

Look at these sentences.

> The fish belong to them.
> They keep **their** fish in a big tank.

There is often used to begin a sentence. *There* also points to a place. It points to a place far from the speaker.

Look at these sentences.

> **There** are twenty fish in the tank.
> Please put the can on the shelf over **there**.

PRACTICE

A. (Written) Write the word that best completes each sentence.

> **Example:** (They're/Their) not going with us.
> **They're**

1. (They're/Their) job is raising fish.
2. That means (they're/their) experts.
3. That is (their/they're) fish tank.
4. Look at all the fish in (they're/there)!
5. The ones over (their/there) are glass catfish.
6. (They're/There) easy to see through.
7. You can see (their/there) insides!
8. I think (there/they're) interesting to watch.

B. (Written) Write each sentence. Correct the words that are not used correctly.

> **Example:** Making kites is there hobby.
> **Making kites is their hobby.**

9. Their making a dragon kite now.
10. They're dragon kite has twenty round sections.
11. On the first section, there painting a dragon face.
12. Their is going to be a Kite Festival on March 5.
13. They will take there dragon kite they're.
14. They're kite may be the best kite of all.
15. They hope there kite will win a prize.
16. They're friends will cheer for them.

APPLY

Write three sentences about a group of friends flying kites. Use *they're, their,* and *there* in your sentences.

13 MORE BASIC SKILLS

Using *Your* and *You're, Its* and *It's*

> In the sound-alikes *your/you're* and *its/it's,* the first word in each pair is a possessive pronoun. The second word is a contraction.
>
> Possessive pronouns: <u>Its</u> flag waved. <u>Your</u> hat came off.
> Contractions: <u>It's</u> your turn. No, <u>you're next</u>.

It's your turn. No, you're next.

Your and *you're* are sound-alikes. *Its* and *it's* are sound-alikes, too. The words in each pair sound alike. They are not spelled alike. They have different meanings.

You have learned that *your* and *its* are possessive pronouns. Possessive pronouns never have apostrophes. You know that *you're* and *it's* are contractions. What tells you that *you're* and *it's* are contractions?

Your means "belonging to you." *You're* stands for "you are."

Look at these sentences.

Your desk is near mine.   **You're** my best friend.

Try replacing *your* in the first sentence with *you are.* If *you are* does not fit in the sentence, use *your,* not *you're.*

Its means "belonging to it." *It's* stands for "it is."

It's my turn to wash the dog.

Its bath day is today.

In which sentence can you replace one of the sound-alikes with *it is?*

Be careful when you use these sound-alikes. Use *it's* only when the words *it is* fit in the sentence.

PRACTICE

A. (Written) Write the word that best completes each sentence.

> **Example:** I know (you're/your) answer is right.
> **your**

1. I stopped by (you're/your) house today.
2. (You're/Your) mother said that you were not at home.
3. (Its/It's) a free day at the museum.
4. You wanted to see (its/it's) new exhibit.
5. (Its/It's) an exhibit of pictures of other planets.
6. (You're/Your) interested in astronomy.
7. (Its/It's) exciting to see pictures taken by spacecraft.
8. I told (you're/your) mother I would see you later.

B. (Written) Write each sentence. Correct the words that are not used correctly.

> **Example:** You're canoe is green.
> **Your canoe is green.**

9. White-water canoeing is you're parents' hobby.
10. You're parents showed me their canoe.
11. It's name is Silver Fish.
12. You're parents said the river is best in spring.
13. It's water is at it's highest point then.
14. I heard that your going on a trip with them.
15. I hope your not frightened by the fast water.
16. Be sure to wear you're helmet and life jacket.

APPLY

Write four sentences about a lion tamer and his lion. Use *your, you're, its,* and *it's.*

Review the Basics II

A. Irregular Verbs
Choose the form of the verb that best completes each sentence. Write the sentence. *(pages 256–257)*

1. May was (taken/taking) a walk in the woods.
2. She (find/found) something on the ground.
3. A baby bird had (fallen/fell) out of its nest.
4. May was afraid an animal might (eat/ate) the bird.
5. She was worried that the baby had not (ate/eaten).
6. It could not (grow/grown) without food.
7. Then the parent birds (find/found) the baby.
8. They (taken/took) some food to the baby.

B. Avoiding Double Negatives
Write the word that best completes each sentence. *(pages 258–259)*

1. There wasn't (nothing/anything) wrong with the car.
2. They didn't find (any/no) treasure in the wreck.
3. Taro didn't meet (anyone/no one) on his way home.
4. I'm not going (nowhere/anywhere) in this weather.
5. George Washington wouldn't (never/ever) tell a lie.
6. We don't have (anything/nothing) to do today.
7. It doesn't (never/ever) snow in Hawaii.

C. Pronoun-Verb Contractions
Write the two words that make up each contraction. *(pages 260–261)*

1. I'd
2. you've
3. she'll
4. it'll
5. she's
6. he'd
7. they're
8. we'll
9. we've

D. Using *They're, Their,* and *There*

Write the word that best completes each sentence.
(pages 262–263))

1. (There/They're) is a strange planet in space.
2. The people (their/there) live upside down.
3. (They're/Their) feet are up in the air.
4. (There/Their) heads are down near the ground.
5. They have to walk on (their/they're) hands.
6. (They're/Their) always falling over.
7. The people pedal bikes with (their/there) hands.
8. (Their/They're) very good at upside-down biking.
9. They never wear shoes (there/their).
10. They wear thick mittens on (they're/their) feet.
11. They use (there/their) toes for dialing a phone.
12. (There/They're) very clever people.

E. Using *Your* and *You're, Its* and *It's*

Write the word that best completes each sentence.
(pages 264–265)

1. (You're/Your) going to play on our team.
2. (It's/Its) name is the Ward Avenue Wonders.
3. We heard that (you're/your) batting is great.
4. (You're/Your) going to be our catcher.
5. Here are (your/you're) catcher's mitt and mask.
6. (Its/It's) a good day for a game.
7. (Its/It's) starting time is 2:00 P.M.
8. We are glad that (you're/your) able to play.
9. (Your/You're) brother might play, too.
10. (Its/It's) good that you both play well.

Words That Organize

Organizing words show how one thought fits with another. They are used to start sentences.

Some organizing words help with *time order.* They give order to events or thoughts. Such words as *first, next,* and *last* are time-order words.

Notice the time-order words in this example.

> **First** I thought it was a cloud's shadow. **Then** I thought it might be an eclipse. **Finally** I remembered I was wearing sunglasses.

The term *in addition* is a different kind of organizer. It signals that more facts or thoughts will be added. Use *finally* or *in conclusion* for a last statement.

You know that good reasons are facts that support an opinion. When you want to persuade someone, use good reasons. Organizing words can give order to your reasons. In the next paragraph, the reasons are in order. First there is an opinion. Then facts are used to persuade.

> I think that we all should live in tall buildings. **For one thing,** a tall building can hold more people than a low one can. **For example,** if four people can live in a one-story house, twelve people can live in a three-story house. **Also,** a tall building takes up less land. **Thus,** there is more land for parks. **In conclusion,** I think tall buildings are better than low ones.

Notice the use of commas in the paragraph. With most organizing words, use a comma if they start a sentence. Do not use a comma when time-order words start a sentence.

WORD BANK

first
second
next
last
also
however
thus
therefore
finally
for example
in addition
in conclusion

PRACTICE

A. (Written) Write each sentence. Add commas after the organizing words.

> **Example:** For one thing litter can be harmful.
> **For one thing, litter can be harmful.**

1. For example pets can be cut by broken glass.
2. Besides rough metal can hurt people.
3. Thus litter is not healthful.
4. In addition fires can start in piles of paper and rags.
5. Also litter is ugly.
6. Therefore we must work together to end litter.
7. For one thing it is our town.
8. On the other hand we all must help.
9. In conclusion we must plan an anti-litter campaign.

B. (Written) Add organizing words to these reasons. Make the facts fit together. Remember to use a comma after an organizing word that starts a sentence, unless it is a time-order word. Write the new paragraph.

    I think cats are nicer than dogs because cats do not bother people. Cats do not have to be taken for walks. Cats give themselves baths. Dogs may be friendlier than cats. Many people do not like dogs to jump on them. Cats take up less space in an apartment. Cats make better pets than dogs do.

APPLY

    Write four reasons why the color green is better than purple. Or choose two other colors to write about. Use organizing words.

Writing an Opinion Paragraph

An opinion is the way someone thinks or feels about some event or thing. A fact can stand by itself. It does not need a person. Facts are true pieces of information. Most often a fact can be proven in some way.

You can prove many facts yourself. Your senses help you. For example, your senses have taught you that ice is cold and fire is hot.

You can accept some facts as true because they have happened many times. You know that boiling an egg will make the egg hard. You know that because it has happened over and over. You do not have to prove it.

Read this paragraph.

I think spinach is a healthful food. Everyone should eat spinach. For one thing, spinach has no fat in it. In addition, spinach contains vitamin A. Also, spinach has almost as much calcium in it as milk. Therefore, spinach is good for you. We should eat spinach.

Now ask yourself these questions:

What is the opinion? What are the facts?
Do the facts support the opinion?
Are the reasons good ones? Are they important?
Does the final statement restate the opinion?
Does the opinion paragraph persuade?

What is your opinion about the paragraph? Can you support your opinion with facts?

PRACTICE

A. **(Oral)** One sentence in each pair is a fact. One is an opinion. Identify each one.

> **Example:** a. No one likes fried grapes.
> **a. opinion**

1. a. I think that fourth-graders should have jobs.
   b. I know three fourth-graders who have jobs.

2. a. I think I am a good joke teller.
   b. People laugh when I tell jokes.

3. a. There were no seats left for the school play.
   b. I do not like the school play.

4. a. Mom helped me fix my bike.
   b. People should help other people.

B. **(Written)** Write an opinion paragraph. Use the opinion for the first sentence. Choose four facts to support the opinion. Add organizing words from Lesson 14. Write your own final statement, or conclusion.

Opinion: The school lunch period needs to be longer.
Facts: It takes ten minutes to get to the cafeteria.
   The meals are too large to eat in twenty minutes.
   The lines to get food are very long.
   The whole school eats at the same time.
   Swallowing without chewing is not good for you.
   The first person is done before the last one has food.

APPLY

Write four sentences about your favorite sport. State an opinion in the first sentence. State three facts that support that opinion. Use organizing words.

A Persuasive Note: Plan, Write, Edit

Have you ever tried to persuade someone to agree with you? You may have persuaded a friend to go somewhere. You may have persuaded someone to taste some food.

One way to persuade is a type of letter. Notes are written to people who can do something to support your opinion. You send a note to someone who can change things. If you wanted something changed at school, you might write to the principal.

In this lesson, you will plan, write, and edit a note to persuade someone to support your opinion.

PLAN

Think about your school or town. Is there something you think should be changed or improved? Is something going to be changed that you think should stay as it is? Think of an opinion you can support. You may want to use the opinion from the Practice B in Lesson 15. Look at the four planning steps. Follow each one.

Step 1: Decide what your opinion is. Who will receive your note? Complete this sentence: *I think that . . . .*

Step 2: Decide the reasons for your opinion. Why do you think as you do? Check your reasons. Is each one a fact? Does it answer the question why?

Step 3: Write your opinion first. You do not need to write a complete sentence. Write your reasons next. Number them. Make sure your reasons are facts that support your opinion. Make sure your reasons will persuade the reader.

Step 4: Think of a final statement or conclusion. It should restate your opinion. Spend extra time on the ending. It should tell what you want someone to remember. A good conclusion is often what persuades the reader.

WRITE

Use this form as a model for your note.

Date:

To: The name of the person you want to persuade goes here.

From: Your name goes here.

Subject: What you want to talk about goes here.

State it in a few words.

Write your opinion and reasons here in paragraph form.

You may need two paragraphs.

Now write your persuasive note. State your opinion clearly. Make sure each reason answers the question why. Check your planning ideas. Include all the important reasons. Use organizing words to connect the thoughts.

If you have too many thoughts for one paragraph, write two. Spend extra time on the conclusion. It will be the last sentence you write.

EDIT

Like all written work, a persuasive note should be edited. "Sense" is the most important thing to look for. The opinion and the reasons must make sense. When you edit, pretend that the note was sent to you. Is it convincing?

✔ Is the opinion clearly stated?
✔ Do the reasons back up the opinion?
✔ Does the conclusion restate the opinion?

Reread the note. Check the form.

✔ Are organizing words followed by commas?
✔ Are negative words used correctly?
✔ Are the verb choices exact?
✔ Are contractions formed correctly?

Before you edit your own work, study the note below. See how each mistake has been corrected.

Date: April 1, 198-

To: Mayor Margaret Cooley

From: Leda Gomez

Subject: Roller skating in parks

I think that special places should be made in parks for roller skating. Now people roller skate on the paths. It's not good for people to skate their. Roller skaters bump into other people and knock them down. Now people have to watch out for roller skaters. If roller skaters had they're own place, their wouldnt be no problems. That is why I think their should be special places in parks.

Now edit your own persuasive note. Copy it in your best handwriting.

Speaking to Persuade

Can you persuade someone? Speaking to persuade is like writing a persuasive note. Your talk must be organized. You must know what you will say. People must see that you believe in what you say. Your belief might help to convince others.

Look at the picture.

What is the opinion of the people in the picture? Give a talk that supports their opinion.

GUIDELINES

1. Plan your talk. Think of two reasons to back up the opinion. Think of an ending that will persuade.

2. Make notes to help you remember each point.

3. Speak firmly and clearly. Look at the people to whom you are speaking.

4. Use your face and voice to tell which reasons are most important.

PRACTICE/APPLY

(Oral) Give your talk to your classmates. Follow the Guidelines.

Unit 6 Test

A. The Verb *Be*

Write the form of *be* that best completes each sentence. *(pages 238–239)*

1. Gary will (be/been) a dancer.
2. He (is/are) studying in a ballet school.
3. Gary (were/was) thrilled by the first ballet he saw.
4. "I (am/are) going to dance like that!" he said.
5. Ballet students (is/are) great athletes.
6. Gary has (be/been) working hard.

B. Linking Verbs

Write the verb from each sentence. Label the verb *linking* or *action*. *(pages 240–241)*

1. The sun is a source of energy.
2. The sun gives heat and light to the earth.
3. Our sun makes life on Earth possible.
4. The sun is hot gases.
5. The gases mix.
6. They are very hot.

Label four columns. Name them *Subject, Linking Verb, Nouns in the Predicate, Adjectives in the Predicate.* For each sentence, list the subject, linking verb, and words in the predicate. *(pages 242–243)*

7. John Glenn was an astronaut.
8. His mission was Mercury/Atlas 6.
9. Now, Glenn is a senator.
10. He is famous.
11. Apollo and Saturn are names.
12. Saturn is a rocket.

13. Apollo was a mission.

14. Earth is a planet.

15. Mercury is tiny and hot.

16. Saturn and Jupiter are huge and cold.

17. Mars is small and dry.

18. Venus is cloudy

19. The moon is a satellite.

20. It is very small.

C. Irregular Verbs

Choose the form of the verb that best completes each sentence. Write the sentence. *(pages 256–257)*

1. A meteor (fell/fallen) to Earth.

2. Rabbits had (ate/eaten) the farmer's beans.

3. The explorers (find/found) a new land.

4. Strange plants were (growing/grow) in the jungle.

5. Aunt Carol (took/taken) us to the ice show.

D. Pronoun-Verb Contractions

Write the two words that make up each contraction. *(pages 260–261)*

1. I'm	5. she'd	9. I've
2. he'll	6. you'll	10. they'll
3. they've	7. we're	11. you've
4. it's	8. you're	12. we'll

E. Writing

Write a paragraph. Persuade your teacher not to give homework on the weekends. Be sure to use facts to support the opinion. Make the last sentence a conclusion. *(pages 272–274)*

Keep Practicing

A. Pronouns
Write each sentence. Replace the underlined word or words with a pronoun. *(Unit 5, Lesson 1)*

1. <u>Dad</u> took Kevin and Tom shopping.
2. <u>Kevin</u> needed a new jacket.
3. <u>Ms. Casey, the clerk</u>, helped Kevin find one.
4. <u>The jacket</u> cost $37.50.
5. <u>Dad</u> bought Tom some new jeans.
6. <u>The jeans</u> cost $12.75.
7. <u>Dad</u> gave Ms. Casey $51.00.
8. <u>The change</u> was 75 cents.
9. <u>Ms. Casey</u> gave three coins to Dad.
10. <u>The quarters</u> were the change.

B. Pronouns after Verbs
Write each sentence. Replace the underlined word or words with a pronoun. *(Unit 5, Lesson 2)*

1. We went with <u>Ed and Jean</u> to the school library.
2. We were helped by <u>the librarian</u>.
3. She showed us how to use <u>the card catalog</u>.
4. We asked <u>the librarian</u> lots of questions.
5. My friends and I looked for <u>books</u> in the catalog.
6. Then we tried to find <u>the books</u> on the shelves.
7. The librarian showed Rosa and <u>Ed</u> the science books.
8. They were all together in <u>one section</u>.
9. Rosa handed <u>two books</u> to me.
10. We used them for <u>a report</u>.
11. Rosa gave the report to <u>Mr. Brooks, our teacher</u>.
12. He read it to <u>the class</u>.

C. Using *I* or *Me, We* or *Us*

Choose *I, me, we,* or *us* to complete each sentence. Write the sentence. *(Unit 5, Lesson 3)*

1. _____ am going to Arizona next summer.
2. Dad and Mom are taking _____ to the Grand Canyon.
3. _____ all will ride mules down into the canyon.
4. My parents and _____ have never ridden on mules.
5. Guides will be riding with _____ .
6. They will take care of the mules and _____ .
7. _____ hope I like riding a mule.
8. Do you think the mule will like _____ ?
9. _____ will be there for three weeks.
10. _____ must carry all our food with _____ .

D. Possessive Pronouns

Choose the form of the pronoun that correctly completes the second sentence in each pair. Write the sentence. *(Unit 5, Lesson 10)*

1. The class will have a craft show. We will show (our/ours) projects.
2. Maria is a potter. Those bowls are (her/hers).
3. She made a tall vase. (Her/Hers) vase is blue.
4. Chan paints. (His/Him) paintings are on the wall.
5. I knit. That sweater is (my/mine).
6. Phil and I worked together. The scarves are (our/ours).
7. Sara and Tim do weaving. These are (their/theirs) placemats.
8. We will invite you to the show. Will (your/yours) class come?
9. My friends make leather vests. They will bring (their/theirs).
10. You would like them. (Theirs/Their) vests are beaded.

E. Clear Pronoun References
Read this paragraph. Write the pronouns and the words
to which they refer. (*Unit 5, Lesson 11*)

One female chimpanzee learned to communicate.
(**1.** She) was named Washoe. Washoe learned to use
sign language. (**2.** It) is a set of hand signals used by
deaf people. Two people trained Washoe. (**3.** They)
began Washoe's training when she was a year old.
Washoe lives with other chimpanzees now. (**4.** She)
has taught (**5.** them) to use sign language, too.

F. *-Self* Pronouns
Use the right *-self* pronoun to complete each sentence.
The pronoun partner is marked. Write the sentence.
(*Unit 5, Lesson 12*)

1. I enclosed an envelope addressed to _____ .
2. Did you fix the bike by _____ , Raquel?
3. A frightened octopus hides _____ in a cloud of ink.
4. Mike found that rare seashell _____ .
5. Rose taught _____ to play the piano.
6. We made _____ a good lunch.
7. Why are all of you sitting by _____ ?
8. Frank and Suki built that treehouse _____ .
9. The robot repaired _____ .
10. I helped _____ to some more soup.
11. Would you like some for _____ ?
12. Pete helped _____ to more punch.
13. Ann made that dress _____ .
14. The Turners painted that house _____ .

G. Information in Encyclopedias

Look at the guide words *coin* and *corn.* On your paper, make three columns. Label them *Before, On These Pages,* and *After.* List each numbered topic according to where it would be found in an encyclopedia. *(Unit 5, Lesson 7)*

coin	**corn**

1. coat
2. Costa Rica
3. colonial
4. cobweb
5. coast
6. Christopher Columbus
7. contact lenses
8. cobra
9. courts
10. coal

11. cork
12. Colorado
13. cotton
14. coin
15. cocker spaniels
16. Cooperstown
17. codes
18. coyotes
19. Coney Island
20. cousins

H. Organizing Notes by Outlining

Write these two WH-questions and notes in outline form. Use the two WH-questions as main topics. *(Unit 5, Lesson 9)*

Who was Charles Richard Drew?
What was Drew famous for?
    Black-American surgeon
    Lived from 1904 to 1950
    Organized first blood bank in U.S. in 1940
    Expert on blood plasma
    Won Spingarn Medal in 1943

You Don't Say!

Both girls in the pictures have won first prizes. Their smiles tell you how they feel. They are happy. Read the description above the pictures.

The writer uses details in the description. The details tell about Jerri as a horseback rider. The writer also tells you that Jerri is happy. But the writer does not *say* she is happy. Find the sentence that describes Jerri's feelings. How do you know Jerri is happy?

Some writers use expressions to tell about feelings. This writer uses the expression "feels as if she is walking on air." It suggests that Jerri is happy.

Write Away!

Jerri won a ribbon for horseback riding. Nan won a ribbon, too. What did Nan win a ribbon for?

Write a few sentences about Nan. Write a few details about Nan as a runner. Use expressions to tell how Nan felt before, during, and after the race, Here are some ideas to help you start. Add some expressions of your own.

She felt as if her feet had wings.
Her heart beat like a motor boat.
Nan felt as if she was racing the wind.

Today Jerri West won a first prize at the fair. She was the best horseback rider in her age group. Jerri has been riding for three years. This is the first time she has won a blue ribbon. Jerri feels as if she is walking on air!

And Then
I was reading
a poem
about snow

when
the sun
came out
and
melted it.

—*Prince Redcloud*

7

Sharing
Information

Review: Sentences

> A *sentence* tells a complete thought. There are four kinds of sentences: *statements, questions, exclamations,* and *commands.*

In Unit 1, you studied *sentences.* You learned that a sentence tells a complete thought. It starts with a capital letter. It ends with a punctuation mark. You also learned that each kind of sentence does a different job.

A **statement** tells something.

A **question** asks something.

An **exclamation** shows surprise or strong feeling.

A **command** gives an order or direction.

Look at these sentences. Notice the punctuation.

Statement: Levi Hutchins had to get up on time.

Question: What did Hutchins do in 1787?

Exclamation: What a great idea, the alarm clock!

Commands: Wake up! Please turn off the alarm.

A sentence has two parts. The *complete subject* tells whom or what the sentence is about. The *simple subject* is the most important word in the subject. The predicate tells what happened. The verb is the *simple predicate.*

Find the two parts of this sentence.

The first alarm clock rang in 1787.

Name the simple subject. Name the verb.

If you need more help with the Practice, look back at pages 10–17.

PRACTICE

A. (Written) Write whether each sentence is a *statement,* a *question,* an *exclamation,* or a *command.*

Example: Did you know that toothpaste was sold in jars?
question

1. People put their brush into a jar.
2. How messy that was!
3. A dentist named Sheffield had a thought.
4. He had seen foods in metal tubes.
5. Can you guess his idea?
6. What a great thought he had!
7. Brush your teeth at least twice a day.

B. (Written) Write each sentence. Draw a line between the complete subject and the complete predicate. Circle the simple subject. Underline the verb.

Example: Some (bulbs) |shine with pink light.

8. A new bulb is brighter than an old one.
9. The first boy at the door knocked loudly.
10. One long leg hung over the arm of the chair.
11. Two hens laid four eggs this morning.
12. Only two bands played music in our show.
13. Today's weather felt too cool for me.
14. Six clips held the stack of papers.

APPLY

What machine or tool do you use often? Write a statement, a question, an exclamation, and a command about it.

Review: Nouns and Pronouns

> A *noun* names a person, place, or thing. A *pronoun* stands for a noun. *Possessive* nouns and pronouns show ownership.

In Unit 2, you studied nouns. You learned that *common nouns* name any person, place, or thing. *Proper nouns* name special people, places, or things.

Name the common and proper nouns here.

Ponce de Leon explored the state of Florida.

You have also learned about singular and plural nouns. *Singular* means "one." *Plural* means "more than one." The rules for forming plural nouns are on page 54.

Possessive nouns show who owns or has something. The rules for possessive nouns are on page 60. Look at this paragraph.

In 1519 **Magellan** left **Spain** with five **ships**. **Magellan's fleet** set out to sail around the **world**. Three **years** later, the **fleet** returned to **Spain**.

Each word in dark print is a noun. Which proper noun shows possession?

In Unit 5, you learned that *pronouns* can take the place of nouns. There are singular, plural, and possessive pronouns. Here is the same paragraph with pronouns.

In 1519 Magellan left Spain with five ships. His fleet set out to sail around the world. Three years later, it returned to Spain.

If you need more help with the Practice, look back at pages 52–61 and 190–217.

PRACTICE

A. (Written) Make three columns. Label them *People, Places,* and *Things.* Write each noun from this paragraph under the correct label.

Juan Ponce de León explored Florida in 1513. Ponce de León had heard stories about a fountain. The fountain's waters could make a person young. Ponce de León searched everywhere for the fountain of youth. Ponce de León never found the fountain. Ponce de León did claim the new land for Spain, Ponce de León's country.

Now make four columns. Label them *Singular, Plural, Common,* and *Proper.* Write each noun from the paragraph above in two different columns.

B. (Written) Use pronouns. Replace eight of the nouns used in the paragraph in the Practice A. Rewrite the paragraph.

APPLY

Write three sentences about the tallest person in the world. Use nouns and pronouns.

Review: Verbs

> A **_verb_** may show an action or tell what someone or something **_is, was,_** or **_will be._** In a sentence, the verb has a tense and must agree with the subject.

In Units 3 and 6, you studied verbs. You learned about the _present, past,_ and _future tenses_ of verbs. The tense of a verb tells the time of the verb.

Look at these sentences.

> The engine **roars.** The tires **spin.**

In the present tense, verbs tell of things that are happening now. Use the _s-form_ of a verb with a singular subject. Use the _plain form_ with a plural subject.

What verb tenses are used here?

> The race **ended** in a tie. The cars **crossed** together.
> Soon they **will race** again. I **shall see** them then.

In the past tense, verbs tell of things that have already happened. In the future tense, verbs tell of things that have not happened yet.

The verbs _am, is, are, was_ and _were_ do not show action. Use _am_ with the pronoun _I._ Use _is_ and _was_ with singular subjects. Use _are_ and _were_ with plural subjects.

> I am in a crew. My sister is in the crew, too.
> My brothers are drivers.
> Our dad was a driver. His brothers were his crew.

If you need more help with the Practice, look back at pages 98–105.

PRACTICE

A. (Written) Write the word that agrees with the subject.

> **Example:** Some animals' eyes (glow/glows) in the dark.
> **glow**

1. These animals (are/is) night hunters.
2. They (need/needs) help to see in the dark.
3. Their eyes (use/uses) a kind of mirror.
4. The eye (return/returns) the light that enters the eye.
5. The light (go/goes) through the eye twice.
6. This (give/gives) the animal more light to see by.
7. The returning light (makes/make) the eyes glow.

B. (Written) Write each sentence. Fill in the blank with the correct form of the verb.

> **Example:** A spider _____ a fly in her web yesterday. (trap)
> A spider **trapped** a fly in her web yesterday.

8. Tomorrow she _____ the fly. (eat)
9. A trap-door spider always _____ in a burrow. (live)
10. It _____ out to catch its food. (rush)
11. We _____ a Venus's-flytrap last week. (watch)
12. That plant _____ shut on a fly. (snap)
13. The fly _____ to get away, but it couldn't. (try)
14. Someday, I _____ a Venus's–flytrap. (buy)

APPLY

Write three sentences telling how people get their food. Underline the verbs in your sentences.

Review: Adjectives and Adverbs

> An *adjective* describes a noun. An *adverb* tells about a verb, an adjective, or another adverb.

In Unit 4, you studied *adjectives* and *adverbs.* You learned that an adjective answers the question *Which ones? How many?* or *What kind?*

What questions do these adjectives answer?

> Eric Heiden is a **fast** skater. He won **five** medals in the 1980 Olympics. Those medals were **gold.**

Adjectives describe what you see, hear, taste, smell, and feel. Name the sense each adjective describes.

> **cold** ice   **loud** bang   **smoky** odor   **sweet** flavor

An adverb answers the question *Where? When?* or *How?*

What question does each adverb answer?

> **Soon** the Olympics will be held. Athletes will compete **there.** Each team will try **hard.**

Adjectives compare nouns. Adverbs compare actions. Add *-er* or *more* to compare two nouns or actions. Add *-est* or *most* to compare more than two.

> The **youngest** swimmer was 12 years old.
> The ocean is **more dangerous** than a pool!
> Penny Dean swam **faster** than any person.
> She swam **most quickly** of all other swimmers.

If you need more help with the Practice, look back at pages 144–151 and 162–167.

PRACTICE

A. (Written) For each sentence, write the adjective and the question it answers.

> **Example:** The highest mountain in the world is Mount Everest.
> **highest—What kind?**

1. The mountain is in two countries.
2. Hilary and Norgay were the first climbers.
3. Those men climbed it in 1953.
4. Five people have climbed Everest twice.
5. Four women have reached the mountain's top.
6. A brave man skied down Mount Everest.
7. He had to climb the huge mountain first.

B. (Written) Write the adverb in each sentence. Then write the question it answers.

> **Example:** We will go on a very long bike trip.
> **very—How?**

8. We are supposed to leave tomorrow.
9. Camping gear is everywhere.
10. We must pack it carefully.
11. We will ride hard the first day.
12. Who can ride fastest?
13. Jan will ride farther than I.

APPLY

Write three sentences about a sports event. Underline the adjectives you use. Circle the adverbs.

5 BASIC SKILLS

Review: *Have, Do, Be*

> The words *have, do,* and *be* are irregular verbs.
> These verbs and their forms may be used as *main verbs* or as *helping verbs.*

The verbs *have, do,* and *be* have many forms. You have learned to use them as main verbs and as helping verbs.

Use *have* with a plural subject. Use *has* with a singular subject. Use *had* with both plural and singular subjects.

Look at these examples.

> We **have** a world almanac.
>
> Our teacher **had told** us about almanacs.

Use *do* with a plural subject and *does* with a singular subject. Use *did* with both plural and singular subjects. *Doing* and *done* must be used with helping verbs. *Do* and *did* never have helping verbs. Look at these examples.

> We **were doing** our geography homework.
>
> Soon we **had done** it all.

Use a helping verb before *be, being,* and *been.* Use *is* or *was* with singular subjects. Use *are* or *were* with plural subjects and with the pronoun *you.* Use *am* or *was* with the pronoun *I.* Look at these examples.

> I **am** studying the western United States.
>
> The almanac **has been** a great help to me.

If you need more help with the Practice, look back at pages 116–123 and 238–243.

PRACTICE

A. (Written) Write the form of *have, do,* or *be* that is used in each sentence. Label it as a *main verb* or as a *helping verb.*

> **Example:** A thesaurus is a kind of word bank.
> **is—main verb**

1. A thesaurus has words in it.
2. The thesaurus does not give word meanings.
3. A thesaurus has a very special use.
4. Perhaps you are writing a paragraph.
5. You have used one word too many times.
6. Other words have a similar meaning.
7. These words are listed in the thesaurus.

B. (Written) Choose the form of the verb that correctly completes each sentence. Write the sentence.

> **Example:** I have (done/did) a report on rivers.
> **I have done a report on rivers.**

8. I (has/have) looked up rivers in the encyclopedia.
9. It (were/was) full of information.
10. We (is/are) looking for the almanac.
11. The almanac (have/has) a list of rivers.
12. The almanac (did/done) not have maps in it.
13. The atlas (have/has) maps showing the rivers.
14. I had (done/did) my report.

APPLY

Write three sentences about a time when you used a dictionary. Underline the forms of the verbs *have, do,* and *be* that you use.

Editing a Paragraph

A good paragraph is written with care. Remember what you have learned. There are many rules for writing well. A good paragraph should be interesting. It should be clear and easy to read.

Editing can make a paragraph clearer. You should ask questions about your writing. Did you say what you wanted to say? Look at each sentence. Are any words missing? Does each sentence make sense?

Study the following paragraphs. They have been edited. See how each error was corrected. Read the Guidelines on page 297. Each one matches a correction. Tell which guideline matches each correction.

I Want to Fly

For a long time, I have wanted to fly. Flying seems like it it might be great fun. I don't mean that I wants to fly in an airplane or soar in a hang glider. I want to fly like a bird or buttefly does.

Think of the questions people would ask! think of the surprise when I land next to people. "Where did you come from?" How did you get here?" I wouldnt answer. I would flap my arms and fly away.

As you edit, correct each error you find. Then reread the paragraph. It should be clear and say what you mean. The Guidelines on page 297 will help you edit your work.

PRACTICE/APPLY

A. (Written) Edit this paragraph. Correct the seven mistakes. Write the edited paragraph.

The Lapps is an ancient people. For many years, lapps have herded reindeer. Reindeer travel from forests in sumer to pastures in winter. In the past, families spent all there time following the reindeer. They lived in tents. They does not follow the reindeer all the time now. Them live in villages today.

B. (Written) Find the mistakes in this paragraph. Two words do not belong. One verb is incorrect. Write the edited paragraph. You will have six sentences.

in may, people in Hong Kong hold a bun festival. Tall towers are made from poles the towers are covered with sugared buns Some towers is 75 feet high. People to race to go after the buns. anyone who gets a a bun will have good luck.

Kinds of Test Questions

Questions are a kind of puzzle. In order to answer a question, you must understand it. There are usually clues to the answer. You should look for clues to two things.

What form should the answer have?
What information should the answer give?

There are two kinds of questions. These are Yes-No questions and WH-questions. Yes-No questions ask for a simple, short answer. Often you need a complete sentence.

Look at the answer to this question.

Is gold found in California?
Yes, gold is found in California.

A WH-question asks *who, what, when, where, why,* or *how.* WH-questions may ask for short answers. But often the answers must be more complicated.

Look at this WH-question and answer.

What happened after the discovery of gold?
After gold was discovered, a gold rush began. Then people went to California to find gold.

Some questions do not look like questions. They are hidden in sentences that do not end with a question mark. Yet, they are asking for facts. Look for clue words in these sentences. The clue words tell what form of answer to use. They help you know what facts to give.

Find the clue word in this example.

Name three states where gold is found.

PRACTICE

A. (Written) Write *WH-question* or *Yes-No question* for each sentence.

> **Example:** What is graphite?
> **WH-question**

1. Is graphite a soft mineral?
2. Where is graphite found?
3. How many graphite mines are there in America?
4. Is graphite used as the lead in a pencil?
5. Why is a pencil lead called "lead"?
6. What is the newest use of graphite?
7. Is graphite used in power plants?

B. (Written) For each hidden question, list word clues that tell what form of answer to use and what information to give.

> **Example:** Name three precious gems.
> **Name—three gems**

8. List the stones in order of weight.
9. Describe how sand looks and feels.
10. Explain how to tell real oak trees from pine trees.
11. Circle the names of four states.
12. List the states next to an ocean.
13. Tell six uses for copper.
14. Discuss the importance of good food.
15. Draw a line under each vegetable.
16. Put a checkmark next to each fruit.
17. Cross out each even numbered answer.

APPLY

Choose four items from the Practice B. Turn each item into a Yes-No or WH-question. Write the questions.

Giving Complete Answers

Questions give clues that tell what an answer should look like. Sometimes, an answer is a single word. An answer may be a list of words. An answer may be a line under a word or a circle. It may also be a whole sentence or paragraph. You must look for clues that tell what answer to give.

Most often an answer should be a whole sentence. Giving a whole sentence is important. The answer gives a clue to the person who reads it. It tells which question you are answering. This is helpful if the answers are numbered incorrectly.

Which answer gives a clue to the question?

> Arkansas   Little Rock is in Arkansas.

An answer can also help you make sure of your ideas. It gives you a chance to edit your answer. Rereading a complete statement is a quick check of your thoughts. You may find a mistake.

For Yes-No questions, your answer will restate the question. For WH-questions, use some of the words from the question in your answer. Then add more information to complete the answer.

Look at these questions and their answers.

> Is Albany the capital of New York State?
> Yes, Albany is the capital of New York State.
> What is the capital of Alaska?
> Juneau is the capital of Alaska.

What fact was added to answer the WH-question?

PRACTICE

A. (Oral) Give a complete answer to each question.

> **Example:** What is your favorite fruit?
> **My favorite fruit is an apricot.**

1. Can you wiggle your ears?
2. How many brothers or sisters do you have?
3. Where were you born?
4. Who is your favorite movie or TV star?
5. Did you eat an egg for breakfast today?
6. Do you like to play softball?
7. What day is today?

B. (Written) Read the questions and answers given. Write each answer as a complete sentence.

> **Example:** Where do koala bears live? (Australia)
> **Koala bears live in Australia.**

1. What are the names of the five Great Lakes? (Erie, Huron, Michigan, Ontario, Superior)
2. Why did eighty thousand people go to California in 1849? (because gold had been discovered there)
3. Where is the Empire State Building? (New York City)
4. Name three kinds of apples. (Macintosh, Baldwin, Cortland)
5. What did people in the Yap Islands use for money? (stone discs with holes in them)
6. How much water is needed to grow a pound of rice? (two thousand quarts)
7. Is the Nile the longest river in the world? (yes)

APPLY

Write three questions. Exchange questions with a classmate. Answer your classmate's questions.

Ways to Solve Problems

Solving problems is like answering questions. There are different ways to get an answer. Some problems are solved one step at a time. They are solved by *trial and error.*
You might solve this problem by trial and error.

> **Problem:** Move only one checker. Make two rows of four checkers each.

First you try one solution. If that does not work, you try another, until you find the answer.

Some problems are solved by *reasoning.* You must think carefully. Use what you know about the problem. Think about possible solutions. Then decide which one makes the most sense to you.

Use reasoning to solve this problem.

> **Problem:** Which line is longer?

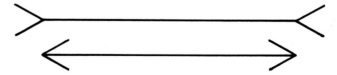

Other problems are solved with *imagination.* Use the same steps as in reasoning, but add some new idea. Some thought may be new just for you. Or, a thought may be totally new. It may be new to the world.

Use imagination to solve this problem.

Problem: Sue lost a coin down a grating. She cannot get her arm through the grating. How can she get her coin?

One method of solving a problem may be better than another. Ask yourself which method is best to use.

PRACTICE

(**Written**) Tell how you would solve each problem: *trial and error, reasoning,* or *imagination.*

1. As I was sailing on the sea, these puzzling questions came to me. "How many fish will fit in my net, if it is dry? If it is wet? And should I catch them in the sea? Or buy them at the grocery?"

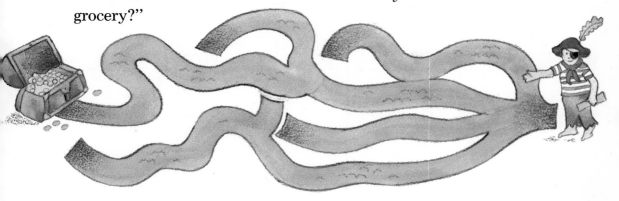

2. What path must the pirate take to get to the treasure?
3. Your kite is hung up in a tree. The branch is too high to reach. The tree seems too hard to climb.

APPLY

Write three or four sentences telling how you would save your kite in number 3.

10 MORE BASIC SKILLS

Review: Irregular Verbs

> The spelling of an *irregular verb* changes. Do not add *-ed* to form its basic parts.

In Units 3 and 6, you studied verbs. You learned that regular verbs and irregular verbs are alike in many ways. You also learned how they are different. You do not add *-ed* to form the basic parts of irregular verbs. Review the *irregular verbs* you have studied.

Basic Parts of Irregular Verbs

Present	Present + ing with a helping verb (am/was)	Past	Past with a helping verb (have/has)
go	going	went	gone
run	running	ran	run
come	coming	came	come
see	seeing	saw	seen
fall	falling	fell	fallen
eat	eating	ate	eaten
find	finding	found	found
grow	growing	grew	grown
take	taking	took	taken

Two verb forms need helping verbs. Use *am, is, are, was,* and *were* with the *-ing* form of the verb. With what form do you use *have, has,* or *had?*

If you need more help with the Practice, look back at pages 120–121 and 256–257.

PRACTICE

A. (Written) Write the form of the verb that best completes each sentence.

> **Example:** Our class (<u>went</u>/gone) to an apple orchard.
> **went**

1. Some parents (<u>come</u>/came) with the class.
2. When we got there, we (<u>seen</u>/<u>saw</u>) many trees.
3. Apples were (<u>growing</u>/grown) on all the trees.
4. Some apples had (<u>fallen</u>/fell) onto the ground.
5. Each of us (<u>took</u>/taken) a basket.
6. Then we all (run/<u>ran</u>) into the orchard.
7. I (<u>found</u>/find) a tree with yellow apples.
8. After I had (ate/<u>eaten</u>) one, I picked more.

B. (Written) Use the correct form of the verb to fill each blank. Write each sentence.

> **Example:** Alice _____ a white rabbit with a watch. (see)
> **Alice saw a white rabbit with a watch.**

9. "_____ here, Rabbit!" Alice called. (come)
10. She _____ after the white rabbit. (run)
11. Suddenly, she was _____ down a hole. (fall)
12. She _____ herself in front of a tiny door. (find)
13. She _____ a drink from a small bottle. (take)
14. Before she knew it, she had _____ tiny. (grow)
15. She _____ through the door after the rabbit. (go)

APPLY

What was the strangest sight you ever saw? Write three sentences about it. Use some of the irregular verbs from this lesson.

Review: Contractions

Contractions **are formed when a verb and another word are combined. An** *apostrophe* **replaces any letters left out of the new word.**

In Units 3 and 6, you studied contractions. You learned that a *contraction* is a short way of writing two words. Forms of the verbs *have, do,* and *be* can be used in contractions. You must join them to *not*. Pronouns and verbs can also be joined to make contractions.

Which words form these contractions?

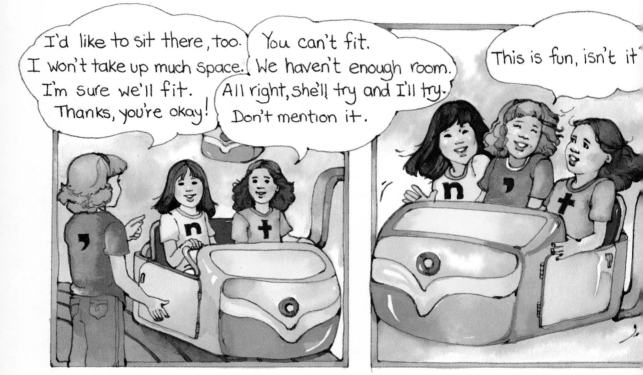

When you form a contraction, remember to replace dropped letters with an apostrophe (').

If you need more help with the Practice, look back at pages 114–115 and 260–261.

PRACTICE

A. (Written) Write the words that form each contraction.

    Example: he's
           he is, he has

1. weren't   **5.** they're   **9.** I'd

2. can't   **6.** he'll   **10.** doesn't

3. we've   **7.** I'm   **11.** won't

4. wouldn't   **8.** she's   **12.** haven't

B. (Written) Make a contraction of the underlined words. Rewrite each sentence.

    Example: I am learning many things in math class.
           I'm learning many things in math class.

13. Here are some of the things I have learned.

14. An odd number is the number that is not even.

15. These numbers are not even: 1, 3, 5, 7, 9.

16. An odd number can not be divided evenly by 2.

17. If a number can be divided evenly by 2, it is even.

18. Straight lines do not have a beginning or an end.

19. Adding "up" or "down" does not change the sum.

APPLY

What have you learned in math. Write three sentences telling what you have learned. Use contractions.

Review: Building Sentences

> **The basic parts of a sentence are the simple subject and predicate. A sentence is often improved by adding details to these parts.**

In Unit 1, you studied sentences. There and in other units, you learned to improve your written work. You know that details can be added to a sentence. They make it grow. They improve it. To add details, ask questions. Answer them with adjectives and adverbs. Make your sentence answer the questions.

See how this sentence can be improved.

> Amy ran. **Where?** to the store
> **When?** yesterday
> **How?** quickly
> **Why?** for a loaf of wheat bread
> Yesterday, Amy ran quickly to the store for a loaf of wheat bread.

When the answers to the questions are added, the sentence tells more. It is improved. When you write a sentence, always try to improve it.

Look at these sentences.

> Maria takes lessons.
> Maria takes piano lessons after school.

What other questions would add different details?

If you need more help with the Practice, look back at pages 168–169.

PRACTICE

A. (Written) Add a detail that answers the question. Make each sentence grow.

> **Example:** Toads hop. (How?)
> **Toads hop quickly.**

1. Mom made soup. (What kind?)
2. Thunder rumbled. (When?)
3. Cameras clicked. (How many?)
4. Kathy raced. (Where?)
5. Dolphins leaped. (Which ones?)
6. Mice nibbled. (What?)
7. Propellers turned. (How?)

B. (Written) Make each sentence grow by adding at least two details. Write the new sentence.

> **Example:** Raindrops sparkled.
> **Small raindrops sparkled in the sunshine.**

8. Spiders spun webs.
9. Birds sing songs.
10. Leaves rustled.
11. Bees buzzed.
12. People clapped.
13. Seals tossed balls.
14. We tiptoed.

APPLY

Choose three sentences from Practice A. Make each sentence grow in a different way.

13 MORE BASIC SKILLS

Review: Correcting Sentences

> **A sentence may be improved in many ways. One way is to correct *double negatives*. Another way is to correct errors in *sound-alike* words.**

WORD BANK

no
not
nobody
nothing
nowhere
no one
none
never

In Unit 6, you studied negative words. You learned that a *double negative* is two negative words used in the same sentence. A negative word and a contraction with *n't* can form a double negative. Remember that *n't* stands for *not*.

Remember how to fix double negatives.

> **Incorrect:** We couldn't find Ana nowhere.
> **Correct:** We could find Ana nowhere.
> **Correct:** We couldn't find Ana anywhere.

To fix a double negative, take out one of the negatives.

Some words sound alike but are spelled differently and have different meanings. If you are not sure which word to use, think about the meaning of the words.

REMINDERS

1. *They're, you're,* and *it's* are contractions.
2. *Their, your,* and *its* are possessive pronouns.
3. *There* may begin a sentence or point to a place.

If you need more help with the Practice, look back at pages 258–259 and 262–265.

PRACTICE

A. (Written) Correct each sentence in two ways.

> **Example:** Raya won't go nowhere without her dog.
> **Raya won't go anywhere without her dog.**
> **Raya will go nowhere without her dog.**

1. Their sister hasn't never played the drums.
2. You won't have none of the soup.
3. None of us didn't see that new movie.
4. There aren't no holidays this month.
5. No one didn't feed the cat today.
6. I didn't pass no one in the race.
7. We couldn't get nothing to eat.

B. (Written) Correct the words that are not used correctly. Write each sentence.

> **Example:** Their are many different kinds of roller coasters.
> **There are many different kinds of roller coasters.**

8. Its the biggest loop coaster.
9. You're favorite kind are big wooden coasters.
10. My brother rode on they're roller coaster.
11. Some coasters their don't go anywhere.
12. They carry you back to there starting point.
13. It's coasters go faster than "The Beast" at King's Island.
14. Its the longest coaster in the world, too.
15. I would love to go their and ride on "The Beast."

APPLY

Write two sentences about your favorite amusement park ride. Use sound-alike words correctly. Then write two sentences about your least favorite ride. Use negative words correctly.

Group Discussions

Some problems can be solved by trial and error. For some we use reasoning or imagination. A fourth way to solve a problem starts in a group. A *discussion* can help to answer questions or solve problems.

Having a good discussion takes practice. You must be a good listener *and* a good speaker. If you follow these rules, you can have a good discussion.

Study the Guidelines.

GUIDELINES

1. Follow these rules when speaking.
   Speak loudly and clearly.
   Stay on the subject and tell your ideas.
   Look at other group members when speaking.
2. Follow these rules when listening.
   Pay careful attention to what is being said.
   Think about how the ideas fit the subject.
   Do not make noise when others speak.
   Ask questions if something is not clear.

Your class may want to discuss different ways to solve a problem. First, choose a recorder. The recorder will write down each idea for solving the problem. Then each solution can be discussed.

Ask these questions about each idea.

> Does it really solve the problem?
> Does it cause other problems?
> Is the solution something you really could do?
> How is this solution better than others?

PRACTICE

A. (Written) Think of possible solutions for these problems. Think about why you believe your solution will work. Make notes about each problem.

1. Your class needs a tape player, but there is no money. How could you earn the money to buy one?
2. Some students do not return library books. What can be done to make sure that books are returned on time?
3. The school lunch room is very noisy. If the lunch room were quieter, it would be a more pleasant place to eat. What can be done?

B. (Oral) Choose a problem from Practice A. Work in a group. Present your solution to the problem. Listen to other students' solutions.

APPLY

What problems have you heard of or read about in the news? Think of one. Write the problem in three sentences.

Writing a Problem-Solution Paragraph

Read the notes from your group discussion. How can the notes be put into a paragraph. How will you put the ideas in order?

In a problem-solution paragraph, the problem is in the topic sentence. Each detail sentence gives a solution. If one solution is tried and works, it is put in the last sentence.

Read this paragraph.

Some students do not bring back library books on time. Pam said that the library should not lend books if students have not returned books. Yukio thought that high fines might help. Mark said that someone could visit students' homes to get the books back. Ann's solution was to post a list of names on the door. The names would be erased when the books were back.

What is the problem? The problem is in the topic sentence. What solutions are given? They are in the detail sentences. The solutions are written in the order they were given in the group. No solution was tried.

You may want to tell how your group felt about each idea. Be polite when you tell how you feel about a person's idea. Tell how you feel about just the idea. Give reasons. Do not talk about the person who gave the idea. If you do not like an idea, give a reason. Do not just say, "That is a bad idea."

This is how the group felt about some ideas.

We did not like the idea about high fines. That might make students just keep the books! We did not like the idea about posting a list of names. That would embarrass students. They would not want their names on a list for everyone to see.

PRACTICE

(Written) Use the notes from your group's discussion in Lesson 14. Write a paragraph. Follow these steps.

1. Write what the problem is in a topic sentence.
2. Write detail sentences to tell the solutions that were discussed.
3. Write the solution chosen by the group.
4. Write at least two reasons for the choice.

APPLY

Choose one of the suggested solutions from the group discussion. Write three sentences telling why you like or do not like that solution.

16 COMMUNICATING

A Summary: Plan, Write, Edit

A *summary* tells the important points of an action or a plan. All the details are put into one or two paragraphs. In this lesson, you will plan, write, and edit a summary of a group discussion. In Lesson 14, your group discussed solutions to a problem. You may write about that discussion. Or you may plan to discuss a different problem.

PLAN

Look at the picture. What problem do you see? Write the problem in a sentence. Think of ways to solve it. List as many solutions as you can.

Get together in a group. Share your notes with the group. Make a large list of everyone's thoughts. You may think of more to add as you talk. All these ideas will be in the first paragraph of the summary.

Discuss all the solutions with your group. Try to agree on one. Decide how to carry out that solution. Make notes. These notes will become your second paragraph.

WRITE

Reread your notes from the group discussion. Use them to write your two-paragraph summary.

The first paragraph should tell the problem and all the solutions. Begin with a statement of the problem. Write the suggested solutions in an order. You may write them in the order in which they were given. Or, you may want to list them in order from the worst solution to the best.

The second paragraph tells which solution the group agreed to try. It also gives the details for the plan. Begin the second paragraph with a statement of the plan your group agreed upon. Give at least two reasons why that solution was chosen. Write detail sentences telling how the plan will be carried out.

EDIT

Now that you have written your summary, you need to edit it. Pretend that you did not take part in the discussion. Keep your notes nearby. You may want to check them.

Read your summary. Does it tell what the group discussed? Are all the ideas presented? As you read, ask more questions.

✔ Does the first paragraph tell the problem?
✔ Are all solutions stated correctly?
✔ Does the second paragraph tell what the group decided?
✔ Are reasons given for the decision?
✔ How will the plan work?
✔ Does each sentence make sense?

Read your summary a second time to check the form.

✔ Is the first line of each paragraph indented?
✔ Does each contraction have an apostrophe?
✔ Have you used any double negatives?
✔ Are sound-alike words used correctly?
✔ Does each sentence begin with a capital letter and end with a correct punctuation mark?
✔ Are all proper nouns capitalized?

Before you edit your own summary, practice on this one. Tell how to correct each error. There are four errors in the first paragraph and five in the second one.

It's hard to cross High and market Streets because of the traffic. The city could install a traffic light stop signs could be put up on all four corners. The city could have a traffic officer they're. The school could post crossing guards.

The group decided to trying to get crossing guards We wrote a letter to Principal cone. We said that their wasnt no help for children crossing those streets. The principal liked our idea. Crossing guards will be trained and posted.

Now copy your own summary in your best handwriting.

17 COMMUNICATING

Sharing the Results

The whole class may want to know about your group's discussion. An oral report is a good way to tell the whole class at once. Look at your notes. Use the notes about the problem and the solutions offered. End with the solution you chose. Give reasons for the decision.

GUIDELINES

1. Stand still.
2. Speak in a loud, clear voice.
3. At times, look up at those who are listening.
4. Stress the main problem. Give the final solution.

PRACTICE/APPLY

(Oral) Choose a problem to solve. Discuss your ideas with a classmate, your teacher, or a friend. Report the results of your discussion to the class.

1. School lunch is dull. Students waste food. Some do not eat at all.
2. In some families, both parents work outside the home. There are not enough helpers for school trips.
3. Because of budget cuts, art class might be cut.

Keep Practicing

A. The Verb *Be*
Write the form of *be* that best completes each sentence. *(Unit 6, Lesson 1)*

1. We have (been/were) told about cheese.
2. Cheese (is/are) a soft, tasty food.
3. Cheese (is/are) good for you.
4. It can (is/be) made from milk.
5. First, the milk (is/are) cooked.
6. Then the cheese (is/were) poured into a form.
7. Soft cheese can (be/being) spread on toast.
8. We (were/was) happy with the taste of this food.

B. Linking Verbs
Write each sentence. Underline the linking verb. Draw an arrow from an adjective in the predicate to the subject. Circle a noun in the predicate. *(Unit 6, Lessons 2 and 3)*

1. Ruth's favorite pets might be strange.
2. One pet is a snail.
3. The snail's home is a jar.
4. Its favorite food is lettuce.
5. Ruth's other pets are funny.
6. They are guinea pigs.
8. Their noises are piglike.
9. A guinea pig is a rodent.
10. Ruth's guinea pigs can be friendly.
11. Ruth is an animal lover.
12. Her pets were large and small.
13. A horse was the largest pet.
14. The horse's name was Carrots.

C. Irregular Verbs

Choose the form of the verb that best completes each sentence. Write the sentence. *(Unit 6, Lesson 9)*

1. Strange things have (fell/fallen) from the sky.
2. Lumps of hay (fall/fell) on England in 1977.
3. People in Russia (found/find) coins falling from the sky.
4. During a storm in France, tiny toads were (fallen/falling).
5. People later (find/found) toads in their hats.
6. In 1897, a rain of seeds (fell/fall) in Italy.
7. Some seeds were (growing/grows).
8. Chunks of meat (fallen/fell) in Kentucky.
9. Two men (ate/eaten) some of the meat.
10. People thought birds had (ate/eaten) it.
11. Have you (find/found) any strange things?
12. Nothing (fell/fallen) in my yard.

D. Avoiding Double Negatives

Write the word that best completes each sentence. *(Unit 6, Lesson 10)*

1. Oil spills aren't (no/any) good for water birds.
2. The birds can (ever/never) get the oil off their feathers.
3. No bird (can/can't) live with oil-covered feathers.
4. At one time, nobody (wasn't/was) able to help the birds.
5. None of the birds (weren't/were) saved.
6. People didn't (never/ever) give up trying to help.
7. Rescue teams search until no birds (are/aren't) left.
8. Workers wash the birds until no oil (isn't/is) left.
9. Not all birds (are/aren't) saved.
10. We should try not to spill (no more/anymore) oil.

E. Pronoun-Verb Contractions

Change the underlined words in each sentence into a contraction. Write the sentence. *(Unit 6, Lesson 11)*

1. <u>It is</u> not a good idea to tease a dragon.
2. <u>We are</u> going to put on a magic show.
3. Luis says that <u>he will</u> become a great ballplayer.
4. Do you know where <u>they have</u> gone?
5. <u>I had</u> just gotten into the tub when the phone rang.
6. <u>You will</u> make new friends in your new school.
7. <u>She has</u> just won a prize in math.
8. If you do not feed the cat, <u>I will</u> do it.
9. <u>You are</u> the best singer in the chorus.
10. I hope <u>they will</u> invite me to their party.

F. Using *They're, Their,* and *There*

Write the word that best completes each sentence.
(Unit 6, Lesson 12)

1. Six couples changed (<u>their/they're</u>) lives for a year.
2. They left (<u>they're/their</u>) homes to live in a village.
3. (<u>There/Their</u>), they had to make everything.
4. They lived (<u>there/their</u>) like others had lived long ago.
5. (<u>They're/There</u>) was no electricity or running water.
6. They grew food and made (<u>their/there</u>) own dishes.
7. They cooked (<u>their/they're</u>) food over open fires.
8. A television crew made a film of (<u>their/there</u>) life.
9. Now (<u>they're/there</u>) back home.
10. (<u>There/Their</u>) lives are not the same.
11. (<u>They're/Their</u>) happy to be (<u>their/there</u>).

12. (There/Their) children learned things, too.

13. They learned how special (their/there) homes are.

G. Reasons—Facts and Opinions

Read each question and the answer given. Write *good reason* or *poor reason* for each. *(Unit 6, Lesson 8)*

1. Can I ride my bike? You cannot ride because the tires are flat.

2. Why must I shine my shoes? I want you to.

3. Why do you play softball? Softball is a good sport to play. It gives me exercise. My friends play, too.

4. Why do you play tennis? Everyone should play tennis.

5. Why do some monkeys climb trees? Because they do.

6. Why do stars twinkle? Stars do not really twinkle. The light is constant. It comes a long distance. To our eyes, it appears to blink.

7. Why do we call army ants by that name? We call them army ants because of the way these insects travel in large groups.

8. Why must we sleep at night? Because that's when we must sleep.

9. Why does the wind blow? The wind blows because hot air rises. Cool air then blows into that spot.

10. Why are pickles green? Because its a good color.

11. Why does the sun rise in the east? The sun rises in the east because of the way the earth spins.

12. Why can't I visit my friend's house? I don't want you to go.

13. Can I go swimming? No, you can not go swimming because you will miss your dentist appointment.

14. Why do tigers have stripes? Tigers have stripes to help them stay hidden in the jungle.

Something Extra

Good References

Dictionaries are very useful. They give word pronunciations, spellings, and meanings. A word entry may tell the history of a word. It may list synonyms and antonyms for a word.

Here are some words from a dictionary. Each word was listed as a synonym or an antonym for some other word. The word *tight,* for example, is an antonym for *loose.*

tight	surprised	revealing	new	water
over	inner	gradually	amazed	unfolding
first	tiny	taking	day	

Can you think of other synonyms or antonyms for the words in the list?

A Mixed-up Poem

Read the poem on the next page. It does not make sense. Replace each underlined word with the correct synonym or antonym from the list. To help you, use the clues beside the lines. Rewrite the poem.

One is <u>surprised</u>   (synonym)
By a <u>land</u>-lily bud   (antonym)
<u>Folding</u>   (antonym)
With each passing <u>night</u>, (antonym)
<u>Giving</u> on a richer color (antonym)
And <u>fresh</u> dimensions   (synonym)

One is not amazed,
At a <u>last</u> glance,   (antonym)
By a poem,
Which is as <u>loose</u>-closed (antonym)
As a <u>small</u> bud.   (synonym)

Yet one is <u>amazed</u>   (synonym)
To see the poem
<u>Quickly</u> unfolding   (antonym)
<u>Hiding</u> its rich <u>outer</u> self, (antonym, antonym)
As one reads it
Again
And <u>under</u> again.   (antonym)

What is the title of the poem? (*Clue:* What is
a flower that is just waking up?)

● Unfolding Bud

Handbook

GRAMMAR/USAGE

SENTENCES

A **sentence** is a group of words that tells a complete thought. (page 10)

> The moon stays near the earth.

A **statement** tells something. A **question** asks something. An **exclamation** shows surprise or strong feeling. (page 12)

> Tools have many uses.   Were tools ever used as money?
> That TV tower is falling!

A **command** gives an order or a direction. Some commands also show strong feeling. (page 12)

> Pass her the paper.   Don't sit on that chair!

A **Yes-No question** needs a yes or no answer. (page 34)

> Did you see the film?   Yes.

A **WH-question** asks *who, what, when, where, why* or *how.* (page 34)

> Who is in the play?   When does it start?

The **subject** of a sentence tells whom or what the sentence is about. (page 14)

> Black holes | are stars that have collapsed.

The **complete subject** includes all the words in the subject part of a sentence. The **simple subject** is the main word in the subject part of a sentence. (page 14)

> The hottest stars | are blue.

A **compound subject** contains two or more subjects that share the same predicate. (page 28)

> Oil, gas, coal, and wood | keep us warm.

The **predicate** of a sentence tells what the subject does, is, or has. (page 16)

Fish|live in water.   Fish|are quiet.   Fish|have scales.

The **complete predicate** includes all the words in the predicate part of a sentence. The **simple predicate** is the main word in the predicate part of a sentence. (page 16)

The starfish|is not really a fish.

A **compound predicate** contains two predicates that share the same subject. (page 30)

The earth|spins like a top and moves around the sun.

Subjects and verbs must agree. Use the *s*-form of the verb with singular subjects that mean *he, she,* or *it.* Use the plain form with *I, you,* or plural subjects. (pages 100, 196)

Bill rides horses.   They plant wheat.

A **helping verb** must agree with its subject. (pages 116, 122, 238)

I have finished my work.   Did Tony help you?

PARTS OF SPEECH

Nouns

A **noun** names a person, place, or thing. (page 52)

singer   beach   coin

A **singular noun** names one person, place, or thing. A **plural noun** names more than one person, place, or thing. (page 54)

gardener→gardeners   box→boxes   mouse→mice

A **common noun** names any person, place, or thing. A **proper noun** names a particular person, place, or thing. (page 58)

man→Ray   city→Tucson   house→White House

A **possessive noun** is a noun that shows ownership. (page 60)

> Singular: the dog's tail
>
> Plural: the dogs' tails, the women's books

A, an, and *the* are **articles.** They mark nouns. Use *a* or *an* with singular nouns. Use *the* with singular or plural nouns. Use *a* before consonants. Use *an* before vowels. (page 73)

> a ship   an oil tanker   the tugboats

This and **these** point to nouns nearby. **That** and **those** tell about nouns farther away. (page 74)

> This plant needs water.   Those plants in the den need sun.

Words That Point to Nouns
a an the
this that
these those
some
several
many

Pronouns

A **pronoun** stands for one or more nouns. *I, you, he, she, it, we,* and *they* are used as the subjects of sentences. (page 190)

> Bob wrote a poem.   He wrote a poem.

Some pronouns may be used after an action verb. *Me, you, him, her, it, us,* and *them* are used after verbs. (page 192)

> Gilda asked the teacher.   Gilda asked her.

A pronoun must agree with the noun it replaces. Replace a singular noun with a singular pronoun. Replace a plural noun with a plural pronoun. (page 196)

> The car wouldn't start.   It wouldn't start.
>
> The birds flew south.   They flew south.

A **possessive pronoun** takes the place of a possessive noun. A possessive pronoun does not use an apostrophe. (page 210)

> Mother's book is missing.   Her book is missing.

Some pronouns end in *-self* or *-selves.* Such a pronoun is used as a partner with another pronoun or noun in the sentence. (page 214)

> The plane lifted itself from the runway.

Verbs

A **verb** is the most important part of the predicate. An **action verb** tells what someone or something does. (page 98)

> The plane <u>soared</u> into the clouds.

Other verbs do not show action. They tell what someone or something *is, was,* or *will be.* (page 99)

> I <u>am</u> a student.   Ron <u>is</u> a cook.   Pat <u>was</u> a dancer.

A **present tense** verb shows an action that is happening now. Some present tense verbs end in *s.* (page 102)

> I <u>walk</u> to the park now. He <u>walks</u> with me.

A **past tense** verb shows an action that already happened in the past. Most past tense verbs end in *ed.* (page 102)

> I <u>walked</u> to the park yesterday.

A **future tense** verb shows an action that has not happened yet. However, the action is expected to happen. Future tense verbs use *will* or *shall.* (page 102)

> I <u>shall walk</u> tomorrow.   Sam <u>will walk</u> with me.

The present tenses of **have** and **be** have different forms. (pages 116, 238)

> <u>Have</u>: I have, you have, he/she/it has, we/you/they have
> <u>Be</u>: I am, you are, he/she/it is, we/you/they are

The past tense of **be** has different forms. (page 238)

> <u>Be</u>: I was, you were, he/she/it was, we/you/they were

A verb that helps another verb is called a **helping verb.** The helping verb comes before the main verb. (page 104)

> helping verb   main verb
> You <u>can</u> <u>ride</u> the subway home.

Used as a main verb, the word **have** means "to own." *Have, has,* and *had* are also used as helping verbs. (page 116)

> Our town <u>has</u> a beach.   The sea <u>has</u> eroded the dunes.

Always Helping Verbs
can shall may could should will would might

Sometimes Helping Verbs
am is are was were have has had does do did

Use a helping verb before *be, being,* and *been.*

> Helen <u>will be</u> ten years old on Friday.
> I <u>am being</u> quiet about the birthday party.
> Helen <u>has been</u> my friend for years.

The **basic parts** of a verb can help you form verb tenses. There are four basic parts of a verb. (page 118)

Present	Present + ing with helping verb am/was	Past	Past with helping verb have/had
call	calling	called	called
live	living	lived	lived
stop	stopping	stopped	stopped
cry	crying	cried	cried

The **present** and **past parts** of verbs are used alone. (page 118)

> I <u>work</u> every day.   They <u>worked</u> yesterday.

Use **am, is, was,** or **were** with the *ing*-form. (page 118)

> Beth <u>is</u> changing jobs.   We <u>were</u> looking for work.

Use **have, has,** or **had** with the fourth part. (page 118)

> You <u>have</u> tried hard.   Paul <u>had</u> finished everything.

The spelling of an **irregular verb** changes. The basic parts of irregular verbs do not end in *ed.* (pages 120, 256)

> I <u>fell</u> on the ice again.   I <u>went</u> home.

Linking verbs do not show action. A **linking verb** states that a subject *is* or *was* something. It links the subject with a word or words in the predicate. (page 240)

> Carla <u>is</u> a stunt performer.
> Her stunts <u>are</u> exciting.

Irregular Verbs

Present	Present + ing (with helping verb)	Past	Past (with helping verb)
am/is/are	being	was/were	been
break	breaking	broke	broken
come	coming	came	come
do/does	doing	did	done
eat	eating	ate	eaten
fall	falling	fell	fallen
find	finding	found	found
go	going	went	gone
grow	growing	grew	grown
have/has	having	had	had
know	knowing	knew	known
run	running	ran	run
see	seeing	saw	seen
take	taking	took	taken

Adjectives

An **adjective** is a word that describes a noun. Adjectives can tell *which ones, how many,* or *what kind.* They can tell how things look, sound, taste, smell, or feel. (pages 144, 148)

<u>wet</u> streets   <u>few</u> cars   <u>gray</u> skies   <u>soft</u> breeze

An adjective is used to compare things. To compare two things, use **-er** or **more.** The word *than* is also used. To compare three or more things, use **-est** or **most.** (page 146)

That pond is <u>deeper</u> and <u>more colorful</u> than this one.
That bird is the <u>quickest</u> and <u>most graceful</u> of all birds.

The adjectives **good, bad, many,** and **much** change form when they are used to compare things. (page 150)

good→better→best   bad→worse→worst
many→more→most   much→more→most

Adverbs

An **adverb** tells more about a verb, an adjective, or another adverb. An adverb tells *where, when* or *how.* Many adverbs end in *ly.* (page 162)

> The band passes <u>nearby</u>.
> It will begin <u>very</u> soon.
> The music is <u>really</u> loud.

Sometimes a group of words acts as one adverb. (page 164)

> We visited the harbor <u>after the storm</u>. (when)
> Three boats had sunk <u>beneath the pier</u>. (where)
> We could raise them <u>with a crane</u>. (how)

An adverb can be used to compare actions. To compare two actions, use **-er** or **more.** To compare three or more actions, use **-est** or **most.** (page 166)

> That car moves <u>faster</u> and <u>more carefully</u> than mine.
> He was the <u>happiest</u> and <u>most friendly</u> guest.

USAGE PROBLEMS

A **sentence fragment** does not tell a complete thought. It is only part of a sentence. (page 10)

> <u>Fragment</u>: in the bay   <u>Sentence</u>: We sailed in the bay.

A **run-on sentence** contains two or more complete thoughts that should not be connected. (page 32)

> <u>Run-on</u>: Lake George has many types of fish and there are
>   also a number of islands in the lake.
> <u>Corrected</u>: Lake George has many types of fish. There are
>   also a number of islands in the lake.

This, that, these, and **those** are never used with the word *here* or *there.* (page 74)

> <u>Incorrect</u>: This here book is funny.
> <u>Correct</u>: This book is funny.

Use **many** to describe things you can count. Use **much** to describe things that are hard to count. (page 150)

> Many people enjoy canoeing.
> There is too much sand in my garden soil.

Sometimes a pronoun is used with a noun in a compound subject or after a verb. Put the pronoun last.
(pages 190, 192)

> Laura and he went to the fair.
> Tom showed Maria and me his pet.

I and **we** are pronouns. Use them in the subject. **Me** and **us** are pronouns. Use them after a verb. (page 194)

> I walked to school.   We walked to school.
> The bus took me home.   The bus took us home.

Be sure each pronoun makes clear whom or what you mean. (page 212)

> Confusing: Carla and Susie went to her house.
> Better: Carla and Susie went to Carla's house.

A pronoun should not follow and repeat a noun. (page 216)

> Incorrect: Babe Ruth he hit sixty home runs.
> Correct: Babe Ruth hit sixty home runs. Or: He hit sixty
>   home runs.

Avoid using **two negatives** in one sentence. (page 258)

> Incorrect: We won't never get home.
> Correct: We won't ever get home. Or: We will never get home.

CAPITALIZATION

A **sentence** begins with a capital letter. (pages 10, 22)

> Coins are different weights and sizes.

A **proper noun** starts with a capital letter. (page 58)

> Andrew Wyeth   Yellowstone National Park   Labor Day

An **abbreviation** begins with a capital letter if it is a short way to write a proper noun. (page 66)

> Wed.   Jan.   Dr.   Ave.   Del.

Postal abbreviations use two capital letters with ZIP Codes. (page 66)

> Elma, WA 98541   Simon, WV 24882

Abbreviations of time use two capital letters. (page 66)

> A.M.   P.M.

The first word in the **greeting** and in the **closing** of a letter begins with a capital letter. (page 68)

> **D**ear Kim,   **S**incerely yours,

The pronoun **I** is always written as a capital letter. (page 190)

> Janet and **I** took a cab.

The speaker's first word in a **quotation** begins with a capital letter. (page 178)

> Ron asked, "**D**o you want to play tennis?"

PUNCTUATION

End Punctuation

A **statement** ends with a **period (.).** (page 12)

> Mustard plants produce seeds.

A **command** may end with a **period (.).** (page 12)

> Call me today.

Most **abbreviations** end with a **period (.).** (page 66)

> ft.   pt.   St.   Ind.   Mr.   Wed.

Some abbreviations do not have periods. (page 66)

> mph   km   FL

A **question** ends with a **question mark (?).** (page 12)

> When does winter begin?

An **exclamation** ends with an **exclamation mark (!).**
(page 12)

> Sue won the race!

A **command** that shows strong feeling ends with an
exclamation mark **(!).** (page 12)

> Don't shake the ladder!

Comma

Put commas **(,)** after the first and second words in a **list** of
three words. (page 28)

> Jupiter, Mars, and Venus are planets.

Put a comma after the **yes** or **no** when you answer a Yes-No
question. (page 34)

> Was the film interesting? Yes, it was.

Put a comma between a **city or town** and its **state.** (page 70)

> St. Louis, MO 63166   Houston, TX 77001

Use a comma in a **date.** Put it between the day's date and
the year. (page 70)

> Jan. 3, 198—   July 27, 198—

Use a comma after the **greeting** in a friendly letter. (page 70)

> Dear Will,   Dear Aunt Ruth,

Use a comma after the **closing** in a letter. (pages 70, 83)

> Your pal,   Truly yours,

Use a comma after **organizing words** that begin a sentence.
(page 268)

> For example, we went to a museum.

Colon

Use a colon after the **greeting** in a business letter. (pages 82–83)

> Dear Mr. Sanders: Dear Professor Acorn:

Apostrophe

Use an apostrophe (**'**) to form singular and plural **possessive nouns.** (page 60)

> Singular: Wanda's boat
> Plural: the cats' fur, the geese's wings

Use an apostrophe (**'**) to form a **contraction.** The apostrophe takes the place of the missing letters. (pages 114, 260)

> is not→isn't   they have→they've   you will→you'll

Quotation Marks

Use quotation marks (**" "**) around a speaker's exact words. (pages 160–161)

> Gina asked, "Did it rain today?"
> "It only drizzled," answered Pete.

Dialogue

If a speaker tag comes first, use a **comma** to separate the speaker tag from the quotation. (pages 160–161)

> Angel said, "It's made of glass."

If a speaker tag comes last, use the **end punctuation** that belongs with the quotation, unless it is a period. If it is a period, change the period to a comma. (pages 160–161)

> "I think it looks pretty," said June.
> "What do you think it is?" asked Ted.

SPELLING

Plurals

To form the plural of most nouns, add **-s** or **-es.** (pages 54, 56)

> car→cars (simply add -s)
> wish→wishes (add -es to nouns ending in *ch, sh, ss, zz, x,* or *s*)
> berry→berries (change *y* to *i* and add -es)

To form the plural of many nouns ending in **f** or **fe,** change the *f* or *fe* to *ve* and add *-s.* For a few nouns ending in *f* or *fe,* simply add *-s.* (page 56)

elf→elves   knife→knives   reef→reefs

To form the plural of some special nouns, change their forms completely. (page 56)

foot→feet   woman→women   mouse→mice
child→children

Possessive Nouns

To form the possessive for a **singular noun,** add an apostrophe and *s* **('s).** (page 60)

Carol's arm   the bird's wing

To form the possessive for a **plural noun** that ends in *s,* add only an apostrophe **(').** (page 60)

the elves' workshop   the students' books

To form the possessive for a **plural noun** that does not end in *s,* add an apostrophe and *s* **('s).** (page 60)

the men's feet   the mice's ears
children's voices

Verbs

To form the *s*-form of many verbs, add **-s** or **-es.** (page 100)

open→opens (simply add *-s*)
tax→taxes (add *-es* to verbs ending in *ch, sh, ss, zz, x,* or *s*)
cry→cries (change *y* to *i* and add *-es*)

To form the past tense of most verbs, add **-ed** to the plain form of the verb. (page 102)

walk→walked (simply add *-ed*)
pave→paved (drop final *e*)
try→tried (change *y* to *i*)
trip→tripped (double final consonant)

To form the *-ing* form of most verbs, add **-ing.** (page 118)

> walk→walking (simply add *-ing*)
> make→making (drop final *e*)
> sit→sitting (double final consonant)

The past tenses of irregular verbs change spellings. (See Handbook page 332.)

Adding *-er* and *-est*

Add *-er* or *-est* to many **adjectives** to compare things. When an adjective ends with a consonant letter and *y,* change the *y* to *i.* (page 146)

> friendly   friendlier   friendliest

When an adjective ends with a final *e,* drop the *e.* (page 146)

> rare   rarer   rarest

When an adjective ends with a short vowel and a single consonant letter, double the final consonant. (page 146)

> hot   hotter   hottest

To compare actions, add *-er* or *-est* to **adverbs** that do not end in *ly.* (page 166)

> soon   sooner   near   nearest

When an adverb ends with a consonant letter and *y,* change the *y* to *i.* (page 166)

> early   earlier   earliest

When an adverb ends with *e,* drop the *e.* (page 166)

> late   later   latest

Contractions

A contraction is a word made from two other words. An **apostrophe (')** takes the place of missing letters. (pages 114, 260)

> I am→I'm   cannot→can't   we have→we've

Common Spelling Errors

They're, their, and **there** sound alike but have different meanings and spellings. (page 262)

> They're collecting stamps. (contraction of *they are*)
> Their stamps are rare. ("belonging to them")
> There are a million stamps. (begins a sentence)
> The stamps are *there*. (points to a place)

In the sound-alikes **your/you're** and **its/it's,** the first word in each pair is a possessive pronoun. The second word is a contraction. (page 264)

> Your car is unlocked. Its lock is broken.
> You're driving the car. It's time to go.

VOCABULARY

Synonyms are words that have almost the same meaning. (page 252)

> all—everything   laugh—giggle

Antonyms are words that have opposite meanings. (page 252)

> noisy—quiet   sold—bought

The endings, or **suffixes, -er** and **-or** can change words into nouns. (page 72)

> visit + -or = visitor   speak + -er = speaker

The **suffixes -able, -ful, -ish, -less,** and **-y** can be used to change base words into adjectives. (page 156)

> wash + -able = washable   skill + -ful = skillful
> clown + -ish = clownish   cloud + -y = cloudy
> seed + -less = seedless

The **suffix -ly** can change base words into adverbs. (page 162)

> quick + -ly = quickly   peaceful + -ly = peacefully

A **prefix** is a word part. It is added to the beginning of a word. It changes the word's meaning. (page 248)

in- + correct = incorrect   un- + able = unable
re- + place = replace   mis- + use = misuse

Homonyms are words that sound alike but have different meanings. (See Handbook page 340.)

WRITING

The Steps

Plan: When you plan something to write, you decide *what* you want to say and *to whom.*

✔ Think about the readers. What do they need to know? Make notes about the ideas you need to cover.

✔ Make notes about details you want to include. Be sure they support your main ideas.

✔ Check all your facts.

Write: When you write something, you try to say what you mean as clearly as possible.

✔ Remember any special Guidelines or Reminders.

✔ Use your planning notes to help you write complete sentences. Be sure you say what you want to say.

✔ Put your sentences in an order that makes sense.

Edit: When you edit something, you look for any problems that might confuse your reader(s).

✔ Read what you wrote. Make sure it says exactly what you want it to say. Is there a logical order? Does it tell everything the reader needs to know?

✔ Check for any mistakes in grammar.

✔ Check for any mistakes in punctuation and spelling.

✔ Copy your edited work in your neatest handwriting.

Some Forms
Paragraph (pages 38, 130)

Topic sentence — Money has many forms. Coins and paper are common **Indent** — forms of money. Tools, beads, and shells have also been used **Detail sentences** — as money. Gold and silver bars are still used as money. Today, even plastic is a form of money. The credit card is made of plastic.

Business Letter (page 82)

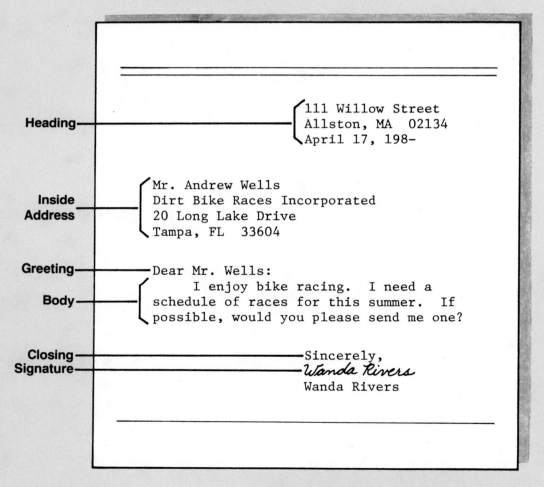

Heading
111 Willow Street
Allston, MA 02134
April 17, 198-

Inside Address
Mr. Andrew Wells
Dirt Bike Races Incorporated
20 Long Lake Drive
Tampa, FL 33604

Greeting
Dear Mr. Wells:

Body
I enjoy bike racing. I need a schedule of races for this summer. If possible, would you please send me one?

Closing
Sincerely,

Signature
Wanda Rivers
Wanda Rivers

Envelope (page 70)

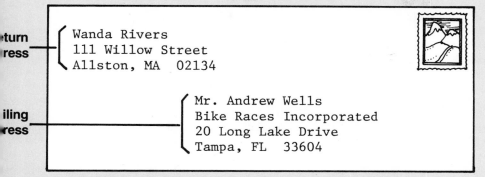

return
address

Wanda Rivers
111 Willow Street
Allston, MA   02134

mailing
address

Mr. Andrew Wells
Bike Races Incorporated
20 Long Lake Drive
Tampa, FL   33604

A Persuasive Note (page 272)

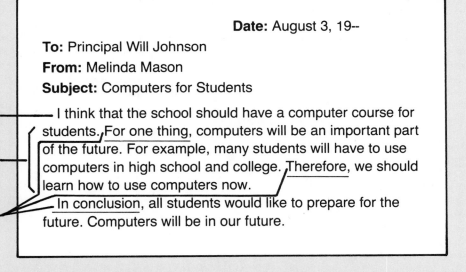

Date: August 3, 19--

To: Principal Will Johnson
From: Melinda Mason
Subject: Computers for Students

opinion

I think that the school should have a computer course for students. For one thing, computers will be an important part

reasons

of the future. For example, many students will have to use computers in high school and college. Therefore, we should learn how to use computers now.

sizing
words

In conclusion, all students would like to prepare for the future. Computers will be in our future.

Improving Sentences

Two sentences with the same subject may often be combined. Use **and** to combine such sentences. (page 30)

> Most parks are free. Most parks have sections for baseball and tennis.

> Most parks are free <u>and</u> have sections for baseball and tennis.

Nouns can be added to improve sentences. (page 76)

Expanding the subject: Sara, my sister, fishes.

Expanding the action: Sara, my sister, fishes on Saturday.

The use of **interesting** and **exact verbs** can improve sentences. (pages 108, 128, 250)

Dull: The bird flew above us.

Interesting: The bird soared above us.

Adjectives of sight, hearing, taste, smell, and touch improve descriptions. (pages 148, 154)

Smoke rose from the fire.

Thick, gray smoke rose from the scorching fire.

Adverbs add details that tell **how, when,** or **where.** (page 168)

The shuttle was launched.

The shuttle was launched safely at sunrise in the desert.

LISTENING / SPEAKING

Listening

1. Sit quietly
2. Look at the speaker.
3. Listen for the main idea.
4. Listen for details.
5. Do not interrupt or make noise.
6. Save your questions for the end.

Speaking

1. Plan your speech carefully. Be organized.
2. Make notes about your important points.
3. Stand still.
4. Speak loudly, slowly, and clearly.
5. Look at the people to whom you are speaking.
6. Look up from your notes.

More Practice

Sentences (pages 10–11)

Number your paper from 1 to 10. Read each group of words. Write *S* if the group of words is a sentence. Write *F* if the group of words is a fragment.

1. Tops are popular toys.

2. Most tops have shapes like pears.

3. Are wood.

4. Some are made from plastic.

5. Have metal tips.

6. A few tops even sing.

7. Popular in Japan and China.

8. Top spinners can do many tricks.

Change each fragment above. Write sentences.

Kinds of Sentences (pages 12–13)

Correct each sentence. Some sentences need a capital letter. Some sentences need a punctuation mark. Write *S* if the sentence is a statement. Write *Q* if it is a question. Write *E* if it is an exclamation. Write *C* if it is a command.

1. look there

2. did you see that

3. what is that big gray thing

4. it is a giant squid

5. It must be close to 60 feet long

6. squid eat fish

7. some people eat squid

8. have you ever eaten squid

9. Here, taste this

10. Not me

Subjects and Predicates (pages 14–15, 16–17)

Write each sentence. Underline the complete subject. Circle the simple subject.

1. Moving air is wind.
2. A nice gentle breeze keeps you cool on a hot day.
3. Gale winds blow trees down.
4. The wind dries the clothes hanging on the line.
5. A steady wind makes the windmill move.

Write each sentence above. Underline the complete predicate. Circle the simple predicate.

Compound Subjects (pages 28–29)

Combine each group of sentences. Make one sentence with a compound subject.

1. Bees can sting. Wasps can sting.
2. Fruit trees need pollen. Some field crops need pollen.
3. Bees bring pollen to plants. Wasps bring pollen to plants. Butterflies bring pollen to plants.
4. People could not live without insects. Plant life could not live without insects.

Compound Predicates (pages 30–31)

Join each group of sentences. Make one sentence with a compound predicate.

1. Insects have three body parts. Insects do not have a backbone.
2. Spiders have two body parts. Spiders are not true insects.
3. Ants are social insects. Ants often live together in the ground.
4. Ants collect seeds. Ants store the seeds in nests.

Correcting Run-on Sentences (pages 32–33)

Correct each run-on sentence. Write the new sentences.

1. Pioneers marked trails on trees and footpaths were "roads."

2. Some people made roads of wood and they traveled in wagons.

3. Turnpikes appeared in the 1880s and railroads were unheard of.

Yes-No and WH-Questions (pages 34–35)

Number your paper from 1 through 4. Write *WH* if the question is a WH-question and *Yes-No* if it is a Yes-No question.

1. What is your name? **3.** Is the sun out today?

2. How are you feeling? **4.** Do you enjoy picnics?

Writing: A Paragraph (pages 42–44)

Plan, write, and edit a paragraph of directions. Tell how to tie a bow or make a sandwich.

Nouns (pages 52–53)

Label each noun *person, place,* or *thing.*

bridge   brother   window   school
nurse   park   pen   baby

Write each sentence. Circle the nouns in each sentence.

1. The first books were clay tablets.

2. Inventors in China made the first paper.

3. William Caxton published the first printed book in England.

Singular and Plural Nouns (pages 54–55, 56–57)

Write each singular noun. Then write its plural form.

beach   goose   box   party   thief
tooth   child   lunch   wish   bakery

Common and Proper Nouns (pages 58–59)

Write each sentence. Add capital letters to each proper noun. Underline each common noun.

1. We visited boston, massachusetts, on labor day.
2. We took a train from rhode island.
3. Our trip took about an hour.
4. In boston uncle fred met us at the station.
5. He bought us lunch at a restaurant near the harbor.
6. After lunch we visited the museum of science.
7. The library was on boylston street.

Possessive Nouns (pages 60–61)

Change each group of words. Write a possessive noun to give the same message.

1. the house belonging to Dr. Singer
2. the house belonging to the Singers
3. the bike belonging to Chris
4. the antlers of the deer
5. the tools of the carpenter
6. the money belonging to Alice
7. the pots of the cooks

Abbreviations (pages 66–67)

Number your paper from 1 through 10. Write the abbreviation of each underlined word.

1. <u>November</u> 14, 1984
2. Buffalo, <u>New York</u>
3. 15 Apple <u>Road</u>
4. <u>Doctor</u> Alice Winston
5. Galveston, <u>Texas</u>
6. <u>Thursday</u> night
7. 11 (<u>at night</u>)
8. Pete Lyons, <u>Senior</u>

Punctuating Letters and Envelopes (pages 70–71)

Write each letter part correctly. Use commas where needed.

1. Dear Susan
2. Palm Desert CA 92760
3. Your friend
4. Dec. 4 1984
5. Dear Mr. Pointer
6. Sincerely
7. Seattle WA 98115
8. June 16 1984

Noun Endings (page 72)

Add the correct suffix (*-er* or *-or*) to change each word into a noun. Write the nouns.

1. climb
2. talk
3. pitch
4. sail
5. visit
6. develop
7. edit
8. act

Using *A, An,* and *The* (page 73)

Write each sentence with the correct article.

1. (A/An) apple has a core.
2. (The/An) core contains seeds.
3. (An/The) oranges are picked twice (a/an) year.
4. (A/An) crate holds many oranges.
5. Unlike (a/the) apple, (a/an) orange has sections.
6. Stores will sell (a/an) single orange.

Using *This, That, These,* and *Those* (page 74)

Choose the correct word in each sentence. Use the clues *nearby* and *away* to help you. Write the sentences.

1. (That/Those) trees are oaks.
2. (This/These) flowers are daisies.

(away) 3. (This/That) concert yesterday was good.

(nearby)	**4.** (This/That) light doesn't work.
(away)	**5.** (This/That) bulb doesn't fit.
(nearby)	**6.** (These/Those) shoes are too large.
(away)	**7.** (These/Those) songs were very old.
(nearby)	**8.** (This/That) bike is new.

Using *Some, Many,* and *Several* (page 75)

In each sentence, the word *some, many,* or *several* points to a noun. Write that noun.

1. Many insects share the world with us.

2. Some insects damage crops.

3. Several types of insects build colonies.

4. There are many bees in a colony.

5. Worker bees do several jobs.

6. Some beetles attack rose bushes.

Expanding Sentences Using Nouns (pages 76–77)

Make these sentences grow. Add nouns and any other words you need.

1. Mike hoed.	**6.** Rosa picked.
2. I cut the lawn.	**7.** Ron cooked.
3. We raked.	**8.** Maria made.
4. The flowers wilted.	**9.** Jackie poured.
5. Alice watered.	**10.** Everyone enjoyed.

Writing: A Letter (pages 84-86)

Plan, write, and edit a letter to a friend. Tell why you are writing. Make sure that you put all parts of the letter in the correct places. Punctuate each letter part correctly. If you need some help, read pages 84–86.

Verbs (pages 98, 99)

Each sentence contains a verb. Write the verb. If it is an action verb, write *A* next to it.

1. A dolphin is a small whale.
2. Some dolphins follow ships.
3. Dolphins eat fish and squid.
4. Some dolphins perform tricks in aquariums.
5. Dolphins are very smart.
6. Some trained dolphins toss balls through nets.
7. Dolphins talk with each other.
8. They make sounds through their blowholes.

Subject-Verb Agreement (pages 100–101)

Write each sentence using the correct form of the verb.

1. Pets _____ much care. (need)
2. A pet dog _____ like a close friend. (act)
3. Beagles _____ by smell. (hunt)
4. One kind of hound _____ by sight. (hunt)
5. Greyhounds and whippets _____ . (race)
6. A sheepdog _____ cattle or sheep. (guard)
7. Some working dogs _____ sleds. (pull)
8. Terriers _____ good watchdogs. (make)

Verb Tenses (pages 102–103)

Write each verb. Label each one *present, past,* or *future.*

1. Lobsters live on the bottom of the ocean.
2. Many people choose lobster as their favorite seafood.
3. Once, lobsters almost disappeared.
4. People trapped too many lobsters.

Write the past tense form of these verbs.

1. learn   3. float   5. carry   7. trip
2. marry   4. carve   6. tag   8. produce

Helping Verbs (pages 104–105)
Write these sentences. Underline the complete verb. Circle the helping verb.

1. Lemon trees can grow twenty-five feet tall.
2. The trees will have blossoms most of the year.
3. Some trees may produce fruit for fifty years.
4. Growers should protect the trees from the cold.
5. Growers have harvested lemons ten times each year.
6. Did Columbus plant the first lemon tree in the Americas?

Contractions with _Not_ (pages 114–115)
Write each sentence. Use a contraction for the underlined words.

1. It has not rained for a month.
2. We will not use the lawn sprinkler.
3. The mayor does not allow the use of sprinklers.
4. I do not waste water.
5. I would not want this dry weather all year.
6. We did not expect such a dry spell.

Verb Forms (pages 118–119)
Think of the form of the verb that completes each sentence. Then write the sentences.

1. We are (go) on a camping trip.
2. We have (purchase) a dome tent.

3. I am (use) a back pack.

4. We have (hike) the trail before.

5. This year, we are (plan) a trip into the mountains.

6. We have already (fill) our backpacks.

7. Sam and I are (leave) on Sunday.

The Verb *Have* and Irregular Verbs (pages 116–117, 120–121)

Decide whether the verb *have, has,* or *had* will best complete each sentence. Then write the complete sentence.

1. Anne _____ a crystal radio now.

2. Crystal radios _____ no batteries.

3. I _____ built one last year.

4. It _____ only a two-mile range.

5. Anne's radio _____ a fifty-mile range.

6. She _____ entered it in the science fair.

Choose the form of the verb that best completes each sentence. Then write the sentence.

1. We (went/gone) to the track meet.

2. This year, my sister (ran/run) at the meet.

3. Next week, she is (run/running) in a marathon.

4. We are (go/going) to the marathon.

5. I have not (saw/seen) a marathon before.

6. Runners are (come/coming) from many states.

The Verb *Do* (pages 122–123)

Choose the verb that best completes each sentence. Then write the sentence.

1. (Do/Does) computers have brains?

2. A computer (do/does) have a brain.

3. Some computers (<u>do/does</u>) the work of hundreds of people.

4. We are (<u>doing/done</u>) a project with computers.

5. We have (<u>doing/done</u>) some interesting things.

Writing: An Order Paragraph (pages 130–132)

Plan, write, and edit a paragraph about an event you recently saw or took part in. It should have a beginning, middle, and end. Tell the details in the correct order. Use the Word Bank on page 112 to help you. Remember to start your paragraph with a topic sentence. Read pages 130–132 if you need more help.

Adjectives (pages 144–145)

Add at least one adjective to each sentence. Write each new sentence.

1. The spaceship shot across the sky.

2. The boat sliced through the harbor.

3. The cry of an owl floated through the forest.

4. Horses raced around the track.

5. A bus carried children.

Using Adjectives That Compare (pages 146–147)

Choose the correct word to complete each sentence. Write each sentence.

1. That film was (<u>more/most</u>) interesting than the other one.

2. It had the (<u>more/most</u>) exciting space scenes I've ever seen.

3. The spaceship was the (<u>bigger/biggest</u>) one in all the space movies ever made.

4. Its landing deck was (<u>larger/largest</u>) than New York City.

5. The movie seemed (<u>shorter/shortest</u>) than three hours.

Details and the Senses (pages 148–149)

For the sense listed, add an adjective. Write the new sentence.

1. Miko saw a mountain. (sight)
2. My lunch made me thirsty. (taste)
3. The flower attracted bees. (smell)
4. I borrowed Karen's sweater. (touch)
5. The jet woke me. (hearing)

The Adjectives *Good, Bad, Many,* and *Much* (pages 150–151)

Decide which form of the adjective will best complete each sentence. Write each sentence.

1. The book was (good) than the movie.
2. There are (many) films this summer than last summer.
3. The (good) film of all is about a friendly space creature.
4. Some say that it is the (much) important film in ten years.
5. The (bad) film is about corn plants taking over the world.
6. It is (bad) than the one about the tomato rulers of Mars.

Punctuating Dialogue (pages 160–161)

Write these sentences. Put in quotation marks and other punctuation where needed.

1. What are you doing this summer asked Joan.
2. I'm working at the town pool said Mari.
3. Joan said I'll be working there too.
4. Mari asked Are you a lifeguard?
5. Yes, I passed the test last week said Joan.

Imagine a conversation between yourself and a friend. You are talking about your plans for the summer. Write the conversation. Use quotation marks correctly.

Adverbs (pages 162–163)
Write the adverb or adverbs in each sentence. Write the question each answers. (Where? When? How?)

1. We visited the zoo yesterday.
2. The lion trainer was carefully feeding the lions.
3. They roared loudly.
4. We crept closer.
5. The trainer quietly opened the cage door.
6. Then two of us ran away.

Adverbs for *When, Where,* and *How* (pages 164–165)
Add a group of words to each sentence to answer the question. Write each sentence.

1. Alan and Lynn hiked. (Where?)
2. They saw a bear. (When?)
3. Alan whispered to Lynn. (How?)
4. They crept. (Where?)
5. She took five pictures. (How?)

Using Adverbs That Compare (pages 166–167)
Choose the adverb that best completes the sentence. Write each sentence.

1. Of all the jets, a supersonic jet travels (faster/fastest).
2. It flies (higher/highest) than a regular jet, too.
3. Rockets move (more/most) quickly than jets.
4. Of all vehicles, rockets fly (farther/farthest) into space.
5. A rocket climbs (more/most) rapidly than a jet.
6. Some rockets roar (more/most) noisily than others.
7. Who launched a rocket (earlier/earliest) of all countries?

Building Sentences by Adding Details (pages 168–169)

Add details to each sentence. Answer the question that follows each sentence. Write the sentences.

1. The moon disappeared. (Where?)
2. The car stopped. (How?)
3. The lions snarled. (How many?)
4. The storm battered the coastline. (What kind?)
5. Gulls soared. (Where?)
6. Some boats cruised. (Where?)
7. The fire began. (When?)
8. The fire spread. (What kind? Where?)
9. Jim baked a pie. (What kind?)
10. The books were valuable. (How many? What kind?)

Writing: A Story (pages 176–178)

Plan, write, and edit a story plot about one of the characters and scenes in the list. Or make up your own characters and scene.

1. Mark and Susan lost on a hike through the desert
2. Carlos and Maura floating on a raft towards a waterfall
3. Jess and Wilma in a city of the future ruled by an evil leader
4. Carrie and Bill in a leaky boat in the middle of a large lake

Think about the problem your characters have. Write about the problem at the beginning of the paragraph. In the middle of the paragraph, tell what the characters do to try to solve their problem. At the end, tell what the characters do that solves their problem. For more help, read pages 176–178 again.

Pronouns (pages 190–191, 192–193)

Think of a pronoun to take the place of the underlined words. Then write each sentence.

1. <u>Ellen and I</u> went on a whale watch.
2. A boat took <u>Ellen and me</u> to the whales.
3. The skipper spotted <u>a group of whales</u> about a mile away.
4. Then <u>the skipper</u> slowly steered <u>the boat</u> toward the group.
5. He asked <u>Ellen and me</u> to remain very quiet.
6. <u>The boat</u> came to a stop about fifty feet from <u>the whales</u>.
7. <u>Several whales</u> made a quick forward roll.
8. <u>That roll</u> allowed <u>Ellen and me</u> to see the whale's entire body.

Using *I* or *Me*, *We* or *Us* (pages 194–195)

Choose *I, me, we,* or *us* to complete each sentence. Write the sentences.

1. Al and _____ are good friends.
2. Al's mother took Al and _____ to the ball game.
3. _____ all sat in the bleachers.
4. Later, Al's mother asked both of _____ to get autographs.
5. _____ each got three autographs.
6. After the game, Al and _____ bought his mother a baseball cap.

Pronoun-Verb Agreement (pages 196–197)

Choose the verb that agrees with the subject in each sentence. Write the sentences.

1. Sue and I (<u>works/work</u>) together on a science project.
2. We (<u>is/are</u>) building a model solar house.
3. I (<u>am/are</u>) making the roof.
4. Solar cells (<u>form/forms</u>) the roof.

5. Solar cells (use/uses) light from the sun.
6. Sue (is/are) making a solar battery for inside the house.
7. The battery (store/stores) light energy.

Possessive Pronouns (pages 210–211)
   Choose the pronoun that correctly completes the second sentence in each pair. Write the completed sentences.

1. The class had a food sale. (It/Its) goal was to pay for a trip.
2. Karen made a pie. (Her/Hers) pie had raisins and apples.
3. Pablo brought a cake. That large one is (him/his).
4. I created some new cookies. That is (my/mine) tin of cookies.
5. Gene and Betty made a salad. That salad is (their/theirs).
6. The sale was a hit. (Our/Ours) class will go on a trip.

Clear Pronoun References (pages 212–213)
   Choose the word that best completes each sentence. Choose the pronoun if the meaning is clear. Then write the sentence.

1. John lent his bike to Willie. (He/Willie) liked the bike.
2. Paul helped Anne decode the message. (He/Paul) knew the code.
3. Rita and Jane made breakfast. (She/Rita) fried the eggs.
4. Jim sold a ticket. (It/The ticket) was for the school play.
5. Ted saw Jim. (He/Ted) waved.
6. Sara sang for Ms. Lee's class. (They/Ms. Lee's class) enjoyed it.

-Self Pronouns (pages 214–215)
   Use the correct *-self* pronoun to complete each sentence. The pronoun partner is marked. Write the sentences.

1. I asked _____ that same question.
2. John taught _____ chess.

3. You should study the offer _____ before you accept it.

4. We entered _____ in the Monster Contest.

5. A plane won't fly by _____.

6. They considered _____ the best players in the league.

Too Many Pronouns (pages 216–217)

Correct the following sentences. Each contains a pronoun that repeats the noun. Write each corrected sentence.

1. The parade it will be the best one of the summer.

2. Bands they are coming from many states.

3. My sister and I we plan to go early.

4. Sara she knows a good spot for watching it.

5. Many floats they will be in the parade.

Writing: A Report pages 224–226)

Plan, write, and edit a brief report. The topic should be one that interests you. Write several WH-questions about the topic. Then choose two to answer. Find details and facts that answer the two questions. Write a separate paragraph for each of the questions. Begin each paragraph with a topic sentence. Then write detail sentences that support each topic sentence.

The Verb *Be* (pages 238–239)

Use a form of the verb *be* to complete each sentence. Write your sentences.

1. Horses have _____ people's helpers for centuries

2. Most horses _____ gentle and trainable.

3. Horses can _____ good friends.

4. Some horses _____ excellent racers.

Linking Verbs (pages 240–241, 242–243)

Write each sentence. Underline the linking verb. Draw an arrow from any adjectives in the predicate to the subject. Circle any noun in the predicate.

1. Spring is beautiful.　**3.** A colorful season is fall.
2. The grass is green.　**4.** A cold time is winter.

Irregular Verbs (pages 256–257)

Complete each sentence. Use the correct verb form. Write the sentence.

1. Have you ＿＿＿ the missing pack of giant carrot seeds? (find)
2. Last year, we ＿＿＿ carrots ten feet high. (grow)
3. The tall stalks ＿＿＿ during a rainstorm. (fall)
4. We ＿＿＿ the seeds and hid them away. (take)
5. I have never ＿＿＿ any of those giant carrots. (eat)
6. You ＿＿＿ one last year for a whole week. (eat)
7. We must ＿＿＿ that pack of seeds. (find)
8. Do you think they could have ＿＿＿ from the shelf? (fall)
9. Has anyone ever ＿＿＿ carrots that large? (grow)
10. I ＿＿＿ a story in a record book about tall carrots. (find)

Avoiding Double Negatives (pages 258–259)

Rewrite each sentence so that it is correct.

1. I didn't want to do nothing today.
2. The teacher hasn't never given us homework.
3. I don't never want to play chess again.
4. Don't none of you know the answer?
5. We can't go nowhere this weekend.
6. I can't eat no more pie.

Pronoun-Verb Contractions (pages 260–261)

Change the underlined words in each sentence into a contraction. Write the sentence.

1. <u>We have</u> asked for a recount of the votes.
2. <u>It will</u> be a week before the final results.
3. <u>He had</u> won the first election count.
4. Now <u>she will</u> probably win.
5. <u>They have</u> demanded a new election.
6. <u>You will</u> watch all the ballot boxes.
7. <u>I have</u> asked everyone to be fair.
8. Now <u>we are</u> going to conduct a fair election.
9. <u>She is</u> willing to help us.
10. <u>He has</u> agreed to the new rules.

Using *They're, Their,* and *There* (pages 262–263)

Write three sentences. Use *they're, their,* and *there* in the sentences.

Using *Your* and *You're, Its* and *It's* (pages 264–265)

Write four sentences. Use *your, you're, its,* and *it's* in the sentences.

Writing: A Persuasive Note (pages 272–274)

Plan, write, and edit a persuasive note about one of the following topics.

1. How and why <u>something</u> in your community should be changed.
2. How and why <u>something</u> in your school can be improved.

Use the steps on pages 272–273 to help you plan and write your note. Use the form on page 273 as a model.

Index

light italic print *(123)* = Review the Basics, Unit Test, Keep Practicing, More Practice
dark italic print ***(123)*** = Handbook

When. *See* Adverbs, *where, when* and *how;* News story.

Where. *See* Adverbs, *where, when,* and *how;* News story.

Who. *See* News story.

WH-questions, 34–35, 206–207, 224–226, 298–299, *327, 347*

Writing

comparison and contrast in descriptions, 186–187

comparison poems, 94–95

completing forms, 48–49

figurative language in descriptions, 282–283

general guidelines, *341*

similes, 94–95, 234–235

models, 38–39, 80–81, 82–83, 126–127, 128–129, 172–173, 174–175, 220, 221, 222–223, 270, 273, 314–315, *342–343*

See also, Business letters; News story; Paragraph, of action; Paragraph, of directions; Paragraph, order; Paragraph, writing about an event; Paragraph, writing an opinion; Paragraph, writing a problem-solution; Persuasive note; Report; Story; Summary.

Yes-No questions, 34–35, *37,* 298–299, *327, 346*

Your and **You're,** 264–265, 267, 310–311, *340, 341, 362*

ZIP Code, 66–67, 70–71, *139, 335, 342, 343*

ABCDEFGHIJ089876543
Printed in the United States of America